THE PORT OF
NEW YORK

AMERICA'S FIRST PORT

"First to be discovered, first to be occupied, first to be fought over for its advantages, first in the world in volume and value of commerce"

THE PORT OF NEW YORK

BY

THOMAS E. RUSH
SURVEYOR OF THE PORT

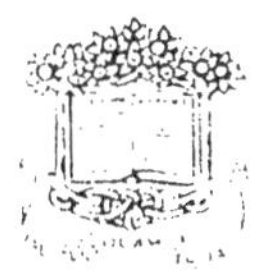

ILLUSTRATIONS
FROM
PHOTOGRAPHS

GARDEN CITY NEW YORK
DOUBLEDAY, PAGE & COMPANY
1920

ACKNOWLEDGMENTS

One of the greatest pleasures in the preparation of this book has been the hearty coöperation received from business men, public officers, and educators. I am especially indebted to

Francis Lee Stuart, Consulting Engineer and President of the International Conveyor Corporation;

Benjamin F. Cresson, Jr., Consulting Engineer, New York, New Jersey Port and Harbour Development Commission;

Calvin Tomkins, former Dock Commissioner of Greater New York;

Ex-Congressman William Kent, member of the U. S. Tariff Commission;

Grosvenor M. Jones, Assistant Director, Bureau Foreign and Domestic Commerce, Washington, D. C.;

R. G. Simonds, Vice President and Treasurer of the Bush Terminal Company.

Marc F. Vallette, LL.D.;

Jeremiah H. Lant, Chief Statistical Clerk, United States Custom House, Port of New York;

Lieutenant Colonel H. S. Crocker, Construction Quartermaster, U. S.A.;

Nelson B. Killmer, Secretary, Jamaica Bay Association;

Several publicists, editors, and educators have granted interviews, recommended incidents of interest, and read parts of the manuscript. Appreciation is expressed particularly to

Alexander R. Smith, editor of the *Marine News* and the *Port of New York Annual;*

ACKNOWLEDGMENTS

Captain Vladimar Lassen, Superintendent of the Scandinavian-American Steamship line;

P. H. W. Ross, President, National Marine League;

William Liebermann, Chairman Committee on Industrial Advancement of the Brooklyn League;

Edgar F. Luckenbach, President, Luckenbach Company, Inc.;

Thomas A. Arnold, member of Atlantic Yacht Club;

John Cotton Dana, Librarian, Newark, N. J.;

William Harris Douglas, President, Arkell & Douglas, Inc.;

Hiram Barney, Director, Parsons Trading Co.;

Henry V. R. Scheel, Division of Planning and Statistics, U. S. Shipping Board;

Lieutenant R. E. Lambert, Supply, Commissary and Disbursing Officer of the U.S.S. *Minnesota*, and Naval Salvage Service;

Mrs. Marian K. Clark, Chief Investigator, Bureau of Industries and Immigration, New York State Industrial Commission;

And to the Institute for Public Service for the services of its director, William H. Allen, LL.D.

THOMAS E. RUSH.

FOREWORD

To MAKE it easier for business men, officials, teachers, and students to understand New York Harbour and to demand the utmost competence of New York as a port, is the main purpose of this book. It is written from the experience and studies of a Surveyor of Customs of the Port, responsible for directing nearly two thousand Federal employees in applying America's policy to the business which enters and leaves America's first port.

First to be discovered, first to be occupied, first to be fought over for its advantages, first in the world in volume and value of commerce, the Port of New York is first in its lessons for America's future and first in immediate importance to world trade.

The third decade of the Twentieth Century will begin with almost half of the colossal foreign trade of the United States of America going out from and coming in through the Port of New York.

Few American citizens are untouched by this port. Civics, history, government cannot do without it. It can be outvoted, but it cannot be outled in ability to help or hamper progress in our country.

The history in these pages is not new except in the use which is made of it, namely, to show that the great population which centres about the Statue of Liberty is not merely America's largest city plus forty neighbouring New Jersey cities, but is America's metropolis and the world's metropolis because it is also a port and the world's greatest port. Oft-told tales about the purchase of Manhattan Island from the Indians for twenty-four dollars, the wooden leg and even more combustible temper of Peter Stuyvesant, the persistence of the primitive instinct to resent customs duties, and the civic blunderings of Tammany and anti-Tammany are here retold for the purpose of driving home the fact that from its earliest settlement, through the centuries of its growing pains to its present predominance, the Port of New York has been first and foremost a port in everything except in the thought of America's statesmen, who gave little attention if any to this important fact.

Stories of its past—the early discoverers, Dutch and English occupiers, pirates, and privateers, attempts to prevent smuggling, growth in commerce, growth in merchant marine, its defences and its value to the nation in war time—throw light upon the road ahead, upon the nation's need for more intelligent handling of America's first port, and upon the unsolved problems of the port. The important improvements are listed under the five agencies responsible for making them: cities within the port area; New York and New Jersey State governments; the Federal Government; the projected bi-state unified port control; and extra governmental agencies through which the public's demands and needs are voiced. Only eternal vigilance by business men, educators, officials, and statesmen, will keep the Port of New York continuously fit for the work which it will be called upon to do for the nation as well as for the world at large

Schools and colleges are urged to teach the vital truths of port management, not for the sake of satisfying an antiquarian interest but to prepare students for future helpfulness. Chambers of commerce, merchants' associations, boards of trade and transportation, and individual shippers are urged to establish complaint and suggestion departments as well as publicity bureaus with respect to America's ports for America's sake rather than for the mere profit which such educational advertising will inevitably bring to the business which centres in ports. Improved facilities are urged for handling commerce—for weighing carloads by the ton instead of by the hundredweight, for lifting huge loads by derricks instead of by hand, for unloading cargoes in one day instead of five—not merely as baits for increasing commerce, but as fundamental necessities for lowering the cost of living and increasing opportunities for American labour.

The new and conspicuous part which our country must take in keeping the world free for Democracy demands that all our ports be world ports. Mistakes, waste, undemocratic policies at these ports will affect not only our own welfare everywhere but the world welfare as well.

In all probability the Port of New York could not, in a generation, lose its leadership, no matter how incompetently it might handle its share of world business. In all human certainty, however, the Port of New York, by failing to correct present glaring deficiencies, and by failing to fill in the gap between its own facilities and the greater facilities of competing ports in Europe and South America, may incalculably injure and hamper American industry and world industry.

Moreover, the holders of property, the doers of business, and the drawers of wages in Greater New York cannot afford longer to blink the fact that every time a great business goes to another location because of New York's mistakes and unattractiveness, the earning power of labour and capital in New York is injured and depreciated.

Statesmanship, business foresight, yes, just plain, ordinary common sense, show that New York must awake to the fact that it is not merely a populous city, not merely a great manufacturing centre, not the much-advertised great white way of allurement, but first and foremost a port.

THOMAS E. RUSH.

New York, January 15, 1920.

CONTENTS

LIST OF ILLUSTRATIONS

THE PORT OF NEW YORK

The Port of New York

CHAPTER I

America's First Port Is Yours

IF EACH of us is a part of all he has met, as Tennyson says, then America's first port is practically a part of every American. Progress made here will make life easier and more enjoyable for the miners of Pennsylvania, the farmers of the Dakotas, and the mountaineers of Tennessee. Obsolete facilities, reactionary policies, and dilatory tactics at the Port of New York will make life less endurable and less enjoyable for the schoolboy of Kansas, the button maker of Connecticut, and the fiction writer of Indiana.

The area most directly conscious of the part which the Port of New York plays in its daily living is shown by the accompanying map. In this area live over six million people, more than 6 per cent. of the country's total population. Any surplus product within this territory for which markets are sought in Europe or Latin-America can be carried to the sea more quickly and more economically through the Port of New York than through any other port. Any articles of commerce from outside our country, such as coffee from Brazil, rubber from the East Indies, gowns from Paris, silver knives from England, can come into any part of this territory more expeditiously and with less expense through the Port of New York.

When forty thousand carloads of freight were congested in the railroad yards of the New Jersey side of this harbour, it meant not only that our allies in Europe and our own soldiers must wait for desperately needed munitions and food, but it also meant that throughout the United States home-town railroad sidings were piled up with freight for which cars were lacking, and that thousands of homes needed food and clothing which could not be obtained until cars at the seaboard were unloaded and returned.

When the rubber makers of Akron and workers of Cleveland read the news in the papers of their own town that the longshoremen or harbour masters or railroad employees of the Port of New York were threatening a strike within twenty-four hours thereafter, they ought to reflect, as perhaps most of them did not, that a tie-up in New York might easily, within a few days, throw out of employment the workers in their own towns.

When the receiver for Brooklyn's Rapid Transit System announces that he will not meet labour leaders or committees representing the union labourers in his employ, his decision affects not merely the sentiment of labourers throughout the land, but also materially affects their prospect of continued labour at reasonably high wages. Similarly, when the Mayor of New York announces, as he did on April 15, 1919, that the receiver has rescinded his refusal to meet with the labour committee and has promised such a meeting, that message bears directly on the earning and collective bargaining prospects of labour from coast to coast.

As stated frequently in these pages, the influence upon the rest of the country's prosperity which is exerted by New York with the neighbouring cities that make the Port of New York is due not merely to the fact that it is our largest port of entry and departure, but also to the fact that it is already a community of more than six million people. Labour difficulties, business deficiencies, governmental short-sightedness in other places may be just as serious in principle, but are less serious in effect because the numbers depending upon the sanity, industry, fairness, and prosperity of six million people at our first port vastly exceed those influenced by any other territorial combination of forces in this country, if not in the world.

No one has ever suggested that any other centre of population in America would displace the Port of New York from its position as

First in commerce,

First in financial operations,

First as arbiter of styles,

First as a magnet for recreation and for what is called "Society,"

First in its educational influence,

First in its news productivity,

First as a publishing centre, and

First in the interest of its editorials.

You may not like New York; you may never have seen it; you may feel sure that you never will see it; you may not, to your knowledge, ever purchase an article from or sell articles in or to New York; nevertheless, in the things you wear, the things you eat and drink, the pleasures you enjoy, the books you read and the moving pictures you see, you are being influenced by what happens there. Every improvement which cheapens the cost of goods handled through this port increases the price of what you sell and decreases the cost of what you buy. It is for this reason that the story of the Port of New York, its past, its present needs and possibilities are discussed here from the broader standpoint of national welfare and not from the narrower standpoint of port prosperity alone.

Since America's first port is yours, since it affects your earnings, your enjoyments, and your opportunities, it is obviously not fair to yourself to leave its management entirely to the small fraction of workers who live at the port itself. If you live in the Middle or Far West, or Far South, or elsewhere outside its limits, you cannot bring your intelligent interest to bear at the polls, except to ask congressmen and senators to vote for needed port improvements; you will probably not feel like writing letters of criticism to city or state officials in some measure responsible for the port; you can, however, materially promote your own interest by informing yourself with regard to port problems, and by contributing to the public knowledge and public discussion of port services. For the same reason that New York business men know that their profits are larger when they please out-of-town patrons, New York and New Jersey port officials are apt to give more heed to praise, suggestion, and criticism from the outside than to the same praise, suggestion, or criticism from within.

CHAPTER II

Birth, Christening, and Youth

"As THE twig is bent so is the tree inclined," applies to America's first port, New York, whose early days were prophetic miniatures of those characteristics by which, in a colossal degree, it is known to the Twentieth-Century world.

Do newspapers, educators, civic agencies, and business corporations quarrel over discoveries and leadership in and for New York? What more can we expect of a harbour of which the Dutch, the Spanish, the French, and the English claimed original discovery!

Are drivers of business trucks and pleasure cars in constant fear of running over pedestrians in congested streets? Blood will tell; the first white man to enter this harbour suffered because he was in constant danger of running down Indian boats filled with sightseers who were characteristically willing to risk a few lives in order to be first to see a new show.

Is this port proud of its polyglot population?

Remember that while still a village it was already polyglot.

It may not be true that there is nothing new under the sun, but it certainly is true that there is very little in and about New York to-day which has not its first cousin of one, two, or three centuries ago. Promoters—and until they proved their case, promoters as wild as any who have recently sought New York capital for developing oil wells in Texas, potash beds in Virginia, or airplane factories in Ohio—persuaded Spanish and Dutch financiers to back voyages of exploration to this harbour. Had O. Henry lived in the year 1523 or 1609 he would have found not one but many a prospectus of fortunes obtainable in the Port of New York which would have made some of his famous gold bricks look like real money. The money grabbers and profiteers of our day can seldom equal the big dividends of 400 per cent. which rewarded the rich and influential backers of Henry Hudson. Even the padrone system, against which our modern reformers were compelled to be vigilant almost to the time of the recent war, had its counterpart in the patroon system of early New York.

Present-day tendencies to concentrate power in the hands of an individual, a commission, or a board is but repeating governmental decrees of the years 1683 and 1686 which dissolved the General Assembly of the province of New York and deprived the people of any further representation in the passing of laws or in taxing themselves. A three-century-old analogy is found in present-day competition between New York City and the Jersey City Meadows which are attracting great industries and rich investments away from the east side of the harbour, in the action of the Indians nearly two hundred and fifty years ago who deserted New York for the better markets in New Jersey, where instead of high taxation there was no taxation at all.

All of which emphasizes the fact that New York began with a desire for commerce; was seized by one nation from another because of lust for commerce; was governed and misgoverned with a view to commerce; and grew to its present stature by serving commerce.

Henry Hudson is the first of a long line of distinguished discoverers who, while contributing to New York's fame, have made themselves famous by rediscoveries. Unlike many others, Hudson attained success without building a family fortune, and held his fame without becoming infamous. For entering this harbour in the year 1609, all Americans must always be grateful to Henry Hudson. At the same time we cannot be fair to history unless we remember two other explorers, Giovanni Verrazano, a Florentine, and Estavan Gomez, a Portuguese, who preceded Hudson by nearly one hundred years.

It was in the year 1523 that Verrazano, the first discoverer, came, saw, and recorded in a letter the earliest known description of the Port of New York and its "curious" inhabitants. At that time all the adventurous speculators of the world, kings, scientists, navigators, and explorers, were looking for a short water route to Cathay. Although a Florentine, Verrazano seems to have been just the kind of man who would attain his objective in New York. He was quite at home in the uncertain waters of the Mediterranean and was particularly noted for daring, initiative, thoroughness, and genius for handling men and situations. With his other accomplishments, he was apparently a good salesman because in the year 1523 he was hired out to Francis I of France as a privateer against the ships of Spain, applying his energies particularly to vessels returning from Mexico laden with treasure confiscated from Montezuma. His biographers finish the picture of a typical New Yorker by claiming that in addition to his salesmanship, privateering and profiteering, exploring, and confiscating, he was of a "benevolent and generous nature."

It was on April 15, 1524, when Verrazano reached Sandy Hook with four boats and fifty men. Like other subsequent discoverers of the harbour, this first discoverer found the people "friendly and unafraid," a trait which has clung to customers and traders in the Port of New York to the days of Get-Rich-Quick-Wallingford.

As these first white salesmen approached the shores of Manhattan, they found paraders "dressed out with feathers of birds of various colours." They came toward the discoverers "with evidence of delight, raising loud shouts of admiration and showing us where we could most securely land with our boat." A squall struck the navigators, who returned to their ship and sailed out of the harbour "greatly regretting to leave the region which seemed so commodious and delightful and which we supposed must also contain great riches, as the hills showed many indications of minerals." The departure was not too hasty for Verrazano to discover that fruits and flowers were growing luxuriantly; that brooks and rivers teemed with fish; that the soil was fertile and growing lavish crops; that game was numerous and varied, and that nut trees were plentiful.

From maps then drawn for a report made to the King of France in July, 1524, we find that Verrazano sailed out between Sandy Hook and Coney Island, along Rockaway Bay, just outside the southern shore of Long Island, to a place now identified as Block Island, where he was prevented from landing by violent weather. It is a coincidence which seems almost prophetic and fatalistic that this agent of big capital seeking conquest found refuge from the squalls of New York in the calm waters of Newport, where by "imitating signs of friendship from the natives, the visitors inspired confidence and gained a welcome which permitted them first to approach near enough to toss hawkes, bells, and glass beads and toys of various kinds," after which the natives, "very much pleased with their presents, boarded the ship without fear." The Newport women were found "very graceful, of fine countenance, and pleasing appearance in manners and modesty."

In and about Newport, the foreign visitors found the climate delightful and the soil adapted to the cultivation of "corn, wine, or oil," while easily obtainable were "apples, plums, filberts, stags, deer, and lynxes." Unlike those of the present day, however, the father and whole families, sometimes as many as twenty-five or thirty, dwelt together in one cabin and lived by hunting and fishing. Without wishing to carry the analogy to unseemly lengths, the following quotation is given to help the New York and Newport of the present day to reflect upon their indebtedness to Verrazano, and to pray for other equally generous historians:

> It seemed to us that they had no religion nor laws, nor any knowledge of a first Cause or Mover; that they worshipped neither the heavens, stars, sun, moon, nor other planets; nor could we learn if they were given to any kind of idolatry, or offered any sacrifices or supplications; or if they have temples or houses of prayer in their villages. Our conclusion was that they have no religious belief whatever, but live in this respect entirely free. All of which proceeds from ignorance, as they were very easy to be persuaded, and imitated us with earnestness and fervour in all which they saw us do as Christians in our acts of worship.

The second discoverer of America's first port was Estavan Gomez, who followed Verrazano in the year 1525. Gomez sailed along the Hudson far above the Palisades and gave it the name of *Rio de las Montanas*—River of the Mountains—which for purposes of poetry and promotion would have served modern New York better than its present name, the Hudson. There is no special reason for remembering Gomez except that he represented a rival prospector and that he himself was a promoter from Portugal.

Thus within a period of twelve months we have Italy, France, Spain, and Portugal assuming credit for the discovery of New York; France and Spain through their capital, Italy and Portugal through their promoting acumen. How natural it seemed, from the first, for New York to be a polyglot city of international competition! To the careful student of discoveries, the name of Gomez suggests the earliest "Baedeker" for the American coast. In fact, it was the Gomez map which Hudson used when he threaded the needle's eye into New York Harbour.

The year 1609, an Englishman named Henry Hudson, and Dutch capital are three sides of a triangle which are indelibly associated in the American mind with the discovery of America's first port. This was eleven years before the *Mayflower* landed at Plymouth Rock, and but two years after the first English explorers landed at Jamestown, Virginia.

Hudson soon progressed into the rôle of an international character, for the reason that when English capital had failed and French capital had refused to sustain his enterprise the Dutch East India Company backed him with its money, its commercial power, and its social influence.

The commander of the *Half Moon* had the vision to anticipate the million or more visitors to America's first port, each year, in finding it "a good land to fall in with and a pleasant land to see." The explorer's verdict was that the newly found country was rich in fur-bearing animals, its waters teeming with fish, its soil "the finest for cultivation that I ever in my life set foot upon, *and the situation well adapted for shipping.*" Hudson guessed better than he knew, too, when, upon his return to Holland, he reported that the hills back of this locality, so well adapted for shipping, might contain "mines of precious metals."

Fortunately for America's development, the merchants of Holland saw immediate profits in abundant furs at slight cost and did not waste their capital and their energies in searching for mineral mines. While the year 1613 was noted for six expeditions sent out from Holland, the following year, 1614, when the Dutch Government granted a charter to the United New Netherland Company for the development of what was then, and for forty years thereafter, called New Netherland, marked the real beginning of systematic trade development. A recognized system of exchange was adopted as a result of which so many beads or so much rum were given for a certain number or kind of pelts, e. g., six wampum to a penny, three hundred and sixty beads to a fathom, etc. The trading basis always insured so little to the Indian that the great profits to the Dutch in furs were a growing incentive for increase in their commercial interest and enterprise.

True to their capitalistic type, the parent charter was taken over by a stronger commercial body after the hazard of pioneering days had passed; under it exclusive privileges were given for trading, making treaties, maintaining courts, and employing soldiers.

The famous trade by which these Dutch exploiters secured all title from the Indians to what is now Manhattan Island for about $24 at present rates took place in 1626. It is not surprising that the Indians preferred beads, buttons, and other trinkets instead of gold coin, when we realize that they had no knowledge of the value of gold coin or its equivalent but an aboriginal delight in beads, buttons, and trinkets.

Three facts we should not forget: the first real estate deal in New York City was for value received, a fair exchange and no robbery; the price paid was in goods, and that price was more for its time than any one could get to-day for this same real estate with only Indians inhabiting it.

For fifty years after 1614, when trade began in earnest at this port, it was New Netherland, farmed out by the Dutch Republic to incorporated private capital known as the West India Company. In the year 1619, exports, practically all in furs, totalled $52,000, and goods purchased, mostly in beads, axes, knives, and gaily-coloured clothes, totalled $45,000. Such totals seem small when we realize that the export trade in furs in 1918 amounted to $25,000,000. Nevertheless, they were enormous for a handful of white men dealing with Indians who depended upon hunger as the main incentive to go trapping and upon their wits, rude stones, and primitive wooden devices for catching the game which the white man wanted.

Shy and fickle, then as now, capital wanted some guaranteed permanence, and obtained in 1629 a charter of privileges and exemptions which established a semi-feudal system of patroons, or feudal chiefs, each with his own "estate" and with much coveted exemption from taxation for ten years. Then as now, big business men thought of taxation as a burden rather than as an investment and cheerfully incurred great expense in the effort to avoid taxes and to conceal their ability to pay the same. In return for the title and privileges of patroon, the wealthy merchants of 1629 and later were under contract to "satisfy" the Indians for the land taken; to plant a colony of fifty persons above fifteen years of age within four years; to provide a minister and schoolmaster for the colony as soon as possible and "until that is done a comforter for the sick,"—a forecast of Manhattan's later leadership in house-to-house nursing, reduction of infant mortality by education of mothers, and universal free schools.

Not satisfied with the apron strings which the West India Company assigned to them, the patroons found fur trading more valuable than colonizing, and scoured the adjacent country up the rivers into the woods and along the shores, with the result that they became involved in a long dispute with the holding company; one privilege after another was taken away from them, culminating finally in the recall of Governor Peter Minuit in 1633.

The first professional clergyman and the first professional schoolmaster came in 1633. The importance attributed by historians to the fact that these two gentlemen were properly accredited, makes us wonder if then as now unfrocked clergymen and unlicensed schoolmasters were seeking a market. For no reason connected with the arrival of these two specialists in human conduct, international troubles began in this same year—the English wanted to trade, the Dutch refused a license, international names were called, the English hoisted their flag and defiantly sailed up the river to Fort Orange, now called Albany. A mere layman in history, with some legal training and slight acquaintance with the give and take of politics, wonders what would have happened if the Dutch, instead of forcing this conflict by denial of a license, had, by giving a license, compelled the English to acknowledge the Dutch sovereignty.

Although modern time sheets and other efficiency devices were not yet introduced in their present refinements, it is interesting to know that two different Dutch governors lost their official positions, the first, Van Twiller, 1639, for failing to keep in close touch with his board of directors, omitting to make written reports with due regularity, producing no profits, and failing to respond to complaints and rumours of mismanagement; and the second, Governor Kieft, eight years later in 1647, for alleged unscrupulous management. From all facts obtainable about the business ethics of those days, Kieft's board of directors meant by "unscrupulous management" a supervision that failed to produce bulging profits.

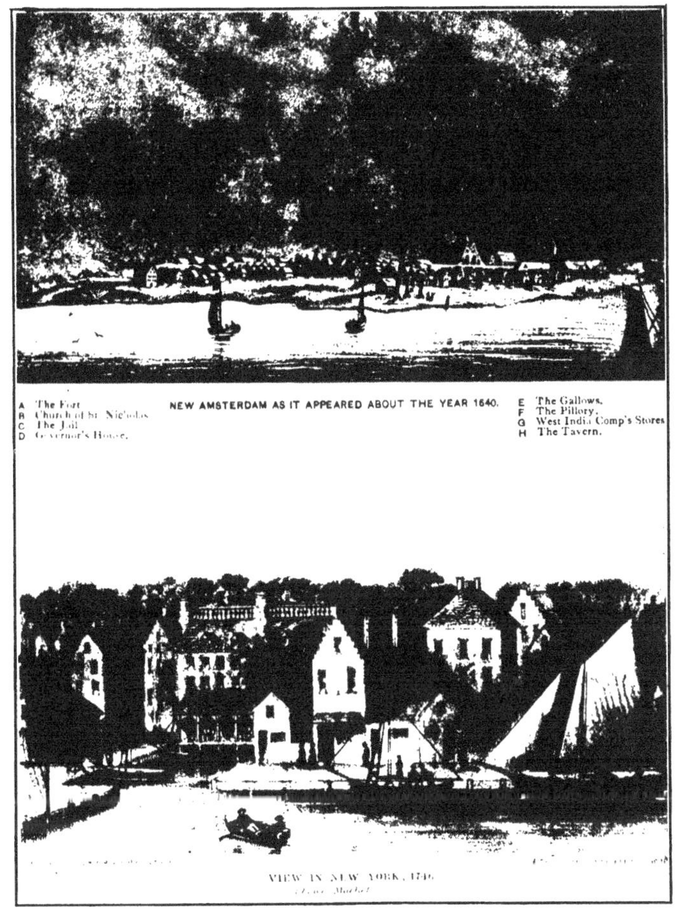

HISTORIC NEW YORK—I

New Amsterdam in 1640 and Lower New York in 1746

HISTORIC NEW YORK—II

McGowan's Pass (located at what was later the northwest corner of Central Park at 110th Street) during the Revolutionary War, and Harlem Bridge in 1861.

By the year 1647, New Amsterdam had approximately 800 inhabitants, not including the near-by Indians. Small in population as the colony seemed, it had Twentieth-Century ideas about self-government, and like the greater population of to-day, watched with jealousy and acquisitive interest the improvements in small hamlets. As Greater New York in our day, with nearly six million people, has gone to Gary, Indiana, with a population of only twenty thousand, for a new school programme, or sought in Dayton, Ohio, for the idea of city manager; so the New Amsterdam of 1647 resented the fact that the new world's metropolis was autocratically governed, while villages beyond the island and across the river were allowed to manage their affairs in town meetings.

When local agitation grew onerous Governor Stuyvesant discovered that he needed the aid of the people; accordingly a representative body, which had earlier been disbanded, was reorganized "in a board of nine men." Then as now authority, jealous of its reputation for originality, found it advisable not to recognize any mistakes. Therefore, instead of taking the original twelve men first requested by the people, or the eight men first granted in 1643, plagiarism was disavowed and prestige protected by choosing nine men. As a matter of fact, the nine men did practically what the eight had done and were just as unwelcome to Peter Stuyvesant.

They had their way, however, in 1653, when magistrates were sworn in and municipalization completed. New Amsterdam was a city; the privilege of moving out of it was granted; surveys of its needs were ordered and within a year, 1654, the first city hall was erected at the corner of Pearl Street and Coenties Slip, a short distance from what was in name as in fact the City Dock. By this time the term city was not a misnomer because there were a little more than a thousand inhabitants. New York's love of monopoly and fear of competition were confessed repeatedly before this year when settlers were permitted "to trade freely with all foreign countries on condition that their vessels should return their cargoes to the Port of New York and that furs should be exported to Holland alone."

Our Dutch forefathers were more particular than present-day taxpayers on the subject of city improvements. In 1662—which, by the way, is the date when New Jersey's side of the harbour officially started on land which now includes Hoboken, Jersey City, and Bayonne—important harbour improvements were made, a small breakwater to protect ships against floating ice and a canal running up to the present location of Broad Street, which was then called the "Heeren-Gracht" or Gentlemen's Canal. When the twenty-one owners of the abutting property were each assessed at three thousand guilders they protested vehemently that they had never asked for the improvement and had never been warned that they must pay for it; because of refusal to pay the tax one or two were imprisoned, but enough refused outright to pay, so that the home company had to assume the expense. Too often indignation shows itself neither by consistent protest nor by the foresight in learning about proposals before it is too late to make the protest effective. The mass meeting method circulates grievances quite rapidly, and this small city insisted that the people who contributed the business were entitled to the rent of the Long Island Ferry, as well as the fees collected at the company's scales, over which all merchandise brought into or carried out of the city had to pass. This bit of history may be sad to relate because it shows that government ownership and municipal ownership are indigenous to Wall Street and American business and are not foreign importations from the Bolsheviki or Soviet movements.

In 1664 military unpreparedness proved an almost fatal luxury; four English men-of-war, carrying a force of several hundred troops, appeared in the harbour and demanded the surrender of New Amsterdam, the fort, the city, the province, and its hinterland.

It was discovered that nearly half the powder in the fort was incombustible; that among his one hundred and fifty regular soldiers and two hundred and fifty of the local volunteer militia Peter Stuyvesant was so unpopular that he could not depend upon them to use even the powder that would explode. He blustered, ordered a defence, distributed spades, shovels, and wheelbarrows, but the business men behind the fort, with an eye to business salvage and personal safety, compelled the fort's surrender. In view of the inexpensive ease of this conquest the victors could afford to be generous to the vanquished and thereupon permitted Stuyvesant and his Dutch soldiers to march out of the city with drums beating and colours flying—August 29, 1664.

The rechristening of the city occurred immediately. The name of New York took the place of that of New Amsterdam, the original name York being derived from the King's older brother and not from an English city; and New

York it has remained, except for a short period of nine years later when the Dutch recovered it and again lost it in 1674. As a matter of fact, the Dutch have never entirely lost their identity in it because Dutch names in New York persist to the present generation, and Dutch commerce has been unremittingly benefited by all improvements in this harbour. From 1664 to 1786 the population of New York increased from approximately fifteen hundred inhabitants to twenty-four thousand inhabitants, and the city from a northern limit of what is now Wall Street, and was then a wall marking the northern boundary, to what is now City Hall Park. Rival cities elsewhere on the new continent also grew up under English dominion during these one hundred and nineteen years and for them the English Government and the English people cherished even a fonder sentiment than for this Dutch step-child.

When the Stars and Stripes were unfurled over the Port of New York, both Boston and Philadelphia led New York in population and commerce. Fortunately for New York, as is shown later, these rival ports refused to indulge in the novelty of running boats by steam, in consequence of which New York attained a decisive lead which quickly became permanent after a New Yorker's statesmanlike project to carry the ocean through the Erie Canal to the Great Lakes had become a reality.

Our present interest in English conquerors of New Amsterdam is exclusively in their treatment of New York as a port. Shipbuilding was started at once; a merchants' exchange was established on a bridge over the canal in Broad Street, which, by the way, was the first time that business here was transacted at regular hours. Fishing and whaling were encouraged and domestic trade with Virginia, Massachusetts, and the West Indies was finally permitted; all of this within ten years by the first English governor, Colonel Francis Lovelace. The second governor, Edmund Andros, saw the future of this commercial centre and gave particular attention to improving the harbour. On December 30, 1675, he procured from his council the adoption of a resolution "that it is a very good and necessary work, not only for ye city, but ye whole government, and of particular benefit to all traders that a harbour be made before ye city of New York." They went further and forbade any one "to cast anchor or grapnet either within or near the sea wall (the present Battery) whereby any vessels might be endangered." For violating this prohibition, a fine of ten shillings was imposed, "halfe to ye town and halfe to ye wharfinger, or havenmeester." Another prohibition that still needs reiteration forbade any person "to cast any dung, dirt, refuse of ye city, or anything to fill up ye harbour, or among ye neighbours (neighbouring shores) under penalty of forty shillings."

The achievements of this "city manager," officially termed Governor of New York, read like the promises of an up-to-date candidate for mayor. Few, indeed, are the municipal or state executives of whatever training or period, of whom biographers can say what has been said of Andros by James Grant Wilson: "He effected a complete reorganization of the militia; repaired the fort and strengthened the defences of the harbour; increased the trade of the province; beautified the city; largely augmented the revenue from the excise; and by a personal supervision of municipal affairs, and an untiring industry gave such a tone to the political and social condition of the people that its effects were apparent fully a century after the period of his incumbency." He built a substantial wharf "convenient for the largest ships to ride at anchor," frankly expressing the opinion that the only wharf they had was not only a disgrace to the city and to the King's government, but an obstruction and a deterrent to trade. He regulated the trade with the Montauk Indians. He permitted ships of all nationalities free access to the Indian tribes of the Hudson far beyond Albany until his principal, the Duke of York, objected to his liberality and forbade all foreigners and even the people of New England from going as far as Esopus or Albany. When, later on, Andros was asked by the King's council for a verbal report, he told them that they must adopt a more liberal policy and even urged the great advantage of trade reciprocity among the different colonies.

Fortunately for the new government the difficulties between New Jersey and New York were threshed out in colonial days. The first open break was in 1678 when an attempt to force all cargoes coming into New York Harbour to enter at the New York Custom House led to friction and resulted in the official seizure by New York customs of all vessels that paid duties at Elizabethtown, New Jersey. The boundary questions were settled by Governor Dongan in 1684. This did not settle the port questions, however, because in 1686 Governor Dongan reported to the home company that the inhabitants of New Jersey were "paying noe Custom, and having likewise the advantage of having better land, and most of the Settlers there out of this Government Wee are like to be deserted by a great many of our Merchants whoe intend to settle there if not annexed to this Government." It was at this time that the Indians left New York because they found a better market in New Jersey, due to the latter's freedom from customs and excise duties. Instead of a New York-New Jersey treaty, such as was proposed in 1919, the competitive method of settling difficulties was adopted, a small fort erected on Sandy Hook, then called Sandy's Hook, and a collector of the port named.

Thus two hundred and thirty years ago we had the nucleus of the present port organization with the recognized steps for docking and for paying taxes, including a collector of the port, and armed forces to enforce the law against smuggling.

To modern Gotham, exercised for years over the question of a garbage disposal plant and aroused in 1919 over the suggestion to substitute incinerator reduction plants for throwing garbage into the sea, it is of passing interest that in 1699 this city of four thousand inhabitants began employing public scavengers. It was high time because both the city and province were sadly "run down at the heels." Waste had interfered with the beaver trade; the port was greatly retarded by factional struggles within the city, English against the Dutch, aristocrats against the common people, Church of England against the Dutch Reformed Church. The improvements instituted under Andros two generations earlier and even the city's defences were already in a state of decay; the military stores were unfit for use; the soldiers' ranks were thinning out and those who remained, insufficiently clothed and equipped. Even public scavengers were some slight consolation for such conditions and for the constant fear of attack by French men-of-war. Long before the benevolent society of Tammany was organized, fifteen hundred pounds, which the state assembly had voted to fortify the Narrows, had been used by the governor to build a country seat on Nutten (now Governor's) Island.

These troubled times, however, proved not to be an ill wind, for they blew to New York immigrants in large numbers, thrifty immigrants coming with agricultural implements and building tools. The new governor in 1710 brought no fewer than three thousand of these Palatines in ten vessels. A waterfront that is receiving immigrants by the thousands will naturally receive special attention for removal of its inconveniences. Staten Island ferry was established in 1713; another ferry from the foot of Cortlandt Street to Jersey followed shortly thereafter.

A frequent disturber of the peace of the harbour, however, was due to the capture of vessels on the high seas by pirates, who, apparently, not satisfied with cruising off shore, actually sailed into the port itself. A deplorable menace to port prosperity and revenue was a slave market opened at the Wall Street slip in the spring of 1711. Only stern fidelity to historical accuracy justifies the admission that there ever was any connection between Wall Street and slave marketing. This great financial street and its intersecting streets soon learned that slave trading had many decided disadvantages, for the traffic increased to such an extent that the white population in the port was in constant dread of revolt by the blacks. Strict laws were passed to prevent them from congregating together or walking out of the prescribed zones.

The first serious attention given to the division of title between what is now the State of New York and what is now the City of New York with respect to land grants included within the Port of New York dates from a grant by Governor Dongan in 1686 under which the State purported to convey all the land between high and low-water mark around the Island of Manhattan, to which was added in 1730 a strip of land four hundred feet wide, lying immediately outside the low-water mark and extending south from Corlear's Hook. This was the first state dock programme and the land was taken for wharfage with the privilege of collecting all dockage fees.

As business progressed and the port's individuality grew, a more complicated organization for supervising the port seemed necessary. Accordingly, on December 13, 1763, an act was passed empowering the governor to appoint one master and three or more other colonists to be wardens of the Port of New York. The duties were substantially the same as they are now: to examine and commission all pilots; to survey all damaged goods on vessels brought into port; to maintain lighthouses and collect tonnage dues; to place and keep in repair such buoys as were thought necessary. This last provision raised a question as to what buoys were necessary to safeguard passage through the Narrows, and the warden's office took immediate steps toward conservation of life and property. "For the safety of vessels coming into and going to sea from the Port of New York, the Master and

Wardens of said port did last week place a large can buoy on the South West spit of the East Bank in eighteen feet water at low-water bearing from the Lighthouse at Sandy Hook," lighted for the first time in 1763.

The office of Port Warden is still a branch of the state government, but the maintenance of lighthouses and buoys and the collecting of tonnage dues have been transferred to Federal jurisdiction.

From the enactment of the English Stamp Act of 1764 to the final departure of the English in 1783, commercial progress practically ceased. The problems of government filled the minds of the royalists and revolutionists alike to the exclusion of all matters of economic policy. Foreign commerce was sidetracked. From protests against "taxation without representation" it was a short step to persistent and continuous demands for home rule, home manufacturing, encouragement of home markets. In these agitations New York was the leader. A decade before the Declaration of Independence New York's merchants countermanded orders for British goods amounting to more than three million dollars; a market for home goods was opened under the exchange in Broad Street; and an organized campaign, or publicity drive as we would call it now, was conducted to stop the use of foreign goods and to insure continuity of coöperation. On April 6, 1765, twenty-four of these home-rule, home-trade spokesmen for a commercial port perfected an organization in the long room at the Queen's Head, now Fraunce's Tavern. This was the first commercial body organized in America and was the legitimate ancestor of our present Chamber of Commerce.

Thus by 1783 the Port of New York, twice born, thrice christened, and variously nurtured through three centuries of growing pains, had reached the stature of twenty-four thousand inhabitants, with an annual trade of ten million dollars. Although second in size to Philadelphia with a population of forty thousand her then surveyor of the dock credits her with receiving and transporting more than six hundred ships in 1770 to Hamburg and Holland alone; with shipping cargoes of wood, corn, flour, and rum to London and Madeira; with sending provisions to the Spanish Main; with exporting bread, peas, rye, Indian corn, horses, sheep, beef, pork, and at least eighty thousand barrels of flour to the West Indies in return for rum, sugar, and molasses. In short, New York had attained the distinction of being "a place of great resort and of very exclusive commerce."

CHAPTER III

Forward Steps Under the Stars and Stripes

WHEN the British evacuated the City of New York one fourth of its area was covered with the blackened ruins of buildings swept by the great fire of 1776, and with temporary wooden huts which had housed the soldiers. The débris of army life was left scattered all over the city. Business had to be reconstructed from the very foundation. It took several years to make an appreciable start because of political and factional differences among the people. Still by 1785 the city was rebuilt and afforded the newly organized Federal Government fairly adequate accommodations.

During the one year when New York was designated as the new nation's capital, the city showed a steadily progressive public spirit. Her dependence upon the State Legislature, even for the exercise of the ordinary municipal privileges, is shown by the charters of the Chamber of Commerce and King's University in the early days. To the first organization the Legislature granted a charter as the Chamber of Commerce of the State of New York; to the second it conferred a charter changing the first name from "King's University" to "Columbia University." This was the period, too, which gave birth to the contentious spirit surviving apparently to the present day between the Board of Estimate of the city and our Board of Education on the subject that education is a state and not a city function. It was in 1789 that a state constitutional convention established the University of the State of New York and provided for state support and establishment of free schools.

Remember that we are describing now a small city whose directory gave only nine hundred individual and firm names actually engaged in commercial enterprises. Nevertheless, in those days the population of 24,000 in one small area made a city of considerable size. While to a great extent the wish may have been father to the thought, it is nevertheless true that the conferences of business men arranged to debate the port's future and their own prospects began to discuss the natural advantages of this port: its accessibility to the farming and trapping lands, northward and westward; and its destiny as a centre for manufacturing, trading, and shipping;

HISTORIC NEW YORK—III

Franklin Market, Old Slip, in 1820, and South Street in 1828

HISTORIC NEW YORK—IV
Cortlandt Street Ferry in 1835, and Jackson Street Ferry in 1861

at any rate, they plunged actively into the development of the port's business, an evidence of which appeared in 1784 when they founded a bank and secured legislation to impose specific duties and establish a custom house.

From the position of the fourth city in importance on this side of the Atlantic, between 1791 and 1800 New York began to outdistance her competitors, gaining first position in 1800. The value of her exports during that decade was $96,000,000. Pennsylvania was a close second with export values estimated at $95,000,000; Maryland, $80,000,000, and Massachusetts, $70,000,000.

In 1787 a great tide of immigration swept the city forward, giving a new impetus to building and other civic improvements. "The streets were cleaned and pavements mended. New business firms were organized and old warehouses remodelled; the markets were extended and bountifully supplied with produce, and stores were filled with fashionable goods. Wall Street, the great centre of interest and of fashion, presented a brilliant scene every bright afternoon."

Progress was not entirely unimpeded, however. The French Revolution, not only commercially, but also politically, had a pronouncedly disturbing effect upon New York. Differences of opinion on the subject of neutrality resulted in the organization of parties more or less violent in their attitude toward each other. People were even harshly critical of the President for not taking sides, and more or less openly tried to arouse public opinion to bring pressure to bear upon him. England added fuel to the fire by an order intended to bring France to terms through starvation, but which reacted with greater force upon American commerce than upon French statesmen. The perils to shipping that arose from this order impelled the United States Government, on March 24, 1794, to declare an embargo of three days on all foreign-bound vessels, to increase the regular military force, and to mobilize 80,000 additional troops.

New York, of course, was vitally affected by all these happenings, and, naturally, found it difficult to decide just how the situation ought to be handled. Further complications arose in 1795 when an epidemic of yellow fever spread through the city from a British frigate entering the harbour with several cases of the disease on board. Although many of the citizens withdrew to the country districts, 732 deaths occurred, and much destitution followed; a new almshouse was completed in this year in Chambers Street, described as "of special use in the emergency," and shortly afterward reported to contain 622 paupers. There was an opportunity, however, to start a library which soon gained one thousand members and five thousand books—the New York Society library, which was then far up town on Nassau Street at the corner of Cedar Street. Public education was encouraged by a state appropriation of $50,000 for the maintenance of free schools for a period of five years.

The year 1795 is a red letter date for this port, because in that year, June 24th, the Jay Treaty was signed which marked the country's admission as a nation "into the world's fraternity of commerce." The immediate effect upon this port was an enormous increase in export trade which had been doubled in 1794 and redoubled in 1795.

By the year 1800 New York had more than 60,000 people, more than twice the number it inherited from the English in 1783, and showed its prosperity by a tearing up and littering of streets in the same manner which has characterized it since it passed its five million mark. Buildings were being erected everywhere; old buildings were being remodelled; streets were opened and improved and sidewalks laid; "the most eligible situation for commerce in the

United States" was credited to it. A contemporary gave his evidence that it was then "importing most of the goods consumed in the best peopled area of the whole country, which contains at least eight hundred thousand persons or one fifth of the inhabitants of the Union." Its reputation abroad earned it the name of the "Tyre of the New World." To foster and to advance with this commerce, there were already three banks, three insurance companies, more than a dozen newspapers, several trade organizations, and hundreds of large private business concerns. Docks were lined with sloops which sailed up the Hudson and along the Sound. A large fishing fleet made its headquarters in the port and each year showed enormous exports of dried and salted fish.

The steamboat, of which New York has been called the cradle, first proved to be a commercial possibility for general travel in 1808, and the Erie Canal, known to be inevitable after 1792 and finally completed in 1825, fixed New York's supremacy. The story of the *Clermont*, designed by Robert Fulton and run from New York to Albany in thirty-two hours in 1807, is known to all Americans. For reducing the time required by sail from four or six days to one and a third days, Fulton and *Clermont* deserve our undying gratitude. For proving that the ocean had no terrors or difficulties which steam could not overcome, by shortening the time from New York to Philadelphia by the sea route, Colonel John Stevens of Hoboken and his *Phoenix* deserve equal credit in the annals of American commerce. Students of business and government may go a step farther, however, and in gracious appreciation place in the halls of fame a model of the little steamboat, eighteen feet long, with a six-foot beam and a twelve-gallon iron pot for a boiler, which, eleven years before Fulton's test, at the rate of six miles an hour steamed around the little toy pond called the "Collect" on the site now occupied by the Tombs prison. New York's interest in John Fitch's demonstration in 1796 as well as her encouragement of the practical application of the achievements of Fulton and Stevens, entitles her to be called the "cradle of steam navigation."

Steamboats up the Hudson, steam ferries to Hoboken, Jersey City, and Brooklyn, steamships to Philadelphia meant a future for steam propulsion of international commerce on all oceans. For the inevitable demands to be made upon it, New York levelled her hills and filled her hollows; laid out new streets scientifically and with sound judgment, parallel east and west, parallel north and south, distinguished from one another by numbers and letters. The toy pond upon which the first steamboat was "demonstrated" was drained, filled in, and "bordered on either side by shade trees and a pleasant street," which is our present wide and busy Canal Street. Lest the people of our day be short-sighted in our city planning and nation planning, let us remember that as early as 1789 it was proposed "to make a public park of this beautiful pond and its shores," but the scheme was abandoned. It was the belief "that New York would never grow within accessible distance of this lonely region," which is now almost the geographic centre of a population of six million souls, and is "way down town" to three million New Yorkers.

Three times between the years 1800 and 1919 America's first port was to have all commerce stopped, and to again be given an idea of what it means to be a seaport without access to the sea. The Napoleonic wars greatly curtailed the business of the port, while the embargo act passed by Congress in 1813 practically ended it. Thereafter, until the close of the War of 1812, building trade gave way to building forts. With volunteer labour new lines of defence were erected on Brooklyn and Hoboken Heights and a garrison of twenty-three thousand men, mostly of state troops, was mobilized to hold them. Experiments with the application of steam to war vessels promptly convinced Congress, so that in 1814 they appropriated $320,000 for the construction of a vessel launched the next year, which in its trial trip to Sandy Hook proved to be unqualifiedly successful. A second time during the Civil War from 1861 to 1865, and again during the recent World War from 1914 to 1918, New York learned what it meant to have undeliverable freight congesting its docks and railroad terminals and its business with the outer world seriously impeded.

From the close of the War of 1812, more particularly with the signing of peace on Christmas Eve, 1814, a period of prosperity began in American shipping and in New York's commercial leadership. First to adopt steam and first to be free to deal with Europe's warring nations, New York like all of our other ports, but particularly New York, grew by leaps and bounds; stores and warehouses, shipping yards and factories multiplied, and ships imported from and exported to the other nations of the world a business rapidly growing in volume and profits. The war with England had taught America the value of home manufacture; and New York was quick to profit by the lesson. Factories of many kinds were opened; demands for their products were augmented by the great tide of immigration which swept in from Europe. Enormous importations of merchandise from Europe beginning in 1816 gave this port a tremendous impetus. During the first period of canal construction from 1817 to 1837, when the State of New York spent ten million dollars in that constructive work—almost the identical amount which had in that same time been spent for public schools—the New York Custom House paid to the United States Treasury $64,000,000 in duties on imposts and tonnage.

The opening of the Erie Canal October 26, 1825, would have given New York predominance among American ports even had it been occupied at that time by only a trade post instead of by a population of 200,000. It was not merely that the Erie Canal was the largest canal in the world, had cost $10,000,000, and had been built without a single day's cessation of work between July 4, 1817, and October, 1825. The canal marked a new era in the history of this port and in the history of America, because it began that which the new barge canal, opening nearly one hundred years later, would completely guarantee, namely, continuous cheaper water transportation from America's richest, most fertile and most productive areas to the markets of the world.

In 1831 the New York & Harlem River Railroad was chartered. Although only a "horse-railroad" it attracted attention as a novelty and served its purpose as a convenience, until it was absorbed in the Hudson River road in 1851. By this time the $33,000,000 which the State of New York had expended on the Erie Canal was already paying big dividends. During this period the freight carried through the Erie Canal to the Port of New York amounted to 10,000,000 tons and was already greater than that at any other port in the world except London. Any day in the year, a writer of the times said, "five hundred vessels could be counted discharging in the docks, or at anchor in the stream. From foreign ports nearly two thousand vessels arrived annually, while twice and a half of that number, engaged in the coastwise trade, ran in and out at the same time." And yet in 1918, at the height of our war commerce, when the whole world needed our foods and merchandise, we were proud of the fact that eight hundred vessels of different nations were used in transporting our troops!

In 1832 New York's payments to Uncle Sam on imports totalled $15,100,000, a little less than two thirds of the total for the remainder of the country ($28,300,000), while in 1918 we had in New York 63.51 per cent. of the entire revenue of the United States.

Out of the calamitous fire of 1835, which raged for three days over an area of fifteen acres and destroyed property worth eighteen million dollars (a trifle more than the loss of the Equitable Insurance Building in 1912), New York learned many lessons and gained many benefits. First, it set about securing a better water supply and constructed the Croton Aqueduct which began to deliver water in 1845. This improvement like its successors, the Catskill and Ashokan Dam developments, secured the port not only against devastating fires but also in helping to prevent equally devastating contagion. Economic historians, by the way, declare that New York's losses from the conflagration of 1835 contributed greatly to the business depression which resulted in the panic of 1837.

The telegraph, the invention of which is too seldom credited to the University of the City of New York, where Professor Morse did his experimental work, and the opening of the first trunk line railroad, the Erie, from New York to Dunkirk in 1851, marked the beginning of two other methods of communication, for which the

Port of New York has later become a national, continental, and world centre. The combination of an unequalled port and unequalled communication by electricity, telegraph, telephone, cable, and rail cannot be excelled. Whatever the new communication through the air accomplishes for commerce, it will utilize the combination of port, railroad, telegraph, and telephone found at their greatest and best degree of efficiency in this port.

The Golden Age of American shipping, at least the first Golden Age, began in the Napoleonic wars and had its climax in 1859, when we had a total tonnage of three and one half million and led the world as shown in the subsequent chapter on Merchant Marine. New York had more than a fair share of this total tonnage and even of the cotton trade to which the ports of New Orleans and Baltimore still offered superior advantages. While the city suffered from privateering and from more disastrous interruptions of trade, she still gained by the blockade which closed the Southern ports. This is proved by the fact that in the year following the war, when the blockade was lifted, New York's commerce dropped $75,000,000, that is, from $229,000,000 to $154,000,000. This increased rapidly, however, until in 1917 its imports and exports were

$3,978,856,464 more than they were before the war in 1860. An inglorious Wooden Age after the Golden Age followed, the story of which is told in another chapter. After substituting iron for wood, we have still to awaken to the fact that leadership must be earned each year anew.

As shown in the chapter on Merchant Marine, while generally commerce in merchant ships rapidly lost ground, the commerce from the Port of New York continued to grow because it utilized all the artificial advantages of capital and business coöperation above enumerated. The transatlantic cable brought us into direct communication with Europe, facilitating the present great system of commercial coöperation which began in 1865.

By the year 1880 New York City's population had increased to two and a half million people.

The electric trolleys, elevated railroads, and subways have taken the place of horse cars; public and private improvements followed one another until the 1920 census will find here a population of six millions, manufacturing interests of enormous magnitude, the centre of education, transportation, communication with the western world, and a sailing port for most of the world's largest steamship lines.

One important achievement in the present century has had a far-reaching effect upon this port, namely, the opening of the Panama Canal in 1914. Thus we return to the first chapter of our book and the search of Verrazano and Hudson for a route to Cathay. An all-water route from any port in the world to every port in the world is now possible through the Panama Canal. Its physical possibilities and commercial advantages enrich the whole world, and not only strengthen all American ports, but also add to the advantages of America's first port—New York.

CHAPTER IV

Piracy and Privateering Abolished

SMUGGLING, to use the language of the underworld, is a "confidence game" or "sneak-thieving," while piracy and privateering might be classified with the activities of "gunmen" and "second-story" burglarizing. Had this chapter been written in the summer of 1914, it would have been necessary to explain the words piracy and privateering. Thanks to thrilling exploits of German sea rovers, later turned into the universal horror of unrestricted submarine warfare, which, like the thug with dagger and bludgeon, springs upon an unsuspecting victim, even American children now know what is meant by piracy and privateering.

To its profit, if not to its credit, America's first port is indelibly identified in the minds of pirate-loving school boys with that best-known of all pirates, Captain William Kidd. As a matter of fact, Captain Kidd owes his fame as much to the pronounceability of his name and to his alleged respectability as to genuine piratical performances. Those who believe that every child is entitled to a short period when above all things he would like to be a pirate like Captain Kidd, really sympathize with the juveniles who suffer great disappointment when they learn the truth about Captain Kidd, namely, that he did not want to be a pirate, never was even a "fifty-fifty" pirate, denied being a pirate, and like some of our up-to-date American revolutionists when haled to court, begged for a chance to prove that he was only faking. Nevertheless, the fact remains that Kidd belongs to America's first port, anchored his ship but a few miles down the Sound, and to this day haunts the northern coast of Long Island, every bit of which has been searched by beach combers for the treasures which a man of his reputation ought to have had. The New York *Tribune* brings the piracy of Captain Kidd pertinently before the Twentieth-Century restaurateurs in an editorial:

Kidd Born Too Early

How fitting it is in a world where things seldom happen as they should that Captain Kidd's old home at Hanover and Pearl streets may be leased by a restaurant! There is always a sentimental interest in seeing property of any sort kept in the family, and here New Yorkers can now enjoy beholding lineal descendants conducting in the old homestead the same business, generally speaking, as that pursued so energetically by their late fellow townsman.

It is evident that times change, and codes of morality with them. Once the world so misunderstood the enterprise and business acumen of the captain that, after making life miserable for him with men-o'-war for five years, in 1701 it finally rounded him up and hanged him in chains in London. But Captain Kidd simply was unlucky to have lived when he did. . . .

Alas! for him, though, he did not wait till to-day to live. And if, reading that his old home may be leased by a restaurant, he should think of coming back to see how the venture progresses, he would be well advised to stay away. Nothing but humiliation could result for him. Were he to come back for a day and march into a restaurant for dinner, as like as not when the bill was presented and he had a good chance to look it over he would feel compelled to go to the management.

"Son-of-a-pirate" is a modern epithet, inelegant but expressive. With the greatest respect for all that New York is, we may still with strict accuracy call her a "daughter-of-a-privateer"; she was found by a pirate. Had Verrazano been captured by Spain, he would have been hanged as a pirate, in spite of his royal partnership with Francis I of France.

From Verrazano's day, 1524, to the present, there have been several war periods when piracy was legitimatized as privateering, and several other periods which accompanied, preceded, and followed war, when piracy was legitimatized only in that esteem which pays obeisance to success.

The first immigrants to New York were Belgian refugees who came out under the Dutch West India Company for the purpose of capturing Spanish treasure from Mexico, and thus repay the Spanish king who had driven them out of their own land. Under the more respectable name of privateering even kings and bishops then joined in the noble sport of piracy; in fact, Captain Kidd's main defence was that he was not acting for himself, but for a company of thoroughly respectable English and American business men and thoroughly respectable nobility and royalty who had fitted out his expedition with the understanding that embarrassing questions would not be asked. Kidd's trouble came from pirating on his own backers instead of pirating for them, that is, to use the vulgar term of our criminal courts, he "held out" on his "side partners."

Seamen credentialed by Peter Stuyvesant in 1647, ostensibly for privateering, actually violated international law and captured a peaceful Spanish vessel in the Caribbean Sea and unblushingly stole "pieces-of-eight and pearls." This was sheer piracy. In fact, the court so considered it, but in view of the necessity of sending a ship to Curacao for a cargo of salt, pardoned the criminals "with the forfeiture of their prize money." After the treaty of Westphalia, 1648, there was no such thing as legitimate privateering by the West India Company, and what was called privateering was undeniable piracy.

New York has the distinction of being the only state which can boast a governor known to have taken part in piracy. This was Governor Fletcher of 1692, who gave commissions to ships to sail the seas ostensibly in behalf of Britannia but actually for the seizure of precious fabrics, spices, gold, and gems from the opulent marts of the Orient, which were taken down to Madagascar Island; there, some putative respectable and honest merchant would act as a "fence" or "receiver of stolen goods," and return to New York with the flag of respectability flying and with no evidence of piracy whatever appearing in the transaction. It was because of the crass stupidity with which he played this game that Captain Kidd came to his ignominious end on a gibbet.

In 1756 there were forty privateers using New York Harbour as a base. In the next twelve years, sixty-nine prizes came into the port and thirty-six condemned ships to other ports. What they thought of their life may be judged by the names they gave to their vessels: the *Dragon*, the *Charming Peggy*, the *Brave Hawk*, *Who'd Have Thought It*, the *Impertinent*, the *Wheel of Fortune*, vessels described by the historian as "small, graceful craft, well armed and well manned, prepared to pounce on the unprotected merchant ships like a falcon on the dove." Between 1704 and 1763 there were no fewer than 185 of these falcons seeking doves; in fact, many of the economic and social fortunes of the present day which determine prestige in Gotham society trace their origin to privateers just as America's shipping goes back to privateering boards and profits.

After our Revolutionary War and during the Napoleonic wars American seamen actually built up the American marine on the business of privateering. At the time of the French and Indian wars, the colonists on the seaboard had already learned that capturing enemy's ships paid good dividends.

So aggressive were our Revolutionary seamen that Lord Howe was seriously criticized for suffering "the rebel merchants to carry on a constant and extensive trade with all their ports," and for failing to permit and to help the Loyalists at New York to destroy the rebel ships in this port. By no means were these rebels satisfied with the profits obtainable in American waters, but were constantly harassing British merchants in the European seas, an example which the Loyalists themselves first envied and subsequently emulated by securing royal commissions to fit out their own privateering expeditions. The Loyalist governor issued as many as one hundred commissions to as many private vessels of war.

It was a privateer, Paul Jones, who established the fighting reputation of the United States Navy, which to this day prides itself on the fact that however doubtful the outcome may seem, "we have just begun to fight." How worthily have our Marines emulated our first admiral, even to epigrammatic sentiments of their song:

> Here's health to you and to our corps,
> Which we are proud to serve,
> In many a strife we have fought for life,
> And never lost our nerve;
> If the Army and the Navy
> Ever look on Heaven's scenes,
> They will find the streets are guarded by
> UNITED STATES MARINES.

Privateering, whether in the Revolutionary War, during the Napoleonic wars, in the War of 1812, or in the Civil War, was profitable only to the privateer. Legitimate shipping clings to shelter, wherever there are privateers, for the business of privateering is to make profits by capturing enemy shipping and not by the protection of home shipping. One of the great accomplishments of the last century is that privateering has been suppressed to a vanishing point, although interrupted for a time by Germany's use of the submarine. The treaty negotiated with Frederick the Great, of Prussia, in 1795, deserves perpetual radiance because it was this document repeated later with England and then with other countries by which the seizure of private property at sea, except contraband of war, has been mutually prohibited. The final agreement of nations to this abolition of seizure was the Declaration of Paris in 1856.

During the Civil War, New York's commerce suffered considerable loss because of Confederate privateering. The *Alabama* and other Confederate ships, which the North insisted upon calling "piratical craft," were fitted out in British ports to prey upon Northern merchantmen. The Chamber of Commerce in New York warned their British colleagues "that the repetition of such acts would not fail to produce widespread exasperation in this country." And such exasperation was produced, and a state of feeling toward Great Britain was developed because of the unfriendly motive which was imputed to England in permitting Southern privateers to fit out ships in their ports, which threatened war and was only appeased by the *Alabama* Arbitration and its results.

Privateering in the recent World War was the subject of much concern in this country, and particularly in the Port of New York, because Great Britain by its Orders in Council asserted the right to stop all ships at sea, neutral or otherwise, suspected of carrying merchandise to or from Germany, although admittedly no actual blockade was declared or maintained. The American Government, while it was neutral, protested against these orders, but after it entered the war on the side of the Allies, nothing more was heard of the protests.

One very successful method of meeting the piratical attacks of the German submarines was by camouflaging our vessels, a description of which appeared in the March (1919) number of the *National Marine* as follows:

Baffling the Undersea Pirate

The World War brought no stranger spectacle than that of a convoy of steamers plowing along through the middle of the ocean streaked and bespotted indiscriminately with every colour of the rainbow in a way far more bizarre than the wildest dreams of a sailor's first night ashore.

Every American ship going across was ordered camouflaged. The Allied nations gave similar orders. So one seldom saw a ship at sea, except neutral vessels, that was not camouflaged in some way. After a good look at them you could see why the sea serpent had the best season last summer he has had since the lamented death of the Baron Münchausen.

Many people seem to be under the impression that the sole purpose of camouflaging a ship was the same as that of the land camouflage used by the army for its guns. That idea is quite erroneous. The purpose of marine camouflage was not to decrease the visibility of a ship at sea—in fact, the bright whites used so frequently in camouflage sometimes made a ship much more prominent than if the neutral grays had been used.

The purpose of the camouflage was to deceive the submarine as to the true course and speed of a ship. It was intended to, and did, upset the calculations of the U-boat commander in determining the right time and place to come to the surface or to fire a torpedo at a possible victim. It often resulted in a submarine emerging in the wrong place where it could not launch a torpedo successfully and was perhaps discovered and trapped.

The effect of good camouflage was remarkable. I have often looked at a ship in the convoy sailing on our quarter and on exactly the same course with us, but on account of her camouflage she appeared to be making right for us on a course at least forty-five degrees off from the one she was actually steering. The deception was remarkable even under such conditions as these and, of course, a U-boat with its necessarily hasty and limited observation was much more likely to be deceived.

Each nation seemed to have a characteristic type of camouflage and after a little practice you could usually spot a ship's nationality by her style of camouflage long before you could make out her ensign. It was no uncommon sight to see vessels bound toward us stern first. The deception was created by the use of false sterns, false bows, and dummy smokestacks and masts. Devices to deceive during the war were legion and that they were successful was evident when the Hun underseas fleet was interned at Harwich underneath the guns of the Grand Fleet.

R. A. Fulton, late Paymaster Lieutenant R.N.V.R., who held official position with the British Convoys, tells us, in an address before the Marine Insurance Club of New York on May 13, 1919, how German piracy was beaten by the convoy plan:

At the beginning of 1915 Germany declared a blockade of Great Britain and Ireland. She declared that on and after February 18th every hostile merchant vessel sighted round the British Isles would be destroyed. She extended also her warning to neutrals, advising them of the danger incurred if found in the so-called "prohibited zone." Germany, however, was kind enough to permit neutral vessels to proceed around the Shetlands, and a special lane to Falmouth was another example of her graciousness. She tried hard, in a manner befitting the Hun, to effectually carry out this blockade, but the whole thing, as far as the blockade was concerned, was a farce and quickly developed into piratical raids of fiendish brutality against the legitimate commerce of the world. The Huns, realizing their failure, later redoubled their efforts, and this increased activity in submarine warfare made it necessary to evolve some scheme to beat the devil at his hellish game, and in

1917 the convoy system was started. While the convoying of merchant ships has been in existence for many years, this was the first organized movement from this side of the Atlantic.

Before the entry of the United States into the war, it was necessary for British ships from these ports to join convoys sailing from Canada. After America's entry the work was greatly facilitated by our being able to send convoys from ports in the United States. Later the Americans got into the convoy game themselves. My remarks on the subject apply to convoys to Europe trans-atlantic, and for you to grasp a slight idea of the magnitude of this work I would point out that ships had to be collected from Canada to Mexico—specially loaded, routed, and equipped. On an average no less than fifty ships a week were dispatched in our convoys from New York alone, and in all nearly 15,000,000 tons of food, ammunition, and supplies, as well as nearly 70 per cent. of the glorious American Army, were safely convoyed across the Atlantic.

In the work of preparing a convoy before sailing, many things had to be attended to. The speed of the ships had to be carefully gone into (this meant systematic inquiries and examinations of logs); we had to be sure she was capable of maintaining a certain speed; the destination was an extremely important item, as well as the cargo, the loading of which on all ships was carefully supervised, and the utmost cubic capacity utilized. Every ship had to be down to her marks with no available space left on board. This was all done against time, for we never allowed a ship to lose an hour if it was possible to prevent it. The question of bunkering was also given careful attention. The consumption of each ship per day at a certain draft on a certain quality of coal had to be carefully worked out. We knew how long she would take on the voyage and, leaving a safe margin, we allowed her to load only so much bunker coal, leaving the balance of what she was capable of carrying to be devoted to cargo capacity of her holds.

You are all aware that you could load a ship down to her marks with heavy deadweight cargo and still leave plenty of space in her 'tween decks—that is what we had to guard against—she had to be full and we had to adjust various commodities accordingly. The interviewing of all captains took considerable time, and everything had to be explained to them. The navy practises manœuvres at sea—a merchant marine had never attempted it. We had to manœuvre a convoy at times in the face of the gravest peril, and they all had to be efficient at the job. Before sailing the wireless was examined and tested, and the gun or guns she carried had to be carefully gone over. Her otters or paravanes, if she carried such, had also to be given our attention.

Just before sailing the captains of the various ships in that particular convoy, to which they had been allocated, met at the convoy office and the whole thing was carefully gone over again. They would receive plans or diagrams of the convoy and their relative positions in it. They would receive not only instructions from the port convoy officer stationed at this port (under whom I had the pleasure of serving), but also from the senior naval officer in charge of the escorting ship or ships, as well as from the commodore, placed on board of one and in charge of the ships themselves.

The work of the Merchant Marine was carried out in a quiet manner. No press representative was present at the numerous scraps to tell through the columns of the periodicals of the heroic efforts of the lumbering tramp against the piratical, bloodthirsty Hun. Fighting to a finish with the ship sinking beneath them, their boats shot away, their decks riddled with shrapnel, their one and only gun blown to pieces—then struggling for their very lives in the water, with the hounds of hell, after jeering at their battle with death, leaving them to their fates. The survivors always received the most careful attention, but even after all this they were not allowed to tell the public of these heroic efforts which would have thrilled the world. The movements of the ships were kept secret and in view of the value of such information to the enemy, the Navy would not permit of any information being given out. One of the worst examples of the Huns' damnable methods was in the case of the *Belgian Prince*, in June, 1917, of which, no doubt, you have all heard. The submarine approached the ship unseen and fired a torpedo, which struck her in the engine room. The engines were immediately put out of commission and the wireless rendered useless. The officers and crew took to the boats and the submarine, breaking surface, ordered them alongside. They were all transferred to her deck, while the Germans destroyed their boat and threw away their life preservers. After questioning and abusing the officers and men, the Germans climbed down into their submarine, the hatch was closed, and gradually she began to move. Slowly she dipped her bow and gradually began to submerge; then, with increasing speed, she disappeared beneath the waves. I shall not burden you with the struggles of the poor souls on her decks. Fortunately, three were able to pick up life belts or wreckage, and these were the only survivors of a crew of more than forty.

It is all very well to be safely tucked away behind heavy armour, a full complement to man the guns—with every device invented to frustrate the Hun but your tramps put to sea with the officers and crew knowing full well that if a Hun spotted them they would have a poor chance. Yet, they carried out their work nobly. They challenged the Hun every time they left harbour and having been torpedoed, they went out again as soon as it was possible to put them on another ship. Their scraps with submarines have added glory to their service. I can assure you that in the great drama of war, in which I believe nearly forty nations took speaking parts, and on the last scene of which the curtain is now falling, the splendid scraps put up by the Allied Merchant Marine were alone well worth the price of admission. . . .

The following account of the sinking of the U.S.S. *Ticonderoga* with a loss of 103 men, on September 30, 1918, is given by the Navy Department:

The U. S. S. *Ticonderoga* sailed from Norfolk for France on September 22, 1918, with a general cargo. She was commanded by Lieut. Comdr. J. J. Madison. At 5:30 A.M., September 30, 1918, a submarine was sighted which immediately commenced shelling her. The first shell set the vessel afire amidships, put the steering gear and wireless apparatus out of commission. The continued firing destroyed the forward gun, killed most of the gun crew, and wounded the Captain. The *Ticonderoga* opened fire with her aft gun and the submarine withdrew to a distance of four miles, but continued shelling. At that time there were but approximately fifty men left on board who were not killed or badly wounded. The life boats were riddled with bullets and the falls broken so that when attempts were made to lower the boats the occupants were thrown into the water and drowned. The survivors in the boats that were successfully launched were made targets of by the submarine, so that but one life boat, containing the Captain and a small number of the soldiers, was saved. A life raft with five wounded lashed to it and seven or eight men was launched by the Second Officer, as the upper deck was at this time awash with the sea. The submarine, after silencing the *Ticonderoga's* guns, fired a torpedo which caused her sinking shortly after.

The submarine came alongside the life boat, questioned the men and asked for the Captain. Medical aid was requested of the submarine but refused. On being told that the Captain was dead, the boat was tied to the submarine, which started off at full speed but the occupants were saved by the parting of the rope. The life raft was shelled but not hit. The Executive Officer was picked up out of the water and the First Assistant Engineer taken from the raft and both were made prisoners on board the submarine.

Later the life boat came near the raft. The Second Officer and a few of the men swam to the life boat and climbed aboard. They then tried for four hours to pick up the raft but on account of a change in the wind these attempts were unsuccessful and the men on the raft were lost.

The submarine remained in sight until 4 A. M. the next day. The boat load of twenty survivors were at sea four days and nights and were eventually picked up by the British S. S. *Moorish Prince* and later transferred to the *Grampion* and landed at New York. They were all very weak and the Captain was in an extremely critical condition.

While other nations did not brutally defy conventions and treaties on the ground which Germany cited to justify invasion of Belgium and the use of unrestricted submarine warfare, the fact remains that convention or no convention, treaty or no treaty, war means piracy and privateering with inevitable interruption and destruction of commerce; that the world's greatest port, New York, and the business world which uses New York must find protection against piracy and privateering by preventing war.

If preventive measures fail us, the conclusion of Herbert Sidebotham, formerly military and naval critic of the Manchester *Guardian* and now service critic of the London *Times*, may still save us, namely, "maintenance of the power to punish an enemy for gross infraction of the law of war and of humanity."

There remains still one salient fact about our merchant marine's future—*neither the World War nor the League of Nations Covenant, nor agreements between America and Britain has reconciled or fused the policies and beliefs of the two empires respecting freedom of the seas.*

Mr. Sidebotham has recently drafted for the *Atlantic Monthly*, of June, 1919, an "imaginary agreement which will reconcile the American and the British traditions of the sea." This imaginary agreement is repeated here to help readers think constructively of one great problem which remains to be dealt with radically:

ARTICLE 1. The law of naval warfare in the future shall vary according as the war is waged with the sanction of the League of Nations, or without its sanction. Wars waged with the sanction of the League are hereinafter styled public wars, and those waged without such sanction, private wars.

ARTICLE 2. In public wars, the full blockade, as practiced by the Allies in this war, shall be permitted. Such wars being waged in defence of the common law of humanity, neutrals have an equal interest with the belligerents in securing their just determination, and they shall therefore contract to give no assistance to the enemy by land or sea, directly or indirectly, but shall enforce a pacific blockade against him.

ARTICLE 3. In private wars, the operations of blockade shall be restricted to the enemy's naval ports and to the service of actual operations against the enemy's armed forces. Commercial blockade in private wars is hereby declared to be abolished, and there shall be full liberty of commercial intercourse between belligerents and neutrals, subject only to the prohibition of trade in contraband of war.

ARTICLE 4. The only lists of contraband which are binding on neutrals shall be lists drawn up by a naval committee attached to the permanent secretariat of the League of Nations, and such lists shall be revised from time to time.

ARTICLE 5. Sinking of merchantmen by belligerents is prohibited, unless it be the only means of preventing a breach of blockade legally established. Merchantmen are good prizes of war only in execution of a judgment of the International Prize Court.

ARTICLE 6. Where ships or cargoes are neutral property, they shall in all cases before condemnation be adjudicated upon by the International Court.

ARTICLE 7. The International Court shall be set up by the Executive of the League of Nations and shall be a permanent part of its machinery.

Not the least interesting of the proponent's reasons for these suggestions is that the same general principles "can also be applied to operations of the belligerents in the air!"

CHAPTER V

Eternal Vigilance Against Smugglers

It is an axiomatic truth that excessive taxation produces extensive smuggling. That is one phase of American history which we should not forget. The Boston Tea Party was the end of a period of smuggling provoked by extortionate import taxes when, to paraphrase Breckenridge's statement of 1861 regarding treason, evaders were numerous enough to make evasion appear to be respectable. Smuggling just before the Revolutionary War was not merely an evasion of taxes, but was a retaliatory act carried out with a fanatical bravado that culminated in the Boston Tea Party. The King's officers often connived at smuggling, while, like the three sacred monkeys of Japan, they saw no evil, heard no evil, spoke no evil. It was not an unknown thing for vessels to unload by day and by night at a cove on Staten Island within a mile of Amboy, where there was a customs representative who made no pretense at molestation. The customs duties of the time were especially

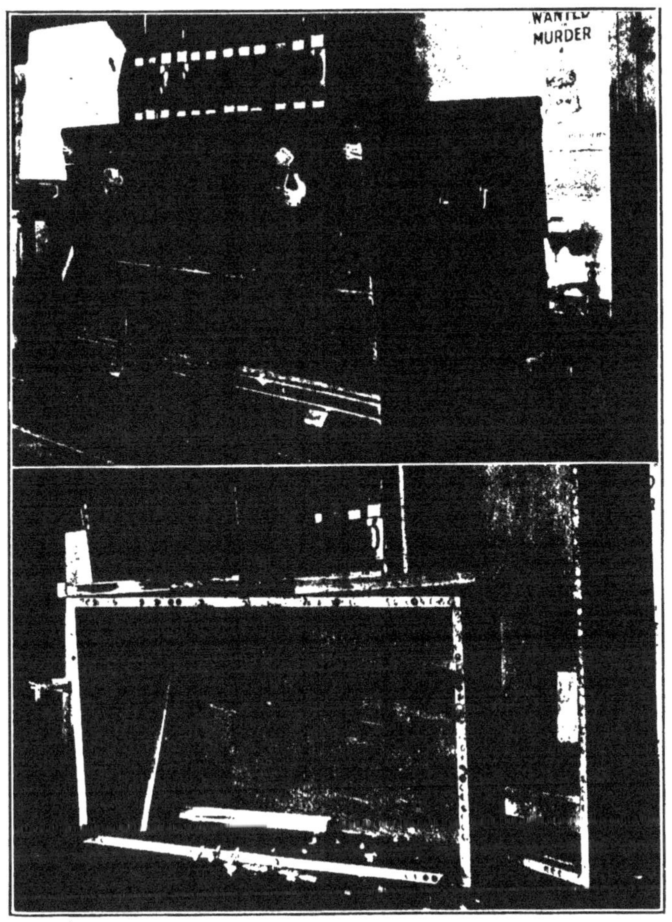

A SMUGGLER'S TRUNK—I

So well constructed that it escaped detection of customs officers both in Holland and New York. Tubes of Salvarsan—2,062 ampules, valued at $30,000—were concealed in perforations, half an inch in diameter, made in the top, sides, and bottom of the trunk, as shown in the lower photograph.

A SMUGGLER'S TRUNK—II
A close-up view of the perforations in the walls of the trunk

APPRAISING INCOMING MERCHANDISE
No package is permitted to pass the customs officers until it bears a "pass label" showing that it has been examined by them

adapted to invite attempts at violation of the law. Furthermore, there was always a certainty of popular approval and support as well as pecuniary profit for successful evaders.

But five of the many instances in connection with the present Surveyor's office in the Port of New York suffice to indicate the need for eternal vigilance against smuggling and suggest that two thousand officers and employees, working day and night, promote compliance with law and obedience to conscience. How much smuggling or evasion of customs and how much theft and other interference with legitimate commerce there might be in this port and how important it is to have enough men of the right competence rather than too few or incompetent men is suggested by these striking instances.

The "sugar trust" paid to the Government nearly three million dollars, which agents of that trust had in effect stolen from the Government by regularly "fixing" the scales so that the actual weight of sugar would be understated. For example, instead of a thousand pounds, the scales would show thirty pounds less, or nine hundred and seventy pounds. Of course a number of unscrupulous employees had to be in collusion with the trust and presumably shared in the profits. There was a general clearing out of all agents who were in any way connected with the frauds. The story was told to the United States Senate, 61st Congress, by Senator Owens in Document No. 60, entitled "Customs Frauds in New York."*

The discovery of these frauds stimulated governmental investigation into the underweighing of all other commodities in the port. The cheese weights, for example, were found to be one third too small! None of the other illegal activities, however, approached in interest the peculations of the sugar trust and Government employees. The Special Agent of the Treasury Department who discovered these practices proved that they had been indulged in for more than a decade. He sustained his charges with adequate proof and subsequently received a moiety of $100,000, and was promoted to the position of Deputy Surveyor.

The second typical incident was the discovery of what is known as the "sleeper" trunks. Information had been received by the Surveyor of the Port that passengers' baggage was passing through the port unexamined. Plans were laid for investigation, but the frauds were so carefully concealed that it required nearly a year of con-

*See pp. 25 and 26, "Impressions of Theodore Roosevelt," by Lawrence F. Abbott.

stant effort and surveillance to break up the practice.

The fraud was cleverly executed. It is an interesting speculation to imagine what might have been accomplished for the world's greater happiness if the study, inventiveness, persistency, thoroughness, foresight, and courage which were involved in this attempt to escape customs had only been spent legitimately. The plan of operation disclosed also a conspiracy between foreign dealers in gowns, lingerie, and other valuable merchandise and their consignees in the Port of New York and various subordinates of steamship companies.

The original plan, which was carried out successfully for many years, was to ship the so-called "sleeper" trunks as "leftover" baggage, ostensibly belonging to passengers who had arrived previously; to carry out this idea, the names of certain previously arrived passengers were selected and the trunks regularly tagged and labelled with their names; the baggage master, who was in the conspiracy, when informed that these trunks were coming on certain vessels, would take pains to secrete them from the observation of the customs inspectors, and when the opportunity favoured would simply deliver them to an expressman for shipment to some point where they would be claimed and reshipped to their ultimate destination.

After the suspicions of the customs authorities were aroused customs guards were placed on the piers to prevent the removal of all baggage which had not been regularly examined by the customs inspector. Substitution of the contents of the trunks was then resorted to. Upon the arrival of the "sleeper" trunks, the baggage master would secrete them on the pier, detach the addressed tags and remove other marks of identification, and transfer their contents to other trunks which he shrewdly substituted. The latter were usually the property of second-class passengers who had not sailed and had abandoned their baggage held by the company for possible claims. This baggage was submitted to the inspectors and represented to contain servants' baggage of "passengers who had previously arrived," and was of very little or of no dutiable value. When the customs officers had left the pier after their usual day's work the original trunks were taken from their hiding-place and delivered to the baggage expressman, also in the conspiracy, who shipped them to a fictitious address in some suburban town. Upon arrival one of the conspirators would claim the trunks at this point and reship them to their ultimate destination. The name "sleeper" trunk was given because the trunk was left on the dock, and permitted to lie there undisturbed, to sleep as it were, until the opportunity arrived to remove the same.

After the scheme had been uncovered by the customs officials, several of the newspapers attempted to give a sensational account of the manner in which these trunks were landed and disposed of by a system known as the "trolley route" which consisted of a trolley being rigged up from a steamer to an adjoining pier where the trunks were landed and turned over to an expressman for delivery.

Arrests were made and convictions obtained, not, however, until more than two million dollars in revenue had been lost.

One of the most dramatic incidents in the history of the port occurred in the early part of February, 1918, when orders were issued from Washington thoroughly to search the S. S. *Nieuw Amsterdam* for poisoned pollen, supposed to have been indirectly transmitted from Germany for the purpose of scattering the same in our great wheat fields in the West and in that way destroying the crops. The precautions taken by the Customs Service in the port required the assignment of 350 men and 50 women, an extraordinarily large number of subordinates to be assigned to one ship. Their investigation was so thorough that it required three days.

During all that time a citizen of Holland, who was in business in Australia and a passenger on that ship, had as part of his baggage 2,062 ampules of Salvarsan valued at $30,000. The trunk which contained the passenger's clothing was made of green cedar wood, at a cost in Holland of $140. It was duly examined, as the baggage of all other passengers was examined, and apparently contained nothing but clothing. Subsequently it was removed to the room engaged by the passenger in one of the hotels in the city and placed near a radiator in the room; the heat issuing therefrom warped the fresh wood; fearing that the heat would crack the ampules, the passenger took the pieces of the trunk apart and removed the drug. These ampules were inserted in various perforations made in the wood at the top, bottom, and sides of the trunk, drilled to a depth of 7 inches and in diameter about one half an inch. The ampules were carefully packed in these holes; they were purchased in Holland for $7,000, apparently having been imported into that country from Germany. The job was so well done that it escaped the detection of the customs authorities in Holland, from whom no export license was obtained; it likewise escaped the rigid scrutiny of the customs officers of this port. Efforts were made to dispose of the medicine to various chemists in this city, and through a patient of one of our city physicians who laid plans for the exportation of the same to Argentine, where it was reported that very much higher prices could be obtained, the fraud was detected, the smuggler was arraigned before the United States Commissioner, fined $250, and the merchandise confiscated.

Under few other circumstances does human nature reveal its best and its worst, its strongest and its weakest characteristics, so clearly and dramatically as when facing the question: "Shall I tell the truth and the whole truth about my dutiable importations, or shall I attempt to deceive my country? Shall I proudly and patriotically pay every cent I owe, or shall I unpatriotically and criminally try to pay less than my share?"

When men and women of international reputation for service in uplift work, church work, women's clubs, and business organizations "take a chance" or condone taking chances on evading customs duties, and when reputable journals, authors, and scenario writers win applause for describing methods of outwitting customs officers, it makes one optimistic about human nature to remember two facts: first, a relatively small percentage of American business men and travellers are willing to resort to using "sleeper" trunks, to claiming foreign residence or citizenship, to wrapping laces around the body, to secreting diamonds in the hair, to sewing long-used and faded labels on spick-and-span, new Paris dresses, or to bribing foreign salesmen to perjure themselves by understating bills and receipts; second, the instinct to evade taxes and to consider tax collectors "fair game" is as old as taxes and taskmasters.

Long before the Christian era began tax evasion was a custom which had grown to such proportions that of the few lessons which His limited time permitted Him to drive home to the Pharisees of His own day, and those of all time, Christ Jesus chose for one lesson the moral obligation to pay one's share of the cost of government; to pay taxes in proportion to taxable property and privileges possessed, to "render unto Cæsar the things that are Cæsar's."

When, as Gibbon the historian tells us, the great "Augustus and his successors imposed duties on every kind of merchandise, which through a thousand channels flowed into Rome—

the then great centre of opulence and luxury—" we know that in ten thousand breasts hope did eternally spring that somehow or other Augustus and his tax-imposing kind might be outwitted.

Tax collecting at ports of the English-speaking world is first mentioned in the Code of Laws enacted by King Ethelred, A. D. 979, to this effect:

> Every small vessel arriving at Billingsgate shall pay to the tax gatherer one oblus (of the value of one penny and a farthing); if of greater tonnage and mast rigged, one denarius (seven and a half pence). If a ship shall arrive and anchor there, four denarii shall be paid to the tax gatherer. Vessels laden with timber shall pay one log to the tax gatherer.

Thus it appears that the first port of entry into the United Kingdom was Billingsgate. Can it be possible that the expression "hurled Billingsgate," meaning epithets, profanity, and vile language, really goes back to the early English method of stating to tax collectors of the first English port what importers really thought about having to pay over part of every load of timber as an import tax?

The nobles who exacted the Magna Charta from King John at Runnymede in 1215 not only secured the guarantees of freedom which we have been teaching in our textbooks, but also secured the abolition of all "evil tolts." Doubtless tolts at that time meant tolls or taxes for bringing goods into England by land or water, which freedom they said they had "by the old and rightful customs." Incidentally, the last five words of the same article in the Magna Charta recalls how, for all time, war conditions have been recognized as exceptional. Even the barons, with the King making concessions to them, wanted port duties removed only "in time of war." Again, in the reign of Edward I in 1279, there appears a suspension of the right to collect customs at ports of entry. In other documents, when these entry taxes are mentioned, it appears that the customs service, despite the lack of recorded evidence, had undoubtedly been in operation since its institution by King Ethelred, and that it was considered important enough to be put under the supervision, or perhaps the monopoly, of such high dignitaries as archbishops and bishops, as well as of earls, knights, and other personages of lesser degree.

The first time that the office of Surveyor of Customs appears is in 1335, the title being Supervisor, not Surveyor. The statute above mentioned indicates that collectors were not permitted to act arbitrarily and tax "what the traffic would bear," but instead were required to use scales and measures which apparently differed according to quantities and sizes of articles to be weighed.

The early name for collector found in 1323 was "Collectors of the King's Customs" and also "Customers." Toward the end of the Thirteenth Century we find the word "Comptroller." That customers and collectors were prevented from owning their own ships and meddling "with the freight of ships" and even from holding life tenure of this lucrative office, all indicates that these early payers of port taxes were not satisfied with total or partial evasion but were seeking to have payment recognized as a just obligation and to put payment on a definitely equitable, provable basis. Thus by 1402, in the reign of Henry IV, we find that "Customs and Comptrollers in every port of England shall abide upon their offices in their proper Persons, without making any Deputy or Lieutenant in their homes, be firmly holden and kept in all points." At the same time, "Customers" were required to "render sworn accounts."

By 1565 duties and obligations were systematized, and what we would now call "port organization" established:

One Customer for the receipt of the Petty Custom on exports.

One Customer for the receipt of the Petty Custom on imports.
One Comptroller.
One Surveyor.

Even at this early date in the history of the customs it is obvious that since its inception it has always been a department of government of the greatest importance, requiring much thought for its proper development as a source of legitimate revenue, itself necessitating as well as giving protection.

Exactly at what time the Customs Service was officially established in the Port of New York is not clear, but it would seem to be under the rule of the Netherlands, in 1642, when Governor Kieft issued a stringent order to the effect that all goods which had not paid legal recognition of the West India Company in the Fatherland or in one of the other Dutch colonies should be charged with the equivalent import duties at New Amsterdam.

The Dutch gave considerable time and thought to the development of the Customs Service, and brought it to a workable state, so that no change was made by the English when they acquired control. They merely built upon the foundation already laid, more clearly defining the method of conduct, and listing more precisely the rules and regulations under which it was to operate.

This is evident in the earliest recorded document relating to the customs dues, which instructs "Mr. Cornelius Van Ruymer, Collector of the Customes in ye City of New York, by order of Colonell Francis Lovelace, Governour, May 24, 1668," that he or his clerk "are to be dayly at ye Custome House from nine in ye morning until twelve at noon. There to receive ye Customes both in and out, as the Merchants shall come and enter, ye Merchant is to make foure Bills, and sign them with his hand, writing his name to them, and ye same time, when you have signed ye Warrant, or one of ye Bills, you are to demand ye Custome, either in kinds at 10 P. Cent. inwards or double ye value of its first Cost in Holland, in Beaver. And likewise outwards for Peltry you are to receive 10½ P. Cent. according to ye vallue in Beaver, for Tobacco one half penny Pr. Pound Ster'g; which is noe more than all Englishmen doe pay. . . . You to tell ye Merchant you are not to give credit. . . . If they do not like your propositions you are not to pass their Bills. . . .

"And lastly pray lett ye Books be kept all in English and all Factoryes and Papers, that when

I have occasion to satisfy myself I may better understand them."

This quaint, but clear, concise, and easily-understood document is typical of the many others that followed, whereby neither the officials nor the people were left in doubt as to the requirements exacted.

These precautions may have been necessary because of the more or less constant agitation that went on in regard to customs duties, leading sometimes to actual uprisings, as in the case of Jacob Leisler, "an importer of liquors and a thriving business man," who stood out against all the constituted authorities, even the representative of the Crown in the Colony, in the payment of duties to a collector of whom he disapproved on religious grounds, rallying to his standard many other merchants, and continuing his opposition until he was taken to England and hanged as a traitor.

The following interesting report of early smuggling is recorded in the minutes of the Common Council:

April 3, 1722. Francis Harrison qui tam ver Diverse Goods and Merchandizes	Francis Harrison, Esq'r, "Surveyor of his now Majesties Customs of the Port of New York . . . did give the Mayor, Recorder and Aldermen . . . to

understand . . . that certain person or persons unknown . . . did import and cause to be imported in a certáin vessel also unknown

29 prospect glasses in tin cases	1 carpenters wooden Square
5 razors	5¼ doz. primers
6 small tin funnells	11 horn books
4 mens felt hatts	1 pair gloves
5 falling axes	½ pound Coffee
22 tin pepper boxes	13 small Books
2 tin cullenders	9 old Books
2 toy looking Glasses in tin Boxes	1½ gross Washed Buttons
2 round wooden boxes	5 penknives
10 Gross Black Buttons	A parcel of prints and Mapps
11 Butchers knives	2 doz. Small Earthen Images
1 doz. Black lead Pencils	11 large Images
24 doz. Wastcoat thread Buttons	2 small Jappand looking Glasses
1 pr. Course Silk Stockins	1 pair Glass Sconces and Nazello
2 Blank books each one quire	100 pound Black pepper in two Baggs
22 red leather Pockett Books	1 leather Trunk
2 Green letter Cases	1 Wooden Box
22 Psalters	6 Ordinary Sadles
5 practice of piety	
12 Testaments	

from the parts beyond the seas . . . and put ashoar without and before any Entry made thereof at the Custom house agt. the form of an act. of General Assembly of the said province.

The goods were proclaimed at 3 successive sessions of the Court & then ordered condemned

⅓ to go to the King
⅓ to Gov. Burnet
⅓ to Francis Harrison, the prosecutor.

Very little or no order characterized the observance of the customs regulations from this time to the Revolutionary War, due directly to the opposition of the Colonists to the tax imposed on tea. During most of that period the Port of New York was in possession of the British, and the continental policy was pursued with respect to customs, an interesting description of which is found in the report of Governor Tryon at London, June 11, 1774:

At this port there is generally one of His Majesty's ships of war stationed near its principal entrance, except during the four Winter Months, when she is obliged, on account of the severe Weather and the Ice, to come to the wharf. The Custom House officers are eight in number: viz., the Collector, Comptroller, Surveyor, and Searcher, Land Waiter, Tide Surveyor and three Tide Waiters; there is also a Naval Officer. The Tide Waiters are mostly employed on Board of Vessels that arrive with dutiable goods, so that there are but three other outdoor officers to look after the business of a very extensive Harbour, lying on two sides of the Town, which is situated on a point between two large Rivers.

As All Articles of Commerce, Provisions and Fuel are conveyed to Town by Water in a number of Small boats,

THE PRESENT NEW YORK CUSTOM HOUSE
On the south side of Bowling Green, in lower New York

NEW YORK CUSTOMS GUARDS

Some conception of the gigantic task of these men, as well as of the prime importance of the port, may be had from the fact that the values of exports passing through the New York Customs District in 1918 was six times that of its nearest rival, Philadelphia, and in imports about four times that of the next in size, the Washington Customs District on the Pacific Coast.

EXAMINING INCOMING BAGGAGE—I

Although every incoming passenger has made a written declaration of taxable articles in his or her baggage, the baggage is very closely examined by customs officers upon the arrival of the ship.

EXAMINING INCOMING BAGGAGE—II

Ingenious devices are sometimes resorted to in order to evade the payment of customs. Diamonds have been found by the customs officers in passengers' tubes of tooth paste, fountain pens, etc.

from Landings that lay on each side of both entrances to the Port, the strict attention of the officers of His Majesty's ship, or the vigilance of the Collector and Comptroller (who speak favourably of their present Outdoor officers) cannot altogether prevent the illegal trade in a port situated as this is; there can be no doubt, therefore, but that assistance different from what the officers have at present would be very necessary, and tend much to the increase of His Majesty's Revenues in this Province.

For the history of the country's awakening to the necessity for ports of entry, for taxes and later for equitable and competent handling of port business, the reader is referred to bibliography entitled "Regulation of Commerce in the American Colonies."

Suffice it here to say that this steady growth in national attention to port service as a matter of necessity and of untold importance to American business is the substantial background against which the striking instances of smuggling are but flickering Roman candles of human weakness and detective skill.

By telling two other instances of attempted smuggling, it is hoped the reader henceforth will use the Roman candles of exciting stories about thieving and lying and cheating to illuminate this background of business procedure and business men's coöperation with the Government.

Shortly after the beginning of the recent war

a "tip" came to the Collector's office to the effect that a certain lady of wealth was about to enter the Port of New York with a large quantity of valuable jewels carefully concealed. This "tip" was merely an anonymous letter, but the Collector, the Surveyor, and all other agents of any importance do not share the contempt which landsmen often claim to have for anonymous letters. On the contrary, experience shows with few exceptions that these anonymous "tips," whether by letter, telegram, or telephone, whether brutally frank or cleverly insinuating, contain more truth than fiction. The fact that this particular "tip" came from an illiterate person, who seemed to have a grudge against the would-be lady smuggler, in no way detracted from the importance of the message.

It required but a few moves, a cable to European agents—of whom our Government always has so many in foreign cities and not infrequently in the stores which give false bills—to verify the main facts in the "tip," namely, that the returning lady had a European son-in-law in the jewellery business. You can imagine the clever lady's surprise when asked by a customs inspector for the jewels which she was bringing home. She indignantly denied possessing them. Finally the inspector, kindly, firmly, but unmistakably assured her that either she must tell where the jewels were or that all of her goods and even her person must be thoroughly examined. Thereupon the possession of the jewels was admitted and a letter produced from son-in-law asking mother-in-law please to care for these jewels during the war. It developed that just as mother-in-law was to board the ship a messenger came bearing a basket of fruit at the bottom of which, to her complete amazement, as stated, she found a box of jewels with the aforesaid letter from son-in-law begging her to act as his steward! A bit of adroit questioning led to a complete confession and to the question which the Custom House never answers: "But, how in the world did you find out?" Surely the way of the transgressor is hard.

The resource of the average smuggler seems to be unlimited as indicated by the experience the customs officials had on February 17, 1920, when the S. S. *Stavangerfjord* was boarded in New York Bay and the inspector in charge examined the declaration of one of the passengers whose name had been recalled by the same inspector as that of a man convicted in the year 1917 of smuggling dental rubber to Scandinavian countries for transshipment to Germany by concealing it in false bottoms of trunks and in Victrolas.

Inquiry by the inspector of the purser of the ship elicited the information that on the previous day the passenger had asked for the return of his declaration and had amended the same by including several other articles among which were three diamonds.

The Acting Deputy Surveyor in charge of the vessel with two inspectors searched the passenger and from his vest pocket removed two fountain pens, one apparently broken in which no ink was found, but a slight rattle convinced the inspector that there was something concealed inside. The passenger was asked what was in the pen and stated "there may be a few pieces of the pen inside." In attempting to get out these so-called fragments, seven diamonds were found. Removing the top of the other pen and finding that it contained ink and did not appear to be suspicious it was returned to the passenger. Subsequently it was re-examined and found to contain four more diamonds.

From the passenger's hand-bag a bath robe was taken and in one of the pockets a handkerchief was found containing a ring with an empty setting for two stones. The bag also contained a tube of tooth paste from which was squeezed out with the contents of the tube two diamonds. Further examination disclosed the fact that in the watch pocket of the passenger's trousers was a diamond ring which he claimed to have purchased in this country some years ago.

The undeclared jewels which were valued at $8,000 were seized by the customs officials and the passenger was arrested and held in $5,000 bail.

CHAPTER VI

Growth in Federal Customs Service

TO THE returning traveller it seems at times as if nobody lived in New York except customs officers. While still several hours from the piers of the port, the ship is boarded by the "customs," well-mannered men in uniform and occasionally well-mannered women, armed with "declarations" upon which the returning citizen or the visiting neighbour from across the seas declares in conscientious detail the articles subject to import tax he wishes to bring into the country. Since an indefatigable Congress, aided by still more energetic manufacturers who never flag in their loyalty to tariff for encouragement of home industries, has done its best to include almost everything that is visible or measurable in the duty list, there is very little which the conscientious passenger does not have to declare. Moreover, since the customs officers cannot appear as courteous as they feel, while rummaging among non-dutiable articles to verify the passenger's declaration of taxable articles, the careful passenger declares everything he or she brings. For reasons which it is apparently very difficult for those outside the Customs Service to understand, the declaration becomes a mere "scrap of paper" when the boat docks, for in spite of all conscientious declaring and of meticulous detail, "milady's" baggage is gone over from top to bottom, just as if she had never declared a thing. Dutiable articles must be paid for, if only ten cents is due; that requires a trip to still another set of customs officers who are legalized to accept payment and who punctiliously give receipts.

While the traveller is wrong in his conclusion that nobody else lives in New York except customs officers, it must be admitted that he usually underestimates their number. Only a small proportion of them give their personal attention to the disembarked passenger, as this and other customs work in the port requires to-day more than two thousand employees as against a total of eight men in the year 1774.

Most travellers never have occasion to deal directly either with the ranking officer of the port, the Collector, or with the special officers on his staff. The men who search your baggage or inspect your imported freight at the dock are under the direction of the Surveyor of the

Drawn from photo by J. F. Garcia

First Custom House in the United States built in 1715 and identified as the Port of Entry for New York, Philadelphia, and many of our great cities when they were in their infancy.

Port, who is responsible for their competence, as well as their courtesy. The exceptions to this rule are the polite gentlemen who formally present the compliments of the Government to distinguished personages on board.

Of the four port officers, Collector, Surveyor, Naval Officer, and Appraiser, the ordinary person coming into the port or bringing in goods has no direct dealing with the Naval Officer and the Appraiser. The Naval Officer is an auditor, verifier of records and vouchers, whose duty it is to check up all branches of the Customs Service. Like the other three officials, he is named by the President with the advice and consent of the Senate. The title Naval Officer is of pre-Revolutionary origin and is said to come from the practice of assigning an officer of the Navy to do this work. The Appraiser, as the name indicates, has to do with values and is an officer of appeal. The Collector not only collects customs revenues and enforces the customs laws, but also enforces the neutrality laws, a duty which proved quite exacting during the recent European war. In general, he is the representative of the Secretary of the Treasury in enforcing any laws and regulations regarding the port. It is he who is responsible for enforcing the country's rules with respect to commerce and navigation, which include the documenting of ships and the enforcement of immigration laws. The duties of the Collector of the Port and the Commissioner of Immigration concur in regard to the alien "head tax," which is paid to the Collector. The immigration officials certify this tax to the Collector, together with the name of the transportation agent responsible for the payment of it. Further, they specify—

(1) The number held for special inquiry.

(2) The number claiming to enter for the purpose of passing in transit through the United States, as to Canada, Mexico, or the Orient.

(3) The number claiming American citizenship.

(4) The number entering for temporary stay, etc.

When this classification is completed the tax is held on special deposit to be refunded or turned in to the Treasury as required by the immigration laws.

The Surveyor is the outdoor executive of the policies for which the Collector is the indoor executive. The Collector names the staff, after which the Surveyor is responsible for superintending and directing them in their work. Under the Federal statutes and the regulations of the Treasury Department the Surveyor must cover the following ground:

1. Superintend and direct all inspectors, weighers, measurers, gaugers, guards, and labourers within the port;

2. Visit, personally or by proxy, all arriving vessels;

3. Report in writing each day all vessels that have arrived from foreign ports on the preceding day, specifying the names and denominations of the vessels and the masters' names, whence arrived, whether laden or in ballast, to what nation belonging, and, if American vessels, whether the masters thereof have or have not complied with the law in having the required number of manifests of the cargo on board;

4. Put one or more inspectors on each vessel immediately after its arrival in port;

5. Ascertain, according to law, the proof, quantities, and kinds of distilled spirits imported;

6. Examine into the correspondence regarding the goods imported in any vessel and the deliveries thereof according to the inspectors' returns and the permits for landing the same;

7. Superintend the lading for exportation of all goods entered for the benefit of drawback, and report whether the kind, quantity, and quality of goods so laden correspond with the entries and permits granted therefor;

8. Test the weights, measures, and other instruments used in ascertaining the duties on imports, by public standards;

9. Certify to the death of any of the passengers or crews on arriving vessels, with the name and age of the decedent and the cause of death;

10. Admeasure American vessels for registry, enrolment of license, and all foreign vessels for the assessment of tonnage dues;

11. Count passengers embarking upon excursion boats between the latter part of May and the early part of September each year, a total of nearly one and a half million in the season of 1919.

12. Police the port day and night, through three hundred and seventy-five customs guards divided into three platoons.

Does this seem a complicated and expensive machinery for just one port and for the Customs Service alone? Please do not forget that we are no longer speaking of the village of New Amsterdam or the New York of Revolutionary days, or even of one city, but rather of the metropolitan district about the Statue of Liberty which has exported in the last three years more than two and one half billion dollars a year, imported more than one and a half billion dollars in merchandise, and collected duties of more than two hundred million dollars a year. Compared with the cost of these collections, which have run as high as two hundred and seventeen million dollars in one year (1907), the cost of maintaining a small army of customs officers is small indeed. When considered with respect to the prosperity of business and social welfare of which the enormous exports and imports are but one expression, the cost is infinitesimal.

That this cost might be justifiably greater was asserted in May, 1919, by Professor L. S. Rowe, Assistant Secretary of the Treasury in charge of customs, who brought to a New York conference of customs officials throughout the country the thanks of the Secretary of the Treasury for having faithfully and efficiently performed during wartime "duties of a delicate and exacting nature" in a way that entitled them "to the gratitude of the country." Mr. Rowe deplored the fact that there are in the Customs Service positions which have not been increased in salary for a period of forty years; that the percentage of men in the Customs Service receiving less than $1,000 per annum is greater than it was fifty years ago; that in the same period the cost of living has so risen that the purchasing power of one dollar is less than one half of what it was when these salaries were originally fixed; and that he regarded it "as little short of a national disgrace that a great country as wealthy as the United States should ask a body of public servants to give the best that is within them to public good and then expect them to live on a pittance."

This is the way that the Customs Service, with the greatest dispatch and with the least possible inconvenience to business, tries to collect the taxes which are decreed by our Congress.

On all steamers which carry passengers, regularly plying between New York and foreign ports, the Surveyor leaves in charge of the purser a quantity of blank Passengers' Baggage Declarations to be used by passengers who come in the first and second cabins, to make the "customs declaration" of the number and character of the pieces of baggage which they are bringing with them. These declarations in pads, each containing fifty, are numbered serially and consecutively, and are generally distributed by the purser or steward to the passengers one or two days before the vessel is due at this port. There are minute instructions in English, French, Spanish, Italian, and German on the reverse side of the declaration as to the proper manner of filling it out, and stating which articles are either exempt or liable for customs duties.

Immediately after the vessel is passed by the Health Officer of the Port at Quarantine, she is boarded by the Surveyor's Staff Inspectors, to whom the purser hands the declarations which he has collected from the passengers. While coming up the bay on the way to the vessel's dock the Staff Officers check off the declarations with the list of passengers to see that all who should do so have made baggage declarations. Each declaration has a perforated coupon attached, numbered to correspond with the declaration. The passenger retains the numbered coupon for purposes of identification on the pier, and when all his baggage is landed he presents his coupon to the Surveyor's Staff Officer on the dock, who has charge of the declarations, and who assigns an inspector to examine the baggage. When the passenger has articles which are liable to duty, a representative of the U. S. Appraiser of Merchandise, who is on the dock for this purpose, appraises the value and states the rate of duty to be assessed. The inspector then takes the passenger and declaration to the Deputy Collector on the dock, who computes the amount of duty and gives the passenger a receipt for the amount paid. The inspector then puts a "pass label" on each package, which permits it to be taken outside the customs lines.

If the inspector does not find any goods liable to duty in the baggage he attaches a "pass label" to each package.

No package, whether it contains dutiable goods or not, is permitted to pass out of the customs enclosure unless it bears a "pass label" showing that it has been examined.

The exits through the customs lines are guarded by customs guards, who see that no package is delivered without such label as it passes through the exit.

Sometimes it occurs that the Appraiser cannot make a satisfactory examination on the dock owing to the quantity or character of dutiable goods, or the question, to be determined later, whether the passenger is "a resident of the United States returning from abroad" or a "resident of a foreign country," in which case the baggage is sent to the U. S. Appraiser's Warehouse, known as the Public Stores, for examination, or pending the determination of the question of residence.

The tariff makes a distinction between the maximum value and character of articles which American residents returning from abroad and foreign residents arriving here are allowed to bring in free of duty. Passengers passing through the United States to foreign countries may send their baggage in bond through the United States. So also may baggage be sent from this port in bond to another port in the United States, the duties to be collected at such port of destination. In these cases the Government takes possession of the goods for purposes of transportation and they are sent under customs seals.

In connection with the importation of merchandise the United States Government has found it necessary for the adequate protection of its revenue from importations to provide so many safeguards and to prescribe so many regulations and legal forms that importers find it convenient to employ customs brokers, whose business it is to pass goods through the customs.

Accompanying the Surveyor's Staff Inspectors the vessel is boarded by a customs officer, also under the Surveyor, known as a Boarding Officer, who certifies to the manifest of the cargo, a list showing the mark, number, and character of

THE EVOLUTION OF NEW YORK'S SKYLINE—I

Above: The skyline at Battery Park, the southern end of Manhattan Island, in 1715. Below: The same view a century later, in 1815

(Lower photograph copyrighted by Brown Brothers)

THE EVOLUTION OF NEW YORK'S SKYLINE—II

Above: A view of lower New York from the tower of the unfinished Brooklyn Bridge on the Brooklyn side of the East River in 1876. Below: A view from the same location in 1915

every package on board the vessel. This manifest is made in duplicate. The original is retained by the captain, who lodges it, with his bill of health and other documents, with the Collector in the Custom House when he "enters" his vessel.

The Boarding Officer gives the duplicate manifest to the Surveyor, who forwards it to the Collector.

Each importer, in order to get possession of his goods, makes an entry of them, after the vessel has been "entered" by the captain. The entry of the goods consists in filing with the Collector a bill of lading and an invoice, the latter sworn to before a U. S. Consular officer in the place abroad from which the goods were shipped. The bill of lading and invoice separately describe each package by mark and number, and the invoice states the prices at which the goods were sold or the market value abroad.

The entry clerks in the Custom House estimate the amount of duties due the Government, on the payment of which, in the case of "duty-paid" goods, the Collector issues a permit, addressed to the inspectors who supervise the discharging and delivery of the cargo from the vessel at her wharf. The importer lodges his permit with the inspectors, who deliver the merchandise on the completion of the necessary operations, for the ascertainment of quantities, which the permit directs shall be performed. These operations include weighing, gauging, or measuring the goods, as the case may be. There are separate units of activity under the Surveyor for this purpose. There are also different forms of entry. Goods entered for consumption must be examined and compared with the invoice by the Appraiser of Merchandise to verify values and quantities. For this purpose a percentage of each invoice is either examined on the wharf or sent to the Appraiser's Warehouse. The permit directs the inspectors as to the procedure.

Goods may be entered in bond for warehousing. In this case they are sent by the inspectors to a designated U. S. Bonded Warehouse, where they may remain in storage for three years at the desire of the importer. Goods may also be entered for immediate transportation to another port in the United States or for transportation to another port and export to a foreign port. In each of these cases the goods are under customs restraint, being forwarded to the Collector of Customs at the interior or coastwise port under customs seals.

	1913	1914	1915	1916	1917
Transfers of merchandise stored in bonded warehouses to bonded manufacturing warehouses	63	60	50	87	85
Export shipments from bonded manufacturing warehouses	3,002	2,395	2,299	2,853	2,442
Warehouse entries .	44,897	30,950	21,159	21,172	20,018
Withdrawals of merchandise from warehouse for exportation by sea .	7,508	8,951	11,910	11,234	10,998
Transshipments from one vessel to another for exportation	21,555	17,840	17,279	17,840	13,854

With the outbreak of war in Europe the duties of the customs officers of this port were immediately augmented and the service necessarily became complex and exacting. These additional duties were discharged, however, by elastic readjustment of parts within the system, without additional legislation or radical changes. To the credit of the staff of employees be it said that their patriotic devotion made possible both protection for this country and services to civilization which before the war would have seemed impossible.

For the President of the United States to declare our nation neutral involved not merely a message which could be telegraphed and printed for the world to read, but included added precautions and at many points new methods on the part of the entire Customs Service, from the Collector to the humblest watchman. Thenceforth our nation's honour was at stake every time we permitted a ship or passenger to enter and every time a ship was given its papers to leave the port.

Before the *Lusitania* sailed for her fated last voyage the Collector of the Port of New York inspected her cargo to test Germany's false charge, as the search proved, that in violation of our neutrality she was laden with guns and ammunition intended to kill German soldiers. When the *St. Paul* sank at her pier, it was the Customs Service which investigated and discovered the cause. It was a customs inspector that discovered who was stealing thousands of pounds of meat from a government transport. Assigned by the Surveyor for this task, he made friends with longshoremen; was let into the secret; spent an evening at a saloon where these men gathered, while in much discomfort they hitched and shuffled to make the meat concealed under their clothes a more comfortable burden to carry, and finally, at the point of a gun, the inspector secured the surrender and confession of the whole group. It was the Customs Service, too, which, at the request of the Army, set about discovering the men within the government service who were disclosing secrets to the enemy. This quest revealed the fact that the United States Government had unknowingly taken into its service, in charge of enemy interned ships, approximately sixty-five former officers and employees of those same German lines to which these ships belonged, thus merely transferring them from the enemy pay roll to Uncle Sam's pay roll.

Another index to the volume of new business created in the Customs Service during the war is the fact that the Surveyor of the Port issued nearly five hundred thousand war zone passes to persons having business within the restricted area; while the important function of viséing passports for persons leaving this country for all parts of the world also became a customs activity.

The following incidents from Civil War times help us to appreciate the many-sided duties of port officers and the interlacing of customs problems with the more general problems and policies of our country and with the politics of the day.

During the Civil War the office of the Collector of the Port of New York was one of the most important public administrative offices connected with the Government, and the naming of the Collector was a privilege greatly coveted by the various political factions, because of the numerous minor appointments included with it.

The daughter of Thurlow Weed, in the biography of her father of which she was the author, writes, page 612, on the subject of a conversation which Thurlow Weed had with President Lincoln in relation to his appointments:

Mr. Lincoln remarked that it was particularly pleasant to him to reflect that he was coming into office unembarrassed by promises. He owed, he supposed, his exemption from importunities to the circumstance that his name as a candidate was but a short time before the people, and that only a few sanguine friends anticipated the possibility of his nomination. "I have not," said he, "promised any office to any man, nor have I but in a single instance mentally committed myself to any appointment; and as that relates to an important office in your state, I have concluded to mention it to you—under strict injunctions of secrecy, however. If I am not induced by public considerations to change my purpose, Hiram Barney will be Collector of the Port of New York." I supposed that Mr. Lincoln, in thus frankly avowing his friendship for Mr. Barney, intended to draw me out. I remarked that until I met him at the Chicago Convention my acquaintance with Mr. Barney was very slight; but that after the convention adjourned Mr. Barney joined us (my daughter and a lady friend) in an excursion down the Mississippi and through Iowa; and that my impressions of him personally and politically were favourable, and that I believed he would make an acceptable Collector. I added that if it were true, as I had heard, that the reply of a well-known and extensive mercantile firm in New York, during an exciting crisis, to Southern merchants who threatened to withdraw their patronage on account of its opposition to slavery, namely, "We offer our goods not our principles for sale," originated with Mr. Barney, it entitled him to any office he asked for. "He has not," said Mr. Lincoln, "asked for this or any other office, nor does he know of my intention."

In an interview which Mr. Barney gave to the New York *World* shortly before his death, commenting upon some of his experiences as Collector of the Port of New York during the Civil War, he said: "President Lincoln appointed me Collector without consulting me and the Senate unanimously confirmed the nomination. The war had just begun and everything was in a turmoil. Although a new collector I had myself to decide almost on the spur of the moment fully fifty cases a day, any one of which was liable to be taken to the Supreme Court. They told me at Washington to do the best I could and they would back me up. When I left office in 1864, completely broken down over its severe work and responsibility, there were at least 3,000 cases pending. My decisions were always sustained by the Secretary of the Treasury, but there were so many new questions coming up all the time that it was impossible to render satisfactory decisions."

During the war the then Italian Minister came one day to see Mr. Barney and said: "Mr. Webb is building two war steamers for the Italian Government and we want to clothe them with steel armour. There is none to be had in this country. We have to import the steel from France and it is about to arrive. I have applied to have it admitted free of duty as the duty will come to $120,000 for each vessel. I have told them that it is no more than a fair return for the use of our dock yards at Civitavecchia, which for a number of years we have placed at the disposal of your Government for storage of naval supplies and repairing your government vessels in the Mediterranean, especially as we are employing an American builder to construct the vessels. It has been worth to your Government $100,000 a year. They are quite willing to admit that armour, but they find no law by which the Government can properly remit the duty. They have sent me to see if you can manage it for us without violating the laws." Mr. Barney thought the matter over and sent for Mr. Webb, the contractor for building the ships, and said: "Mr. Webb, I have a right to establish public stores. I propose to make those vessels public stores where the Italian Government can enter the steel required for armouring the vessels which they are importing from France and withdraw it for exportation, provided you are willing to pay the salary of a government clerk as storekeeper, whom I shall appoint to have charge of the stores. When you are ready to sail you can withdraw the steel for exportation and pay no duty." (Prophecy of a free port.) They were very much disturbed in Washington and gratified at the arrangement, as it was the decision of all to do the fair thing by the Italian Government, and it was accomplished not only without violating any law but in accordance with the law and the practice. Mr. Barney heard nothing more about the affair. The vessels were finished, a trial was made, an excursion at sea, to test their capacities.

"A matter which was the cause of much worry and annoyance to me," said Mr. Barney to the representative of the New York *World*, "was the strife among the office seekers. Actually there were 96,000 applications made to me for places within three months and I had on the average of five hundred calls a day."

The customs officials of the present day are not disturbed by political applications for office as the entire service is now within the protection of the Federal Civil Service Law.

CHAPTER VII

Port Workers' Welfare League

BURNT CORK FUNSTERS OF THE SURVEYOR'S CUSTOMS WELFARE ASSOCIATION!
RED LETTER NIGHT IN THE FUN MAKING LINE!
MINSTREL SHOW AND RECEPTION AT CENTRAL OPERA HOUSE APRIL 23, 1919!
THE COMMITTEE IN CHARGE EARNESTLY APPEALS FOR THE APPROVAL AND AID OF EVERY MAN IN THE SURVEYOR'S DEPARTMENT IN PROMOTING THE SUCCESS OF THE COMING BIG SOCIAL FUNCTION.

Do THE above quotations from the port workers' monthly bulletin seem compatible with the reader's picture of those stern examiners of customs? Please remember that all inspection or all weighing and no recreation or fellowship makes the port worker a listless patriot just as surely as all work and no play makes Jack a dull boy.

A nation which goes around the world to fight for democracy and which has girded up its loins to insist upon democracy in forms and purposes and acts of government cannot afford to have two thousand port workers together in one port without providing means of recreation and fellowship among employees and families who have two important bonds in common, love of America and devotion to their port duties. Therefore, on December 20, 1915, the Surveyor of the Port established what the workers themselves now call "The Fraternal Temple," known as the Surveyor's Customs Welfare Association. A monthly bulletin is issued which circulates among members and now about three thousand outsiders, and it has the second-class mailing privilege. Its nominal editor is the Surveyor; the work itself is carried on by five managers and seven associate editors chosen from the employees; it carries advertising, jokes, poetry, as well as port stories and personalities.

The accompanying photographs tell the story of its service. The Welfare Association of Port Workers is like similar organizations in private business, but has fewer counterparts in governmental services than are needed. The special occasion for starting this welfare work was this:

In September, 1914, when I was appointed Surveyor by President Wilson, there were more than three hundred customs guards, whose work might be described as that of pier policemen; these men were the lowest salaried men in the service and were compelled, accordingly, to seek living quarters in various sections of the city and suburbs where the rents were low. It seemed almost incredible that most of them were assigned to places of work a considerable distance from their homes. Frequently men living in Yonkers and the Bronx were sent to work in Staten Island; men living in Canarsie and Astoria were sent to work in Edgewater, N. J., a distance of more than twenty miles, although there were men available for assignment in the immediate neighbourhood, within walking distance of that work. The carfare expended in going to and from the work was paid by the Government, but the time consumed in travelling belonged to the man himself, for which he received no pay. Here was the first inspiration for real welfare work among port employees. So an order was issued that the men should not be assigned to duty at an unreasonable distance from their homes; the result was not only an economy of more than $5,000 a year to the Government in carfares, but also a considerable saving of time to the employees in travel.

Next, instead of permitting customs guards to have only three full days off in an entire year, a schedule was worked out as a result of which these men now have one day off in every seven days, without any detriment to the service whatever.

A third example of substituting attention for sublime indifference to the ordinary comforts of the men is the change in the reserve room in which the customs guards gather while awaiting assignment. This room was formerly located on the ground floor of the Custom House, in the inside section of the building, where there was no natural light or fresh air. In addition there were more than three hundred steel cabinets for uniforms, each about seven feet in height, ranged alongside of each other around the walls, giving an exceedingly sombre and depressing appearance to the room otherwise poorly ventilated and lighted. And yet at the same time there was a larger and more comfortable room in the Barge Office Building with windows on all sides opening out on Battery Park and the harbour, easily available for the use of the employees, which was exclusively enjoyed by five newspaper reporters. Possession was taken of this space, the reporters moved to another room, and the guards began to experience the beneficent effect of more cheerful surroundings.

On steamship piers there were old-fashioned offices for the customs officials, without ventilation except through the door, with no light except artificial light. We persuaded the steamship companies to relocate and reconstruct the offices, so that the men now work with sunlight and with excellent ventilation, all at the expense of the steamship companies.

A fourth welfare feature was the even distribution of extra compensation or night money. Ships lading and unlading after five o'clock in the afternoon are required to pay the expenses of the customs officers assigned. A full day's pay is allowed where the work is required up to 11 P.M., and a second full day's pay if it continues beyond that hour. More than $100,000 is annually disbursed for this work. About one third of the men in the force formerly had the privilege of overwork which brought this considerable sum. Little chance this discrimination could have had if there had been no pay for overtime! By establishing an equitable system of distributing night work every man in the service is now permitted to enjoy the benefit of the extra money, as against the favoured one third who had the exclusive privilege for years before. After the successful adoption of this system a number of men called on me and told me that although they had been many years in the service, they had never received a single dollar of night money.

The various branches of activity in the service had each its separate organization: there was an Inspectors' Association, a Weighers' Association, a Guards' Association, a Labourers' Association, and so on. Each association vied with the others in the development of lines of demarcation both official and social, so that there was a feeling of superiority among the men in the one class over those in the other classes. To break down these barriers it would be necessary to unite all the men in the service in one organization where each would have equal social and fraternal opportunities with the others, but to compete successfully with organizations already in existence for many years our new organization should give something for nothing. So it was established without dues, initiation fees, or assessments. We selected a subordinate from each of the twelve branches of the service, choosing only those who were prepared to volunteer and who displayed some enthusiasm for the work. We organized the Welfare League, adopted a constitution and by-laws, found available space on the top floor of the Barge Office Building, and there provided a recreation centre with two pool and billiard tables, together with two shuffle-boards, chess, checkers, and dominoes, gymnasium apparatus, shower baths, a piano, and a Victrola. In another room is a library with more than 2,000 books, and an arrangement with the New York Circulating Library which furnishes daily any books applied for by the members. There is also an orchestra and a choral union.

During the stress of hard times and high prices we established a coöperative store where provisions of all kinds were purchasable at wholesale prices, and during the first year of said store we sold 12,000 pounds of sugar at $7\frac{4}{5}$ cents a pound when the market price was 12 cents, and 8,000 pounds of coffee at 19 cents a pound when the market price was 38 cents, besides other commodities at lower prices than that at which they could be purchased in the open market. In the summer and fall of 1919 a food supply committee was established and the Army and Navy surplus food distributed at cost prices to the employees, thus disposing of nearly 700 tons of food merchandise. In addition the Association met the protest of the men in the uniformed service of the Navy against the enormous increase in the price of uniform cloth, by purchasing from the

THE "HALF MOON"

A replica of the famous ship, used in the Hudson-Fulton tri-centennary celebration in 1909. The glory of exploring the Hudson River in 1609 has been accorded by historians to Henry Hudson, but the river was first explored by Giovanni Verrazano, a Florentine pirate hired by Francis I of France, in 1524, eighty-five years before the *Half Moon* sailed up the Hudson.

"THE FRATERNAL TEMPLE"

Known as the Surveyor's Customs Welfare Association, was officially established in 1915 to provide recreation and to promote fellowship among the 2,000 workers in the New York Customs district. The photographs show the billiard room and the coöperative grocery store of the Welfare Association.

Navy at a figure about one half of the present market price 5,100 yards of blue uniform cloth which was allotted to the various members of the force at the very low figure which represented the purchase price from the Navy. Blankets, shoes, raincoats, woollen gloves, hats, underwear, and sweaters which were part of the surplus stock of the Army and Navy were also sold to the members of the Association at the cost price to the Government.

A welfare relief fund of $1,800 was established on July 1, 1916, and increased from time to time by the proceeds of outings, theatre parties, and minstrel shows and by the establishment of life memberships at a total cost of one dollar to each member, and was used for temporary loans in case of sickness of members and for other urgent needs in their families. The total amount of loans made to members of the Association from that date to January 1, 1920, aggregates $36,122.

The trials of delinquents under the old system furnished another chance to do welfare work. The number of trials averaged three a week until the Association was organized. Most of the charges were for absence without leave. It was formerly the custom to prepare written charges to be approved by the Collector and the Surveyor, copies of which were served upon the delinquent, who was required to appear for trial in the Surveyor's Office before a tribunal composed of the Surveyor, the Special Deputy Surveyor, the Deputy Surveyor in charge of the delinquent's own division, witnesses, and a stenographer. My first experience with these cases was ludicrous. One of the Deputy Surveyors complained to me that he had a serious charge to make against a labourer. The charge was that he had been sitting on a box of oranges five minutes, reading a newspaper. Now, under the usages grown up in the service, all the high-salaried officials of the Surveyor's Office would be sitting around a table in great solemnity trying a $2.50 a day labourer for this offence; the decision would be publicly imposed on the man in the presence of his entire division; it would not be the ten days' fine imposed which would hurt half so much as the humiliation of the man before all these officials, the degradation and the shame before his colleagues, making him resentful, not only against the service, but likewise against the man who preferred the charges. Such a system was calculated to break a man's spirit and it did have that effect. Our substitute was this: no written charges were served on that man; I sent for him and we had a heart-to-heart talk alone; I returned him to his job with a reprimand, and he has never had a charge against him since.

In the early part of our welfare work it was reported from Washington that a committee of New York women had been endeavouring to introduce welfare work in another branch of the Government and that one of their first requests was for an appropriation of $12,000. The authorities could not understand why they needed $12,000 to do welfare work in another branch of the Government when the Surveyor's Office of the Port of New York was doing it without cost to the Government. Our explanation is that in the Surveyor's Office *the men themselves* were doing the welfare work, but in the other office *outsiders* were attempting to do it. No department head, no matter how magnetic his personality or how determined his energies, can make a movement of this sort a success unless those affected by it are themselves interested. All he can do is to show them how to start and keep a watchful eye over them in the beginning so that petty jealousies and resentments do not creep in. But once the men get their machine started and realize that they can regulate it themselves, good results are sure to follow.

The welfare spirit seems to have entered into

the daily activities of the men so that their attitude toward one another has completely changed. In fact, every man has proved his right to be called a gentleman in the true sense of Cardinal Newman's definition, "A gentleman is one who never needlessly inflicts pain."

After the entrance of the United States into the recent war our recreation centre was dismantled and all our equipment given to the Young Men's Christian Association and the Knights of Columbus, and by them installed in one of the military camps near by; this gave our members time to apply themselves to Liberty Loan activities with gratifying results. By working together in friendly rivalry we have succeeded in obtaining subscriptions aggregating more than $3,500,000 and we received the actual cash in these drives, doing our own banking. Our subordinates have done all this in addition to their everyday customs work without any extra compensation. The treasurer is an officer in the Welfare League; he has handled the $3,500,000 collected in these drives, and not a dollar of that has been wasted or misspent, and yet he served without bonds; a pretty good record for an $1,800-a-year clerk!

In addition to that activity, we established a 100 per cent. record in the Red Cross and other war relief drives.

Nor was the spiritual side of our members neglected in the League activities during the war period; we organized Military Masses in St. Peter's Church, Barclay Street, February 22, 1918 and 1919, and in the Battery Park on Memorial Day, 1918 and 1919. We also took an active part in the anniversaries of The Lord's Day Alliance of the United States, in the Marble Collegiate Church in this city in November, 1918, and in the Methodist Episcopal Church, Washington, in December, 1919, as well as in the Contennial Anniversary of The New York Port Society, a religious and benevolent organization for the benefit of sailors, in November, 1918.

During Christmas week of the year 1918 in "A Mile of Pennies" movement for a dinner fund organized for the Salvation Army we succeeded in collecting 120,000 pennies, presenting the same to the Salvation Army at our Annual Stag entertainment on the last Saturday of December of that year. In the drive ending May 29, 1919, we organized "A Mile of Nickels" campaign for the benefit of the Salvation Army Home Service Fund and collected nearly $3,000.

The port workers' social activities included not only minstrel shows, theatre parties, and picnics for themselves, but also entertainments given by our minstrel chorus at the army hospitals in and around the Port of New York.

We are not trying to build up a City of Beautiful Nonsense in the Surveyor's Office, and to prove there is more than sentiment in the story of the Welfare League, let the practical commonsense side of it speak:

(1) The average annual sick rate has been reduced from 10 per cent. to 2 per cent.

(2) The record of delinquencies has been lowered from nearly 15 per cent. to 2½ per cent.

(3) Trials for infractions of the rules, with their attendant expenses, have been reduced from three in one week to less than ten in one year.

(4) Good cheer has been put into the hearts of the men.

(5) Their families are more contented and their homes are happier.

(6) The Government has saved thousands of dollars in expenses.

(7) The tone of efficiency has been very materially improved.

This welfare work is described in some detail for the proof it adds that such labour standards as the Covenant of the League of Nations holds up to the new after-war world of 1919 are not merely desirable but eminently and productively practical.

Surely in America we have a right to expect our Government to be a model employer, and a pioneer in ever-growing industrial democracy.

CHAPTER VIII

Giant Growth in Commerce

POETS, tragedians, and historians often tell us that Christian names and family escutcheons have little to do with character. Once in a great while, however, there seems to be something peculiarly appropriate in a name; Mark Twain had Adam and Eve in the "Garden of Eden" agree upon Eve's selection of a name for the Dodo, "because it looked like a Dodo"; Philadelphia has earned its name, City of Brotherly Love, by being indulgent toward exploiting brothers; Oshkosh has earned its place in metaphor and the language of disdain by its very physiognomy; New York City's seal is a reflection of its development. After reviewing the growth in the commerce which has centred in the Port of New York, one is grateful for the premier engineer, the beaver, which all these years has occupied the place of honour in the city's official seal and on the city's flag.

From 1614, when trade began at this port, to 1919, a span of 305 years, we of course expect an enormous growth. It means little to us now to say that when the port was ten years old the exports were $20,000, when it was twenty years old $50,000. What of it? An increase of several hundred per cent., or even several thousand per cent., in the business of a city in the first thirty years of its development is not an unusual result.

The giant growth in the commerce of this port since its destiny as America's greatest port became fixed is natural. Appetite and power to consume are two elements of greatness which must not be forgotten. Given any city of one hundred thousand population that is on a harbour of such beauty that its first white discoverer called it the Bellisimo Lago, and whose subsequent discoverers called it the finest of natural harbours, there would arise a commerce almost out of the clear sky. In the year 1800 the consuming power of the population of the harbour, that is of New York, Brooklyn, Bayonne, Hoboken, Jersey City, and Newark, was an important fact making for commerce and for further growth, regardless of what might be done in the Middle West.

Each succeeding decade, as the population of the port grew to more than six millions by the year 1919, the demands of this population itself

Customs Collection Districts Arranged in Order of Exports for the Years 1914 to 1918, Inclusive

	1914		1915		1916		1917		1918	
	IMPORTS	EXPORTS	IMPORTS	EXPORTS	IMPORTS	EXPORTS	IMPORTS	EXPORTS	IMPORTS	EXPORTS
New York . .	$1,040,300,000	$864,000,000	$931,000,000	$1,193,500,000	$1,191,865,982	$2,332,200,000	$1,338,100,000	$3,053,100,000	$1,251,700,000	$2,616,800,000
Philadelphia .	96,400,000	65,100,000	72,900,000	90,600,000	95,800,000	193,400,000	109,400,000	464,400,000	101,500,000	446,600,000
New Orleans .	89,300,000	193,800,000	79,700,000	209,300,000	90,000,000	211,400,000	104,500,000	303,500,000	117,400,000	381,400,000
Maryland . .	34,400,000	109,600,000	24,900,000	131,900,000	27,800,000	180,700,000	43,900,000	374,000,000	29,100,000	336,300,000
Michigan . .	26,300,000	102,500,000	24,900,000	117,700,000	28,500,000	183,100,000	41,700,000	290,300,000	56,900,000	263,800,000
Washington. .	55,300,000	55,000,000	68,400,000	67,800,000	135,500,000	163,000,000	198,300,000	177,600,000	326,900,000	258,000,000
San Francisco .	67,100,000	63,300,000	76,000,000	81,500,000	113,600,000	94,500,000	144,000,000	142,800,000	269,100,000	211,800,000
Massachusetts.	159,900,000	65,700,000	152,600,000	107,400,000	210,900,000	131,200,000	217,900,000	225,500,000	248,900,000	205,100,000
Galveston . .	12,200,000	258,700,000	10,100,000	230,300,000	7,600,000	190,200,000	8,500,000	266,200,000	15,500,000	195,000,000
Georgia . . .	6,200,000	110,500,000	3,200,000	74,900,000	1,700,000	45,800,000	2,000,000	83,100,000	11,500,000	120,000,000
Buffalo . . .	30,300,000	87,600,000	31,400,000	73,900,000	35,900,000	135,900,000	67,700,000	217,100,000	108,800,000	187,000,000
Chicago . . .	38,600,000	8,600,000	29,400,000	23,500,000	26,500,000	8,500,000	31,100,000	6,000,000	33,200,000	5,500,000

and its capacity for work exacted growth in commerce. In the first decade of the United States of America, New York's total exports were ninety-six millions, or one fifth of the country's total; by the fourth decade they had nearly increased half again and were more than one fourth of the country's total. Just before the Civil War they had reached 28.9 per cent., in 1870 they were 50 per cent., but since that time they have decreased in proportion while mounting in totals. For example, in 1870, when this port had 50 per cent. of the total exports, the money value was nearly one hundred and ninety-seven millions. In 1918, with only 44.1 per cent. of the country's whole, the exports were two billion six hundred and thirteen millions and forty-eight thousand. The record percentage for the last sixty years was 53.8 in 1916, when more than two billion three hundred and thirty-two million dollars was exported. The record fiscal year in exports was the next year, 1917, when more than three billion fifty-three million dollars was exported, or 48.5 per cent. of the country's whole.

For the business man and student wishing to see general tendencies and comparisons by decades these facts are shown in graphic form.

EXPORTS

YEAR	CUSTOMS DISTRICT OF NEW YORK	UNITED STATES	NEW YORK'S PERCENTAGE OF WHOLE
1860	$ 80,047,978	$ 333,576,057	23.9
1870	196,614,746	392,771,768	50.0
1871	222,710,489	442,820,178	50.2
1872	228,510,651	444,177,586	51.4
1873	269,529,299	522,479,922	51.5
1874	304,634,338	586,283,040	51.9
1875	262,433,225	513,442,711	51.5
1876	262,851,576	540,384,671	48.6
1877	282,217,379	602,475,220	46.8
1878	336,493,677	694,865,766	48.4
1879	335,870,295	710,439,441	47.2
1880	392,560,090	835,638,658	46.9
1881	407,181,024	902,377,346	45.1
1882	344,503,775	750,542,257	45.8
1883	361,425,361	823,839,402	43.8
1884	329,883,267	740,513,609	44.5
1885	344,514,761	742,189,755	46.4
1886	314,329,411	679,524,830	46.2
1887	316,347,219	716,183,211	44.1
1888	310,627,496	695,954,507	44.6
1889	319,838,555	742,401,375	43.0
1890	349,051,791	857,828,684	40.6
1891	346,528,847	884,480,810	39.1
1892	413,952,783	1,030,278,148	40.1
1893	347,395,717	847,665,194	40.9
1894	369,146,365	892,140,572	41.3
1895	325,580,062	807,538,165	40.3
1896	354,274,941	882,606,938	40.1
1897	391,679,907	1,050,993,556	37.2
1898	445,515,794	1,231,482,330	36.1
1899	459,444,217	1,227,023,302	37.4

EXPORTS—*Continued*

YEAR	CUSTOMS DISTRICT OF NEW YORK	UNITED STATES	NEW YORK'S PERCENTAGE OF WHOLE
1900	$ 518,834,471	$1,394,483,082	37.2
1901	529,592,978	1,487,764,991	35.6
1902	490,361,695	1,381,719,401	35.6
1903	505,829,694	1,420,141,679	35.6
1904	506,808,013	1,460,827,271	34.7
1905	524,726,005	1,528,561,666	34.5
1906	607,160,314	1,743,864,500	34.8
1907	627,949,857	1,880,851,078	33.3
1908	701,062,913	1,860,773,346	37.6
1909	607,239,481	1,663,011,104	36.5
1910	651,986,356	1,744,984,720	37.3
1911	772,552,449	2,049,320,199	37.8
1912	817,945,803	2,204,322,409	37.4
1913	917,935,988	2,465,884,149	37.2
1914	864,546,338	2,364,579,148	36.5
1915	1,193,581,088	2,768,589,340	43.1
1916	2,332,286,213	4,333,482,885	53.8
1917	3,053,119,504	6,290,048,394	48.5
1918	2,613,048,763	5,919,711,371	44.1

It helps us to realize the gigantic growth in the nation's commerce when we find that not until 1912 did the nation as a whole export as much in value as did the Port of New York in 1918, and that in the four years, 1914 to 1918, the Port of New York alone exported in values more than the entire country exported from 1791 to the

Civil War and during the ten highest years in the last century.

For imports the story is quite the same. Before the Civil War nearly two thirds of the country's imports (65.4 per cent.) came into New York. This rose with fluctuations to the high level of 69.6 per cent. in 1884, and since that time there has been a steady decrease until in 1918 two fifths instead of two thirds, that is 42.8 per cent., of the country's total imports came into this port.

It will come as a surprise to most Americans that even with the increase in prices there was a great increase instead of a marked decrease in imports from foreign countries during the recent war. Instead of gaining in its lead over other American ports because of the European war, as shown in the table on page 130, New York lost steadily. This would not have happened if New York had been able to take care of both incoming and outgoing freight. The Federal Government found it necessary to develop other ports and spent enormous sums upon them as its only means of handling expeditiously the untold quantities of food which it was important for us to get to Europe, while at the same time taking care of the imports which we continued to secure from other nations.

GIANT GROWTH IN COMMERCE

IMPORTS

YEAR	CUSTOMS DISTRICT OF NEW YORK	UNITED STATES	NEW YORK'S PERCENTAGE OF WHOLE
1860	$ 231,310,086	$ 353,047,978	65.4
1870	281,048,813	435,958,408	64.4
1871	348,755,769	520,223,684	67.0
1872	416,162,512	626,595,077	66.4
1873	418,709,493	642,136,210	65.2
1874	376,732,380	567,406,342	66.3
1875	357,136,893	533,005,436	67.0
1876	303,466,910	460,741,190	65.8
1877	298,261,378	451,323,126	66.0
1878	292,797,559	437,051,532	66.8
1879	302,349,053	445,777,775	67.8
1880	459,937,153	667,954,746	68.8
1881	435,450,905	642,664,628	67.7
1882	493,060,891	724,639,574	68.0
1883	496,005,276	723,180,914	68.1
1884	465,119,630	667,697,693	69.6
1885	380,077,748	577,527,329	65.8
1886	419,338,932	635,436,136	66.0
1887	456,698,631	692,319,768	65.9
1888	470,426,774	723,957,114	64.9
1889	472,153,507	745,131,652	62.8
1890	516,426,693	789,310,409	65.4
1891	537,786,007	844,916,198	63.6
1892	536,538,112	827,402,426	64.8
1893	548,558,593	866,400,922	63.3
1894	415,795,991	654,994,622	63.4
1895	477,741,138	731,969,965	65.2
1896	499,932,792	779,724,674	64.1
1897	480,603,580	764,730,412	62.8
1898	402,281,050	616,049,654	65.3
1899	465,559,650	697,148,489	66.7

IMPORTS—*Continued*

YEAR	CUSTOMS DISTRICT OF NEW YORK	UNITED STATES	NEW YORK'S PERCENTAGE OF WHOLE
1900	$ 537,237,282	$ 849,941,184	63.2
1901	527,259,906	823,172,165	64.0
1902	559,930,849	903,320,948	61.9
1903	618,705,662	1,025,719,237	61.5
1904	600,171,033	991,087,371	60.5
1905	679,629,256	1,117,513,071	60.8
1906	734,350,823	1,226,562,446	59.9
1907	853,696,952	1,434,421,425	59.5
1908	688,215,938	1,194,341,792	57.6
1909	779,308,944	1,311,920,224	59.4
1910	935,990,958	1,556,947,430	60.1
1911	881,592,689	1,527,226,105	57.7
1912	975,744,320	1,653,264,934	59.0
1913	1,048,320,629	1,813,008,234	57.8
1914	1,040,380,526	1,893,169,740	54.9
1915	931,011,058	1,674,169,740	55.6
1916	1,191,865,982	2,197,883,510	54.2
1917	1,338,199,355	2,659,355,185	50.2
1918	1,251,386,373	2,945,655,403	42.8

In 1915, when commerce had not readjusted itself after the shock of a world war, there was a drop of two hundred millions, or 9 per cent., in the country's total, and a drop of one hundred and nine millions, or more than 10 per cent., in New York's total. There was a rebound in 1916 which continued for two years, so that the country imported in values in 1918 more than two billions nine hundred and forty-five million dollars, while the Port of New York imported more than one billion two hundred and fifty-one million dollars.

Another way of proving the value of imports at the Port of New York is to show the amount of duties. The first year of this port under American control showed the payment of duties here to be one hundred and forty-five thousand dollars; in six years, two million dollars; in thirty years they had increased to thirteen millions. The highest point before the Civil War was forty-three millions, in 1856; in 1864 they were seventy-eight millions; in the first year of this century they were one hundred and fifty-one millions, reaching the highest point in 1907, or two hundred and nineteen millions, falling back again in 1917 to almost the same figures as in 1900, namely, one hundred and fifty-three millions.

Size is of interest only when it means great numbers of people benefited and large enough profits for handling. Commerce has its value to a port not merely because of the money values, certainly not because of the duties paid the Government, but largely because of the human labour involved in handling it. It is quantity not value which provides work. One hundred million dollars in diamonds would not call for any dock except a spring board, and no ship except a canoe. The increase in tons carried is very marked. In 1791 the tonnage was five thousand, the next year it was fifty-one thousand. This doubled in four years. Just before the Civil War it was counted in millions. For eleven years after 1880 it never reached the million mark, stayed around one million tons for ten years; passed one and a half million in 1905, but waited until the recent war to reach and pass two millions.

Another evidence of growth in commerce which is quite important in its meaning to port happiness and prosperity is the number of different articles that are imported and exported. Two hundred years ago New York was famous for flour, which was called its "staple commodity." It raised so much that it "contrived and invented the act of bolting" by which wheat was converted into flour. One hundred years ago New York was shipping wheat, pork, beef, peas, etc., and importing rum and molasses.

A list of the articles which pass through the Port of New York to-day could comprise a book.

What besides its own consuming power and working power accounts for the colossal growth in this port's commerce? As shown above, the explanations are many: the harbour itself; the introduction of steam navigation, coastwise and ocean; the completion of the Erie Canal; the opening up of the Middle West and Far West and South by America's wonderful railroad systems; the annihilation of time by the electric telegraph and telephone; and the opening of the Panama Canal.

One other cause for this port's continued lead and its continuing growth lies in two simple psychological truths: "nothing succeeds like success," and "to him that hath it shall be given."

With negligible exceptions, such as the Federal rate discrimination against the port, every improvement or invention which has helped competing ports, every progressive step taken by competing inland cities, acts by the vital law of "first come, first served" to help New York City. The rubber industry in Akron, the automobile industry in Detroit, the steel mills in Birmingham, the oil wells in Oklahoma have not, of course, helped New York as much relatively as they have helped these localities, but nevertheless they have enriched New York and have caused growth in her manufacturing; in her financial operations and in her commerce. Similarly whatever good work the Federal Government does through its Department of Agriculture, its Postal Service, its Commerce and Labour Departments and its Bureau of Education, it benefits the Port of New York and causes it to grow. Even the Federal Reserve Bank, which was stated to have been planned to deprive New York of its alleged dominance in national finance, while stabilizing the country's currency and credits, has emphasized New York leadership in her ability to serve the country.

CHAPTER IX

Growth of Our Merchant Marine

We Americans love to stand at the head of the line. When our army was meeting the enemy at Château-Thierry we were proud of this American habit and our Allies were grateful for it. In crises, when once clearly recognized as crises, America has demonstrated ability to fight or work or plan or build so that it would be *first*. We have the tallest office building in the world; we have the highest paid labour in the world; we have innumerable other "first prizes." We indulge in our delight in being first when magazine articles and newspaper editorials tell us that America's first port is the world's greatest port, and that at the close of the war our Merchant Marine leads the world. Fortunately we are warned against over-exultation, because once before America led the world in Merchant Marine and ignominiously lost her leadership until just prior to the recent World War when we were carrying less than 3 per cent. of the world's total commerce.

Part of the story of our Merchant Marine is here retold for the purpose of emphasizing the danger, in fact the certainty, that we shall lose our present leadership and fall back to third or fifth rank unless we avoid our earlier mistakes and use the simple knowledge already in possession of our policy makers.

The period between the close of our Revolutionary War and the meeting of the first Congress under the Constitution in 1789 showed us at a great disadvantage, as a nation, in competing with foreign—chiefly British—ships. In 1789 less than 25 per cent. of our foreign commerce was carried in American ships. The first general act of the first Congress was a tariff act in which provision was made for discriminating in duties in favour of imports in American vessels; later discriminating tonnage dues were adopted. Our Merchant Marine grew, no doubt, as a result of this legislation. Until the outbreak of the Civil War, in 1861, an average of 80 per cent. of our imports and exports was carried in American ships—for a period of seventy-two years. For a long time this proportion exceeded 90 per cent., and at the beginning of the Civil War had fallen to 65 per cent.; but the average was 80 per cent. for seventy-two years. During the period our discriminatory policy was strongest, the largest percentage of our imports and exports was carried in American ships; during the period it was weakest the least percentage was carried in our ships. The policy was suspended, for all practical purposes, coincident with the result of changes in our laws and the adoption of trade treaties with other nations.

From the time of the Napoleonic wars to a period just before our own Civil War, the American Merchant Marine was first in the world's shipping, surpassing all other nations in carrying power and speed, not even excepting Great Britain, the self-declared "ruler of the waves." To attain this preëminence it took nearly two hundred years of lively competition with English shipping which had the advantage of governmental patronage, always doing its utmost to destroy or impede colonial initiative and independence in shipping. Fourteen years before the Port of New York came under British jurisdiction, as early as 1650, the British parliament enacted laws protecting home shipping against the competition of English plantations in America; and up to the time of the Revolutionary War it passed twenty-nine other laws for the purpose of restricting our industry. For example, in 1663, the year before the English took New York, it was ordained that nothing was to be imported into an English plantation "except *in an English-built ship*, whereof the *Master and three fourths of the crew* are English."

The first ship built in the Port of New York, and this means in America, was begun in the year 1614 to replace a Dutch ship burned in the harbour the year before. Although a wee bit of a ship, 44 feet long and 11 feet wide, only a trifle smaller than the present-day life boat, it sailed up and down the Atlantic coast and had the honour of being the first vessel to pass through Hell Gate Channel. Something of New York's spirit is indicated by the change of name, when in place of the burned *Restless* or *Onrust*, the first American-built boat was called the *Tiger*, an animal which has survived the rough political seas for a century until in 1919 the Tammany Tiger rules both city and State.

The first shipbuilding plant was confined to the shore road between the present site of Wall Street and Franklin Square on the line of Pearl Street. Shipbuilders lived near their work, as did all workers prior to the introduction of street-car lines. Very little headway was made until the beginning of the Eighteenth Century. In 1728 shipyards extended along the entire

East River front between Beekman and Catherine streets, and in 1740 there were three other shipyards in the vicinity of Dover Street already called the "Shipyards District." We thought we were doing a land office business when in 1774 wooden ships to the value of $150,000 were built in this port. At that time there were more than 700 ships registered here with about 3,400 seamen.

After the Revolution (1784) investors who sent a ship to China and netted $30,000 on a six months' trip lamented that they had earned but 25 per cent. on their investment. It seems that the experience of other ships led them to expect a full 100 per cent. on a single trip—a faint forecast of the halcyon shipping days of the World War 125 years later. This 25 per cent. profit venture, however, encouraged the sending of several other vessels to China, all of which earned big profits.

The inauguration of the American Merchant Marine dates from these post-revolutionary trips of the years 1784 and 1787. China's trade was sought from necessity, not preference, because the rupture with Great Britain had caused the loss of trade formerly enjoyed by the colonies and forced them to seek markets elsewhere—as the western world's moral boycott on German-made goods after the World War promises to turn Germany's exploitation Russianward. New Yorkers and New Englanders directed their attention to the sea partly because seafaring revived privateering and similar activities during the Revolution, and also because it was harder to make a living from the northern soil than from the sea.

If necessity inaugurated our Merchant Marine, invention gave it the substantial lead which it retained for more than fifty years.

We have already seen how steamboats were invented and tested in 1786, 1791, and 1807, and how the commercial possibility of this invention was proven at just the time when the rest of the world was involved in war, and when as a neutral possessing goods and services needed by European nations, including England herself, our Merchant Marine gained an enviable start.

Even with Americans there is frequently a wide gap between invention or demonstration and adoption. The sailing vessel remained indispensable for decades; in fact, it almost held its own, and at least held an important share of the field, until the combination of iron ships and steam gave Great Britain a lead just before our Civil War, during which period we lost ground steadily because of the necessity for the concentration of all our energies upon our fight for the union.

By the year 1812, just before our second war with Great Britain, shipbuilding was New York City's principal industry, registering 267,000 tons, equal to the tonnage of Boston and Philadelphia combined. The war brought all legitimate shipping prosperity to a sudden end, and in its place came privateering legalized by the declaration of war. Such goods as did find their way to the city were smuggled in through some port on the Jersey coast and were hauled in wagons overland to New York. Enormous profits resulted. Within four months, twenty-six privateers were sent out from New York, and although sailing vessels, they were exceptionally swift, were seldom captured, and with few exceptions returned with great wealth to their owners.

New York gained a good lead in the world contest for sea supremacy by establishing, in 1816, the first packet line to Liverpool—the famous Black Ball Line, founded by local capitalists. At the outset the sailing date was the first of every month, but, as competition developed, an additional sailing date was established on the 16th of the month. The original ships of this line were only four in number, and varied in size from four hundred to five hundred tons; they were immeasurably superior to the old merchantmen in every particular, and consequently aroused such a spirit of emulation that many other lines were soon established, as the Red Star, the Swallow Tail, St. George's, E. E. Morgan's London Line, Spefford and Tiletson's Liverpool Line, and E. K. Collin's Dramatic Line, so that by 1822 the port had a weekly packet service to London, while between 1825 and 1832 three ships were engaged in the trade to Havre, seven to Savannah, ten to Charleston. This list takes no account of the innumerable sailing vessels of all descriptions that made regular trips to all intermediate points of importance on the coast.

The ships used in the transatlantic service were the largest and swiftest that had ever been so employed, making the passage from Sandy Hook to Liverpool during the first nine years in twenty-three days on the average and the return voyage in forty days. Later, some of the packets made the trip in sixteen days, and six of them established sailing records of fifteen days and less.

No ships built abroad could compete with even the earliest of these speedy packets, and the entire country, as well as New York, had the greatest interest in them and their commanders. "No matter what the weather was, ships sailed on the day set, leaving the piers with sails set, and cheered by the multitudes who gathered to see the departure. Tugs were seldom used in leaving or making harbour until after 1835, and long afterward captains took pride in dispensing with their services and in sailing their ships right up to their berths."

The success of the transatlantic lines in 1816 had naturally turned the attention of ship-builders to the possibilities of a similar coastwise service, and accordingly, in 1818, a number of 180-ton sloops began to make regular passages between New York and Boston.

The completion of the Erie Canal, in 1825, gave a tremendous impetus to this commerce: "1,300 sailing vessels entered the port annually and the city's inland trade transported by the way of the Hudson River and the Erie Canal was as great as that of the packet lines."

In 1832, E. K. Collins, who contributed more perhaps than any other man of his time to the development of the American Merchant Marine, opened lines to New Orleans and Vera Cruz, Mexico, which were of incalculable help to the growth of the port. They also encouraged Mr. Collins to establish the Dramatic Line to Liverpool; this, said the New York *Daily Advertiser*, in September, 1836, "added another list of fine ships to the sixteen now built."

Rivalry was so keen that the voyages became real sporting events, large wagers frequently being laid when favourites were entered in a race. In 1837 stakes of $10,000 were put up on the *Columbia*, 597 tons, of the Black Ball Line, and the *Sheridan* of the Dramatic Line, in a race to Liverpool, the former winning in sixteen days, two days in advance of the arrival of her competitor.

Freight rates, naturally, became inflated, as traders were willing to pay extra prices to get their commodities quickly into circulation, and the shipowners readily responded to the new order of things. Fortunes were speedily made by nearly every man having an interest in a line, and this included agents, captains, shippers, and builders; of course a demand was created for larger vessels, so that in 1854 the *Amazon* and the *Palestine*, of 1,800 tons each, were launched by the Morgan Line—the last vessels from their yards, and the largest Atlantic packets ever launched.

The vessels were all of 800 tons and over—enormous for their day, though one eightieth that of the *Leviathan*—constructed in New

York, and added greatly to the American Merchant Marine, as, at the time, the entire number of ships, including those from Philadelphia, was only fifty, with a total tonnage of less than 35,000. The tonnage in the foreign traffic of the whole country was but 753,094, and the packet fleets comprised only a small fraction of this, but they more than made up for this deficiency by the part they played in winning for the new nation the supremacy of the seas.

The British, from whom the lead had been taken, freely acknowledged this superiority, not only with respect to ships, but also in regard to the personnel of the service, "the commanders and officers being generally considered to be more competent as seamen and navigators, and more uniformly persons of education, than the commanders and officers of the British ships of similar size and class trading from England to America; while the seamen of the United States are considered to be more carefully selected and more efficient."

It was also admitted that American ships sailing from Liverpool to New York had preference over English vessels of the same route, because, as more liberal wages were paid the seamen, "their whole equipment was maintained in a higher state of perfection, so that few losses occurred"—a consolation and suggestion in 1919 when American business men are fearing loss of commerce because of America's higher labour cost. The superior compensation attracted the best of the British seamen to the American service, and the quicker and safer hauls were equally strong inducements for the shipper to transfer his patronage. As Spears summarizes the situation in 1837:

> All this is to say that, while twenty-one years had elapsed since the American sailor had won, by good fighting, the right to cross the seas unmolested by foreign warships, his chief competitors openly acknowledged that in the trade between New York and Liverpool (the most important trade route in the world) he had won unquestioned and even uncontested supremacy.

In the meantime, experiments with steam power had continued, its first extensive gains being acquired in the newly developing traffic on the Hudson River. A regular line of steam packets to Albany was established in 1810, extended to a tri-weekly line in 1813, and a line to New Haven and New London was established in 1818. The next year the *Savannah*, a sailing vessel with auxiliary engine, commanded by Captain Moses Rogers, of New York, where she had been built by Francis Fickett, made the first trip under steam across the Atlantic. She sailed from Savannah, Georgia, May 26, 1819, to London in twenty-seven days, eighty hours of which she ran under steam. The *Savannah* was a failure, however, because of her faulty construction; the large space needed for her machinery and fuel leaving so little room for cargo that her engine was taken out. The coastwise service was so satisfactory, however, that by 1830 there were in New York Harbour eighty-six steamboats engaged in that trade.

Some of the most prominent men of the port became interested in shipping; one of them, Cornelius Vanderbilt, at various times between 1829 and 1848 put into operation on the Hudson River and Long Island Sound, after the expiration of the monopoly granted to Fulton and Livingston, fifty steamboats, all owned by him and most of which he had built. Later he established a line of transatlantic packets, proudly advertised as "superior to all competitors."

The American Merchant Marine was thus continually augmented until it reached its zenith in the clipper ship service, brought to perfection by the genius of John W. Griffiths, a young naval architect of New York, who was of the opinion that a ship having "hollow or concave waterlines, especially at the bow, would sail more swiftly than one with ordinary convex lines, no matter how fine the convex lines might be."

Griffiths exhibited a model according to this plan at the American Institute in 1841, and also delivered a number of lectures on the subject, in this way finally generating interest in his idea and securing financial backing to put it into execution. William H. Aspinwall, one of New York's merchant princes, had great faith in the Griffiths plan and, in 1843, ordered a ship of 750 tons to be built in the great yards of Smith & Dimon, of New York, and under the name of the *Rainbow* this ship was launched in January, 1845. She made her maiden voyage to Canton and back in one hundred and ninety-five days, and later broke the record over the same route by sailing out in ninety-two days and returning in eighty-eight days, a total of one hundred and eighty days for the voyage.

The nautical world had been very skeptical about the success of this type of vessel, but, after such a conclusive demonstration, other vessels similar in construction were put into operation as rapidly as possible. A younger sister ship sailed from Sandy Hook for Hongkong on Christmas Eve, 1846, making the out-voyage in one hundred and four days, and the return in eighty-one days. Ultimately, she made the unbroken record from China to New York in seventy-seven days.

Other clipper ships were commissioned as quickly as the shipyards could turn them out, and in this way the shipbuilding industry in New York received such a great impetus that it soon became one of the largest in the world. Philadelphia, Boston, and Baltimore were obliged to adopt the Griffiths type of clipper ship in order to compete with the service from New York, and the majority of these vessels were built by those who had already made a success of their construction.

After the repeal of the British Navigation Laws, in 1849, giving American ships a share of the British tea trade, and admitting American-built ships to British registry, these New York shipyards constructed the best types of the vessels in the English service.

The discovery of gold in California, in 1846, accentuated the boom in shipbuilding in New York, especially of the clipper ship type, as the speedy delivery of cargoes was most important; the vast horde of prospectors which had flocked to that region had to be clothed and fed from the East as nothing but the coveted metal was obtainable on the Pacific Coast in those days.

During this period, from 1850 to 1860, one hundred and sixty clipper ships were built, most of them in or near New York, and the shipyards were put to their utmost capacity to meet the demand for vessels in this service as well as for service overseas. Thirty-one California clippers, built in New York, were launched in 1851. In one of the many races arranged for large stakes between New York and Boston "fliers," New York's clipper, the *Sword-fish,* won in the second best record ever made "round the Horn" to San Francisco—ninety-two days—her competitor's time being ninety-eight days.

So the story of America's Merchant Marine runs through chapter after chapter of adventure, romance, and soul-stirring victories to a triumphant climax—and then suddenly the pendulum swings the other way to the deliberate destruction of all the progress that had been made in the years before.

The sunset of this period of unexampled growth began in 1856. Companies failed because of extravagance. The financial panic of 1857 still further crippled the industry, and the withdrawal of the Federal subsidy in 1858 entirely destroyed the strength of our competition with foreign lines. By the first year of the Civil War we had practically lost our mail,

PERCENTAGE OF OVERSEAS COMMERCE CARRIED IN AMERICAN VESSELS IN SPECIFIED YEARS 1789–1914

Year	Percentage
1789	23.8
1795	90.0
1800	89.0
1810	91.5
1820	89.5
1830	89.9
1840	82.9
1850	72.5
1860	66.2
1870	35.6
1880	17.4
1890	12.9
1900	9.3
1910	8.8
1914	9.7

passenger, and freight traffic from New York to Great Britain, a loss from which the port and the country never fully recovered until the recent World War.

The vicissitudes of our Merchant Marine are reflected in the accompanying diagram which shows the steady growth and decline and also the change in the share of the shipping which left the Port of New York under the Stars and Stripes. A mere glance at this chart shows that the Merchant Marine lines of absolute and relative importance have gone down more often than they have gone up in the days of modern shipping. Accordingly, the question of absorbing concern to Americans to-day is the line-up to stay, or shall we lose the lead which our three years of neutrality during the World War and our possession of invaluable goods gave to our Merchant Marine?

The answer to this question rests entirely with our Congress and our business men within the first two or three years after the signing of peace. If the newspapers and magazines are any criteria to public opinion, we should recognize that the best-informed minds and most constructive talents of the country are being devoted to making sure that the answer shall be: *For the welfare of all the people in the United States of America our Merchant Marine must be henceforth second to none.* Unfortunately, however, the best-informed minds and the most constructive talents are not giving the continuous attention and cumulative publicity to which the dangers and opportunities now confronting our Merchant Marine are entitled. In the latest published list of commercial organizations, only nine titles indicate special interest in port problems and Merchant Marine. Of those nine, four are classified under rivers and harbours and five under ships and shipping. The total membership of the last five is less than 600.

Of what avail are attractively illustrated magazine articles about the "Sea Gate of the Continent," the "Gateway of a Nation," "Clearing House of the World," "The American Merchant Marine, A Programme," "Ships and the Average Man," "The Future of Our Merchant Fleet," etc., if our statesmen in Congress and our energetic business men do not establish "priority" rules for the removal of dangers to shipping and the development of our commercial opportunities under the American flag? Of what avail is the "Call of the Sixth Foreign Trade Convention," presenting in its sessions the following programmes if such vital messages do not reach the people?

THIRD GENERAL SESSION

Friday, April 25th

Orchestra Hall

10:00 A. M.

Session Topic:

The American Merchant Marine

1. Address: **American Shipbuilding,**
HOMER L. FERGUSON
President, Newport News Shipbuilding and Drydock Company.
2. Address: **The World's Merchant Fleets To-day,**
W. S. TOWER,
Division of Planning and Statistics, U. S. Shipping Board.
3. Address: **The Future of the American Marine on the Pacific,**
FREDERICK J. KOSTER,
President, San Francisco Chamber of Commerce.
4. Address: **The Relation of Law to the Development of Our Merchant Marine,**
ERNEST E. BALDWIN, of the New York Bar.
5. Address: **The Relation of Inland Waterways to Foreign Trade,**
JAMES E. SMITH,
President, Mississippi Valley Waterways Association.

Congress Hotel, Florentine Room

Chairman: ROBERT DOLLAR, President, The Robert Dollar Company, San Francisco.
Vice-Chairman: H. F. ALEXANDER, Pacific Steamship Co.

Secretary: C. P. Converse, Secretary Foreign Trade Department, San Francisco Chamber of Commerce.

1. Address: **Marine Insurance,**
   BENJAMIN RUSH,
   President, American Foreign Insurance Association.
2. Address: **Improved Port Service and Foreign Trade,**
   HON. MURRAY HURLBERT,
   Dock Commissioner and Director of the Port of New York.
3. Address: **Freight Forwarding for Export,**
   W. J. RILEY,
   Export Manager, Judson Freight Forwarding Company.

The supreme need now is not for new information, but for the circulation and reiteration of established facts—and of controverted contention until facts agreed upon take the place of controversy—so that "the common man," "the man on the street," "everybody," "the people," become *port-conscious, port-minded, and alive to their personal need for and their personal interest in a national merchant marine* which, while sailing the seas, shall serve a useful end similar to that of the road before their house, the pipes which bring their water, the railroad that brings mail to them and carries their produce to market. Charles M. Schwab, former head of the Emergency Fleet Corporation, says:

We may construct one hundred million tons of ships, but they will have no value to this great nation of ours unless we do what is more important than the construction of ships, and that is to devise the ways and means for their operation. A great merchant marine is essential to the United States for its ultimate success. Its successful operation is not for the benefit of any one man or class of men, or any one branch of business, but it is for the good of every individual citizen of the United States.

I do not care what plan, in the opinion of our great legislators at Washington, may be best for the operation of these ships, so long as they are operated economically and so long as the expense of operation is not borne by any one or few, but by the whole people. No American shipbuilding can be profitable or successful or enlist private capital to-day, as shipping is now operated. The people who constitute the chambers of commerce, the manufacturers of the United States, must raise their voices for the successful operation of our mercantile marine.

Since the purpose of this chapter is to arouse interest and not settle problems, a summary is given of more important statements of facts and suggestions taken from recent discussions by Joseph J. Schlecta, Bernard N. Baker, William C. Brinton, Raymond Garfield Gettell, C. M. Keys, and Gerard C. Henderson:

1. Only profit will attract people to the sea.

2. Americans will not adopt the seafaring life in peace times merely to sustain the glory of the flag or in response to the thrills of romance popularly associated with the seaman's life.

3. Industry and commerce ashore offer opportunities which quite eclipse those open to seamen.

4. Men competent to direct shipping will not accept smaller salaries than offered in other lines.

5. Capital will not accept small profits.

6. Labour will not accept lower standards.

7. Ship repairing is 80 per cent. higher here than in England, Holland, or France.

8. After the war shippers will not pay Americans $250 a ton if the British or Swedish builders will take $200.

9. No one will pay us $20 per ton for space if the British carrier will take $15.

10. We therefore face two alternatives:

1. Reconstruction of our laws so that American capital may buy or build ships wherever the best bargains are (The Panama Canal Act, August 24, 1912, permitted American registry to foreign-built ships, if American-owned and if not more than five years old, but in two years not one ship registered. When the five-year qualification was dropped August 2, 1914, several hundred thousand tons of foreign-built, American-owned shipping came under American registry).

2. Subsidize ships to offset subsidies or bonuses or other advantages granted by other governments to their shipping.

11. New ships to compete in world markets must be of at least 10,000 tons dead weight, and must have speed of sixteen knots (The Shipping Board reported that there are plans for "Lake Ships" from three to four thousand tons; some standardized ships of 8,000 tons called "West Class").

12. Contracts for ships below these two requirements should be immediately cancelled.

13. An educational campaign is needed to provide seamen:

"The American boy is apt to find some position far inland which offers him more in immediate return and future prospects than life before the mast; and yet, if he could be imbued with the vision; if he could be stirred with lust of travel and adventure; if he could see the wide spaces and learn to love the call of the vast; if he could be made to see the romance of it all and the joy that comes from carrying his country's flag to be planted at the crossroads of the world, there would be no trouble in filling the ranks."

14. Sea service must be made attractive, i. e., compensation and opportunities for advancement and development must be increased.

15. The sea calls for large and versatile powers.

16. The sea invites attention.

17. Campaigns of education are needed to awaken interest and pride among laymen in our new maritime position and in the danger of losing it if our present opportunities are not kept abreast and ahead of the times. In 1914 we were a poor third among shipbuilding nations.

18. We need to establish selling agencies abroad.

19. Bunkering accommodations for shipping are needed in foreign ports.

20. After the war we must look to foreign markets as an outlet for war-stimulated manufactures.

21. From this time on trade competition will replace the artificial unity of common war needs among America and its allies in Europe and Latin-America, which will particularly affect new business as with Latin-America, due to the collapse of European shipping during the war.

22. Managerial ability of the highest order must be attractive and held by our maritime commerce.

Thus far there is negligible controversy. The controversy is over the best method of meeting those conditions. The quoted propositions that follow are not stated dogmatically, but in recognition of their currency and their suggestiveness:

1. When peace is declared, Great Britain and America shall have about an equal share of the world's shipping, i. e., 30 per cent.

2. After the war a revival of international exchange of manufactured products will be slow.

3. A decrease in the salary levels will be very slow, if at all.

4. Higher prices will cause a decrease in demand from South America, Asia, and Australia.

5. The volume of world trade after the war will be less than before the beginning.

6. On the Pacific, four Japanese lines which have almost monopolized the carrying trade will continue their supremacy.

7. On all seas our main competition will come from Great Britain unless the terms of peace provide some form of international organization or friendly pooling of interests. In 1914 Great Britain had 30 per cent. and America had 5 per cent. of the world's shipping. Of a total of three and a half billion dollars in American import and export trade only 10 per cent. was carried in American vessels; only 3 per cent. of the world's sea-going shipping was owned by American interests. Of our total shipping 80 per cent. was engaged in Great Lakes and Coastwise trade.

8. After-war competitive conditions will not permit such profits as attracted capital to shipping during the war, such as $21 per ton per manufacture; cotton rates increasing from 35 cents to $6, from signing of labour bill, or nearly 2,000 per cent.; many vessels earned their total cost in a single voyage.

The main open questions which exact early answer by our statesmen and commerce builders are these:

1. Will the Government assume responsibility for maintaining America's first rank in shipyards, shipways, shipyard workers, ships under construction and ships completed during the last war year; with more than 2,000 ships, aggregating 10,400,000 dead-weight tons, under control of the shipyard, plus fifteen vessels, 125,000 tons bought from Japan?

2. Will the Government keep on competing with foreign yards in shipbuilding and go on using its 200 shipyards (where there were 61 before the war) and its 1,000 shipways (where there were 235), and its first rank as a shipbuilding nation (where in 1914 we were a poor third), and with fifteen million tons under contract now building?

3. Shall the Emergency Fleet Corporation continue, and if so, as a public or private agency?

4. Shall the United States Shipping Board continue its policy of trade experiments?

5. Would not national control and "allocation" of shipping be better for us than cut-throat competition?

6. Even if it involved a sacrifice for America, would we forego any temporary advantage we might possess in favour of a greater advantage to world welfare?

7. Should we seek some maritime adjustment with Great Britain so as to utilize the good feeling which has resulted from war-time coöperation, before losing opportunity for amicable settlement?

8. Must we be lured to defend efforts of private interests and partisan politics to arouse mutual suspicion to over-emphasize nationalism in Great Britain and the United States?

9. Is the merchant marine of enough importance to

all American business to justify a government subsidy which will effect any higher cost that conditions of living, of seamen's salaries, and other American restrictions may impose?

10. Can we afford to lower our standards of living and our health several grades in order to increase the competitive ability of our Merchant Marine?

11. Is there danger to our prosperity from abuse on Great Britain's part, or our own country's part, of their respective programmes of maritime imperialism?

12. Is it true that an after-war controversy between America and England over sea power will be "as full of danger to the peace of the world as the period of territorial and dynastic rivalries?"

13. Is it true that by coöperation in their maritime policies Great Britain and America can make "the greatest possible contribution toward world organization and lasting peace?"

In answering these questions we shall be helped by remembering the reasons why our Merchant Marine declined steadily after the Civil War in spite of knowledge they possessed regarding the conditions of a prosperous merchant marine, just as to-day those best informed see what should be done with our present awakening. We lost our lead just before the Civil War because (1) we had obstinately stuck to wood instead of building ships of iron and steel; (2) we were even slow in substituting steam for sails; (3) Great Britain had more developed manufactures; (4) Great Britain had cheaper coal; (5) lack of preference for American ships under our discriminatory laws, and (6) in 1858 the Federal subsidy was withdrawn just when it might have been used to stimulate the kind of progressive shipbuilding which would have been able to survive without government aid. Then the Civil War came with high taxes on shipping, a blockade at Southern ports which meant a general lack of any traffic to carry; and union shipping was frightened from the seas by confederate cruisers fitted out in England's shipyards.

Following the war, eleven different factors contributed to prevent our Merchant Marine from regaining a firm footing:

1. Congress took little interest in shipping—a mistake which is apt to be repeated if those who see the need for both interest and action by Congress and themselves are caught napping.

2. Congress did not allow vessels which had been transferred from the American flag during the Civil War—as a means of fighting confederate cruisers—to be readmitted to American registry—a mistake that is not involved to-day because in the World War it was the American flag under which foreign shipping sought shelter.

3. Congress did not repeal heavy war taxes on shipping until three years after the war closed—perhaps a necessary handicap, but one which should not be retained after the World War unless absolutely necessary, and when considering the necessity, land business should carefully ponder

the certain loss from high taxes on shipping and the possible gains to all American industry from low taxes on shipping.

4. Congress did not allow free importation of materials for constructing wooden vessels until the year 1872 and the free import of steel until 1890—a kind of mistake that it will be easy for Congress to repeat.

5. For twenty years all the reorganization of shipyards was delayed—a mistake which again menaces our shipping.

6. The use of steel on a large scale in building ships was delayed twenty years—there is danger now of trying to save obsolete wooden vessels which earned a debt of gratitude during the war, but which will only be a millstone in international competition after the war.

7. Liberal payments to American vessels for carrying imports were not begun until 1891, twenty-six years after the war—a mistake that could be corrected not by liberal blanket appropriations, but by paying what it costs and all that it costs to render this service on the same theory that the country defrays the cost of maintaining a parcel post department.

8. After the Civil War there was more profit in settling and in developing transportation than in developing a merchant marine, which, of course, led both capital and men away from the sea—a condition that may easily be repeated if our Merchant Marine and its needs are given as little expert analysis as they have been given in the past, and unless the Government fails to insist upon a complete divorce of ships from railroad domination.

9. It was cheaper for American merchants to pay the freight rates charged by foreign carriers than to invest their capital in American Merchant Marine—a condition which those closest to our foreign commerce insist exists to-day and will continue to exist. Whether this is the case of "The wish being father to the thought," i. e., of a desire for subsidy and big profits being father to the claim

that the Merchant Marine is impossible, that big profits cannot with decency and patriotism be discussed on any other basis than the basis of demonstrable facts.

10. There was no large surplus of manufactures after our Civil War needing foreign markets because the total output could be taken care of at home at higher rates—a condition that does not exist to-day, which is perhaps fortunate for a merchant marine because our greater industries are now compelled to look for continued prosperity to outlets in other countries.

In a spirited editorial, P. H. W. Ross urges us to "feel ships":

We never realized why America as a whole had not demanded a merchant marine until one day, a few years ago, in a Western town we met a man who had never seen a ship. He was a Kansan, and a man of intelligence. Fortune had not taken him to the seaboard, so all he knew about ocean vessels was gained from books and pictures.

He wanted to see a ship, but it was not to realize an ideal, like the old man who had not seen Carcassonne; it was pure curiosity. It would have made no difference whether it carried a Dutch, Japanese, British, or American flag; whether it was a coaster or a transocean carrier, a passenger vessel or a freighter.

A man must *feel* ships as well as see them. The greatest ship is vastly more than a mechanical marvel, for it represents powers more far-reaching than engineering achievement. It is a developer of trade, of culture, of advancement in nearly every field of endeavour. It is a promoter of peace and prosperity. It typifies the first step toward sociological development, for the time when men's minds began to be broadened was coeval with the dawn of navigation. The world began to get new viewpoints, which is always a stimulating factor in evolution.

Nations began to exchange things with each other, and the most valuable of these were ideas. When a man gives away an idea he makes himself richer. If the ideas we shot into Germany were less effective than the bullets we shot into Germans, the war effort was wasted.

All of which is to suggest that every patriotic and right-thinking American do his part toward maintaining our Merchant Marine by discussing it on every possible occasion. Keep the subject alive; keep alive to its developments. Talk ships, think ships, *feel ships.*

TABLE OF FACTS ABOUT SHIPPING

Vessels engaged in foreign trade are registered.

Those engaged entirely in coastwise or domestic trade are enrolled and licensed.

Prior to 1864 tonnage of United States vessels was calculated on the basis of 95 cubic feet to the ton.

In 1864 the Moorsom system, inaugurated by the British Board of Trade in the Merchant Shipping Act of 1854, was adopted by the United States Government and the ton register fixed at 100 cubic feet, which is now the basis of calculation by all maritime nations.

Gross tonnage is all material capacity.

Net tonnage is certified spaces eliminated, i. e., engine space, crew space, necessary storeroom space, etc., deducted from gross tonnage.

In other words, net tonnage is space for profit figured on 100 cubic feet to the ton.

Dead-weight tonnage is 40 cubic feet to the ton, average cargo weight.

TABLE OF SHIPS BUILT AND OWNED IN THE PORT OF NEW YORK, 1815–1861

YEAR	TONNAGE BUILT IN NEW YORK	TONNAGE OWNED IN NEW YORK
1815	11,754	278,869
1816	15,743	299,618
1817	11,279	306,221
1818	11,512	233,884
1819	7,715	229,190
1820	5,255	231,216
1821	6,892	236,160
1822	15,567	252,072
1823	13,968	263,750
1824	13,714	281,148
1825	21,350	304,484
1826	22,935	316,289
1827	14,770	346,357
1828	16,331	339,405
1829	7,252	261,704
1830	6,732	256,557
1831	15,738	286,439
1832	16,133	298,833
1833	22,270	323,734
1834	17,368	259,222
1835	......	376,698
1836	16,689	404,814
1837	20,302	410,872
1838	14,330	400,972

TABLE OF SHIPS BUILT AND OWNED IN THE PORT OF NEW YORK, 1815–1861—*Continued*

YEAR	TONNAGE BUILT IN NEW YORK	TONNAGE OWNED IN NEW YORK
1839	16,688	430,301
1840	13,357	414,817
1841	16,121	438,014
1842	18,835	459,474
1843	13,280	496,966
1844	18,025	525,162
1845	26,621	550,360
1846	29,495	572,524
1847	37,591	646,044
1848	57,977	733,077
1849	37,933	796,492
1850	55,525	835,568
1851	71,214	931,194
1852	69,954	1,016,600
1853	68,454	1,149,133
1854	93,590	1,262,798
1855	92,698	1,288,234
1856	49,317	1,328,036
1857	43,118	1,377,425
1858	25,845	1,432,705
1859	15,145	1,444,361
1860	33,484	1,464,001
1861	33,122	1,539,355
Total	1,260,103	28,431,149

The total tonnage of the United States at the close of the fiscal year, 1860–1861, was 5,539,812 tons, of which the State of New York owned 1,740,900 tons, or nearly 30 per cent. of the whole tonnage of the entire country. During the same year the total tonnage built was 233,194 tons, of which there were built in the several districts of the State of New York 46,356 tons, or nearly 20 per cent.

This indicates that, while there were other states producing more largely than the State of New York, there was a rapid concentration of ownership at the Port of New York by purchase.

TABLE SHOWING NUMBER AND CLASS OF VESSELS BUILT IN THE PORT OF NEW YORK, 1860–1918

1860

Ships and barks	4	Sloops and canal boats	92
Brigs	2	Steamers	28
Schooners	15	Total built	141
Total tonnage	23,484.73		

1861

Ships and barks	2	Sloops and canal boats	112
Brigs	00	Steamers	40
Schooners	24	Total built	178
Total tonnage	33,121.85		

1862

Ships and barks	0	Sloops and canal boats	62
Brigs	1	Steamers	45
Schooners	14	Total built	122
Total tonnage	32,627.47		

TABLE SHOWING NUMBER AND CLASS OF VESSELS BUILT IN THE PORT OF NEW YORK, 1860–1918—*Continued*

1863

Ships and barks	5	Sloops and canal boats	322
Brigs	4	Steamers	75
Schooners	13	Total built	419
Total tonnage	77,413.04		

1864

Ships and barks	6	Sloops and canal boats	476
Brigs	5	Steamers	101
Schooners	11	Total built	599
Total tonnage	112,660.12		

1865

Ships and barks	4	Sloops and canal boats	163
Brigs	4	Steamers	59
Schooners	33	Total built	263
Total tonnage	83,763.18		

1866

Ships and barks	2	Sloops and canal boats	60
Brigs	6	Steamers	39
Schooners	13	Total built	120
Total tonnage	37,336.31		

1867

Ships and barks	1	Sloops and canal boats	75
Brigs	0	Steamers	38
Schooners	39	Total built	152
Total tonnage	38,557.81		

TABLE SHOWING NUMBER AND CLASS OF VESSELS BUILT IN THE PORT OF NEW YORK, 1860–1918—*Continued*

1868

Sailing vessels	91	Tonnage	9,546.56
Steam vessels	17	"	14,806.01
Barges	10	"	2,015.28
Canal boats	48	"	3,888.73
Total number	166	Total tonnage.	30,256.58

1869

Ships and barks	6	Sloops and canal boats	57
Brigs	5	Steamers	31
Schooners	24	Total built	123

Total tonnage . . . 28,074.52

1870

Ships and barks	4	Sloops and canal boats	56
Brigs	2	Steamers	28
Schooners	30	Total built	120

Total tonnage 23,860.26

1871

Sailing vessels	76	Tonnage	7,250.95
Steam vessels	21	"	9,630.50
Canal boats	162	"	14,736.65
Barges	56	"	17,711.23
Total number	315	Total tonnage.	49,329.33

Table Showing Number and Class of Vessels Built in the Port of New York, 1860–1918—*Continued*

1872

Sailing vessels	80	Tonnage	4,450.40
Steam vessels	30	"	7,414.28
Barges	27	"	5,791.87
Canal boats	90	"	8,558.77
Total number	227	Total tonnage.	26,215.32

1873

Sailing vessels	63	Tonnage	7,610.60
Steam vessels	66	"	18,193.42
Canal boats	427	"	38,280.72
Barges	45	"	7,460.28
Total number	601	Total tonnage.	71,545.02

1874

Sailing vessels	89	Tonnage	7,532.16
Steam vessels	60	"	25,711.81
Canal boats	196	"	18,929.12
Barges	51	"	11,828.46
Total number	396	Total tonnage.	64,001.55

1875

Sailing vessels	62	Tonnage	7,334.11
Steam vessels	38	"	5,463.71
Canal boats	24	"	2,466.71
Barges	22	"	5,414.59
Total number	146	Total tonnage.	20,679.12

TABLE SHOWING NUMBER AND CLASS OF VESSELS BUILT IN THE PORT OF NEW YORK, 1860–1918—*Continued*

1876

Sailing vessels . . .	63	Tonnage . . .	3,495.97
Steam vessels . . .	23	" . . .	5,353.19
Canal boats . . .	4	" . . .	443.46
Barges	3	" . . .	353.56
Total number . .	100	Total tonnage.	9,646.18

1877

Sailing vessels . . .	44	Tonnage . . .	1,134.87
Steam vessels . . .	20	" . . .	6,408.20
Canal boats . . .	12	" . . .	1,157.93
Barges	6	" . . .	2,518.51
Total number . .	82	Total tonnage.	11,219.51

1878

Sailing vessels . . .	63	Tonnage . . .	3,440.74
Steam vessels . . .	30	" . . .	5,851.56
Canal boats . . .	8	" . . .	748.73
Barges	8	" . . .	1,056.73
Total number . .	109	Total tonnage.	11,097.76

1879

Sailing vessels . . .	76	Tonnage . . .	4,564.45
Steam vessels . . .	33	" . . .	3,062.21
Canal boats . . .	15	" . . .	1,601.86
Barges	11	" . . .	2,036.72
Total number .	135	Total tonnage.	11,265.24

TABLE SHOWING NUMBER AND CLASS OF VESSELS BUILT IN THE PORT OF NEW YORK, 1860–1918—*Continued*

1880

Sailing vessels . . .	53	Tonnage . . .	2,362.19
Steam vessels . . .	40	"	3,831.63
Canal boats . . .	1	" . . .	96.94
Barges	9	" . . .	1,683.70
Total number . .	103	Total tonnage .	7,974.46

1881

Sailing vessels . . .	40	Tonnage . . .	1,662.30
Steam vessels . . .	61	" . . .	8,879.48
Canal boats . . .	14	" . . .	1,481.55
Barges	12	" . . .	2,487.23
Total number . .	127	Total tonnage.	14,510.56

1882

Sailing vessels . . .	57	Tonnage . . .	3,614.99
Steam vessels . . .	57	" . . .	9,517.93
Canal boats . . .	15	" . . .	1,765.50
Barges	29	" . . .	4,830.80
Total number . .	158	Total tonnage.	19,729.22

1883

Sailing vessels . . .	49	Tonnage . . .	2,843.66
Steam vessels . . .	47	" . . .	6,337.31
Canal boats . . .	8	" . . .	920.94
Barges	8	" . . .	1,698.70
Total number . .	112	Total tonnage.	11,800.61

TABLE SHOWING NUMBER AND CLASS OF VESSELS BUILT IN THE PORT OF NEW YORK, 1860–1918—*Continued*

1884

Sailing vessels . . .	60	Tonnage . . .	3,758.37
Steam vessels . . .	48	" . . .	7,069.73
Canal boats . . .	8	" . . .	908.60
Barges	15	" . . .	3,221.00
Total number . .	131	Total tonnage.	14,957.70

1885

Sailing vessels . . .	41	Tonnage . . .	833.54
Steam vessels . . .	43	" . . .	6,407.78
Canal boats . . .	3	" . . .	314.99
Barges	14	" . . .	4,342.47
Total number . .	101	Total tonnage.	11,898.78

1886

Sailing vessels . . .	27	Tonnage . . .	718.23
Steam vessels . . .	29	" . . .	3,176.34
Canal boats . . .	5	" . . .	870.84
Barges	14	" . . .	2,440.02
Total number . .	75	Total tonnage.	7,205.43

1887

Sailing vessels . . .	69	Tonnage . . .	1,252.98
Steam vessels . . .	44	" . . .	6,171.81
Canal boats . . .	2	" . . .	244.54
Barges	34	" . . .	7,165.46
Total number . .	149	Total tonnage .	14,834.79

TABLE SHOWING NUMBER AND CLASS OF VESSELS BUILT IN THE PORT OF NEW YORK, 1860–1918—*Continued*

1888

Sailing vessels	31	Tonnage	331.20
Steam vessels	39	"	3,597.52
Canal boats	2	"	218.17
Barges	50	"	8,848.53
Total number	122	Total tonnage.	12,995.42

1889

Sailing vessels	49	Tonnage	1,383.84
Steam vessels	39	"	4,166.40
Canal boats	10	"	1,023.43
Barges	21	"	4,085.22
Total number	119	Total tonnage.	10,658.89

1890

Sailing vessels	34	Tonnage	2,724.09
Steam vessels	38	"	4,075.01
Canal boats	13	"	1,386.01
Barges	23	"	5,583.65
Total number	108	Total tonnage.	13,768.76

1891

Sailing vessels	84	Tonnage	12,217.12
Steam vessels	64	"	8,704.04
Canal boats	10	"	1,210.68
Barges	38	"	10,203.28
Total number	196	Total tonnage.	32,335.12

Table Showing Number and Class of Vessels Built in the Port of New York, 1860–1918—*Continued*

1892

Class	Number		Tonnage
Sailing vessels	99	Tonnage	1,336.00
Steam vessels	43	"	6,565.75
Canal boats	5	"	541.44
Barges	26	"	6,165.70
Total number	173	Total tonnage.	14,608.89

1893

Class	Number		Tonnage
Sailing vessels	39	Tonnage	621.53
Steam vessels	29	"	2,111.95
Canal boats	5	"	491.38
Barges	13	"	3,193.14
Total number	86	Total tonnage	6,418.00

1894

Class	Number		Tonnage
Sailing vessels	26	Tonnage	373.09
Steam vessels	25	"	5,933.85
Canal boats	3	"	338.67
Barges	9	"	1,707.15
Total number	63	Total tonnage	8,352.76

1895

Class	Number		Tonnage
Sailing vessels	27	Tonnage	418.74
Steam vessels	22	"	1,620.61
Canal boats	00		
Barges	6		1,056.93
Total number	55	Total tonnage	3,096.28

TABLE SHOWING NUMBER AND CLASS OF VESSELS BUILT IN THE PORT OF NEW YORK, 1860–1918—*Continued*

1896

Sailing vessels	23	Tonnage	219.48
Steam vessels	20	"	5,460.76
Canal boats	3	"	295.22
Barges	16	"	4,535.30
Total number	62	Total tonnage.	10,510.76

1897

Sailing vessels	18	Tonnage	446.90
Steam vessels	35	"	1,807.99
Canal boats	17	"	2,158.94
Barges	89	"	21,230.56
Total number	159	Total tonnage.	25,644.39

1898

Sailing vessels	12	Tonnage	123
Steam vessels	26	"	1,953
Canal boats	1	"	103
Barges	28	"	5,694
Total number	67	Total tonnage	7,873

1899

Sailing vessels	20	Tonnage	748
Steam vessels	38	"	5,497
Canal boats	00		
Barges	63	"	12,554
Total number	121	Total tonnage	18,799

TABLE SHOWING NUMBER AND CLASS OF VESSELS BUILT IN THE PORT OF NEW YORK, 1860–1918—*Continued*

1900

Sailing vessels	22	Tonnage	4,894
Steam vessels	42	"	4,977
Canal boats	8	"	1,057
Barges	103	"	27,811
Total number	175	Total tonnage	38,739

1901

Sailing vessels	17	Tonnage	516
Steam vessels	46	"	9,072
Canal boats	11	"	1,277
Barges	104	"	28,143
Total number	178	Total tonnage	39,008

1902

Sailing vessels	15	Tonnage	174
Steam vessels	62	"	6,950
Canal boats	12	"	1,146
Barges	101	"	27,468
Total number	190	Total tonnage	35,738

1903

Sailing vessels	6	Tonnage	1,194
Steam vessels	37	"	5,928
Canal boats	5	"	657
Barges	89	"	24,187
Total number	137	Total tonnage	31,966

TABLE SHOWING NUMBER AND CLASS OF VESSELS BUILT IN THE PORT OF NEW YORK, 1860–1918—*Continued*

1904

Sailing vessels	14	Tonnage	11,766
Steam vessels	31	"	3,943
Canal boats	3	"	303
Barges	105	"	30,291
Total number	153	Total tonnage	46,303

1905

Sailing vessels	10	Tonnage	2,513
Steam vessels	42	"	3,507
Canal boats	9	"	982
Barges	71	"	20,059
Total number	132	Total tonnage	27,061

1906

Sailing vessels	8	Tonnage	2,603
Steam vessels	56	"	7,089
Canal boats	31	"	3,239
Barges	73	"	20,722
Total number	168	Total tonnage	33,653

1907

Sailing vessels	7	Tonnage	1,182
Steam vessels	56	"	8,275
Canal boats	20	"	2,061
Barges	93	"	25,202
Total number	176	Total tonnage	36,720

TABLE SHOWING NUMBER AND CLASS OF VESSELS BUILT IN THE PORT OF NEW YORK, 1860–1918—*Continued*

1908

Sailing vessels	1	Tonnage	8
Steam vessels	47	"	4,990
Canal boats	11	"	1,149
Barges	135	"	38,358
Total number	194	Total tonnage	44,505

1909

Sailing vessels	4	Tonnage	25
Steam vessels	46	"	5,790
Canal boats	7	"	759
Barges	88	"	27,393
Total number	145	Total tonnage	33,967

1910

Sailing vessels	4	Tonnage	1,310
Steam vessels	57	"	7,118
Canal boats	16	"	1,804
Barges	55	"	16,584
Total number	132	Total tonnage	26,816

1911

Sailing vessels	1	Tonnage	9
Steam vessels	28	"	5,902
Canal boats	00		
Barges	51	"	16,231
Total number	80	Total tonnage	22,142

THE PORT OF NEW YORK, ABOUT 1870

Looking southeast over New York Bay, Castle Garden (now the home of the New York Aquarium) in the foreground

SOUTH STREET, NEW YORK, IN 1885

SOUTH STREET, NEW YORK, IN 1920

TABLE SHOWING NUMBER AND CLASS OF VESSELS BUILT IN THE PORT OF NEW YORK, 1860–1918—*Continued*

1912

Sailing vessels	1	Tonnage	11
Steam vessels	37	"	3,152
Canal boats	00		
Barges	31	"	10,236
Total number	69	Total tonnage	13,399

1913

Sailing vessels	00	Tonnage	
Steam vessels	42	"	11,107
Canal boats	2	"	243
Barges	69	"	25,423
Total number	113	Total tonnage	36,773

1914

Sailing vessels	1	Tonnage	5
Steam vessels	35	"	4,769
Canal boats	1	"	146
Barges	81	"	30,283
Total number	118	Total tonnage	35,203

1915

Sailing vessels	1	Tonnage	5
Steam vessels	15	"	3,406
Canal boats	4	"	573
Barges	60	"	22,497
Gas vessels	18	"	290
Total number	98	Total tonnage	26,771

TABLE SHOWING NUMBER AND CLASS OF VESSELS BUILT IN THE PORT OF NEW YORK, 1860–1918—*Continued*

1916

Sailing vessels	00	Tonnage	
Gas vessels	11	"	190
Steam vessels	18	"	3,834
Canal boats	1	"	159
Barges	71	"	27,616
Total number	101	Total tonnage	31,799

1917

Sailing vessels	3	Tonnage	48
Steam vessels	5	"	1,532
Motor boats	40	"	1,498
Barges	91	"	29,232
Total number	139	Total tonnage	32,310

1918

Sailing vessels	00	Tonnage	
Steam vessels	16	"	19,383
Canal boats	5	"	589
Barges	205	"	71,617
Gas vessels	19	"	297
Total number	245	Total tonnage	91,886

GROWTH OF OUR MERCHANT MARINE

TABLE OF DISTANCES

(Nautical Miles)

As Revised by Branch Hydrographic Office
78 Broad St., N. Y.

NEW YORK TO—

Aden	6,528
Algiers	3,619
Ambrose Channel Lightship	20
Antwerp	3,274
Ascension Island (via St. Vincent)	4,539
Bahia	4,096
Baltimore	408
Barbados	1,829
Batoum	5,637
Bermuda	676
Bombay (via Suez)	8,160
Bombay (via Panama)	14,982
Boston (Inside)	281
Boston (Outside)	342
Bordeaux	3,181
Bremen	3,484
Brunswick	745
Buenos Aires	5,868
Calais	3,200
Calcutta (via Suez)	9,830
Calcutta (via Panama)	14,165
Cape Breton	784
Cape Henry	258
Cape Race	1,020
Cape Town	6,720
Cardenas	1,170
Cardiff	2,967
Cette	3,797
Charleston	620
Charlottetown	828
Christiansand	3,660
Cienfuegos	1,646
Colombo (via Suez)	8,610
Colombo (via Panama)	14,112
Colon	1,981
Constantinople	5,052
Copenhagen	3,840
Curacao	1,807
Delaware Breakwater	144
Demerara	2,209
Diamond Shoal Lightship	350
Fayal	2,098
Fire Island Lightship	52
Funchal	2,765
Galveston	1,919
Gibraltar	3,207
Glasgow	3,087
Greytown	2,060
Halifax	580
Hamburg	3,510
Havana	1,170
Havre	3,169
Hong Kong (via Suez)	11,610
Hong Kong (via Panama)	11,190
Honolulu (via Magellan)	13,200
Honolulu (via Panama)	6,686
Hull	3,421
Jacksonville	790
Key West	1,164
Kingston	1,447
Leith	3,081
Liverpool	3,053
London	3,222
Manchester	3,090
Manila (via Panama)	11,580
Matanzas	1,153
Marseilles	3,896
Melbourne (via Suez)	12,599
Melbourne (via Panama)	9,945
Mobile	1,634

TABLE OF DISTANCES—*Continued*

NEW YORK TO——

Montevideo	5,768
Nantucket Lightship	213
Naples	4,155
Nassau	942
Newport News	281
New Orleans	1,730
Norfolk	285
Oran	3,436
Pernambuco	3,696
Philadelphia	230
Plymouth	3,079
Port Antonio	1,406
Portland, Me. (Inside)	335
Portland, Me. (Outside)	395
Portland, Ore. (via Magellan)	13,760
Portland, Ore. (via Panama)	5,887
Port of Spain	1,949
Port Said	5,128
Progreso	1,580
Providence	157
Punta Arenas (via Magellan)	5,890
Quebec (Inside via Rivers and Lakes)	404
Quebec (Outside)	1,315
Queenstown	2,934
Rio Janeiro	4,778
Rotterdam	3,280
Sable Island	668
Sandy Hook	16½
San Francisco (via Magellan)	13,090
San Francisco (via Panama)	5,294
San Juan, P. R.	1,407
Santiago	1,330
St. John, N. B. (Nantucket Sound)	507
St. John, N. B. (Outside)	532
St. Johns, N. F.	1,070
St. Thomas	1,428
St. Lucia	1,791
St. Vincent, C. V.	2,914
Savannah	692
Shanghai (via Suez)	12,360
Shanghai (via Panama)	10,645
Singapore (via Suez)	10,170
Singapore (via Panama)	12,522
Southampton	3,209
Stettin	3,965
Stockholm	3,968
Suez	5,218
Sydney (via Suez)	13,320
Sydney (via Panama)	9,691
Tampico	1,995
Trieste	4,902
Valparaiso (via Magellan)	8,460
Valparaiso (via Panama)	4,637
Vera Cruz	1,973
Wellington (via Suez)	14,230
Wellington (via Panama)	8,522
Wilmington, N. C.	547
Yokohama (via Suez)	13,040
Yokohama (via Panama)	9,677

CHAPTER X

Government Far-Sightedness and Short-Sightedness

"The Mayor is neutral," was the genial remark of Mayor Hylan, Greater New York's mayor, at the public hearing of March 27, 1919, on a proposed port treaty between the states of New York and New Jersey. No more momentous project had ever been brought before any Mayor of New York or any other city. Whether sound or unsound for Greater New York is not the issue here. If unsound, it meant jeopardy to the ability of New York's workers to earn wages, the ability of New York's business to earn dividends, the ability of New York's populace to earn the means of being healthy, prosperous, and progressively happy. If sound it meant more prosperous labour, more prosperous capital and healthier, happier, more prosperous, more ambitious citizenship.

A "League of Cities" about New York Harbour to insure competence and statesmanship in handling port business was important for reasons similar to those which make a League of Nations the dominant factor in the mind of the civilized world to-day.

Who, pray, is under a greater obligation to take sides, to have information, and to have conviction with respect to such a proposition than the elected city officers? To whom is the public entitled to look as confidently as to a mayor elected by a majority never before equalled in any American municipal election? Yet he frankly, though smilingly, admitted and protested that his attitude was not one of exacting inquiry, of presumptions removable only by new facts, of a strong leaning against or for a project which had been worked over for years, but he was "neutral."

What of the other city officials, elected by popular vote to direct the present and protect the future destinies of America's first port? They were reported by the newspapers to be opposed to the treaty. They certainly gave the impression at the hearing of being opposed to it on political and territorial grounds, regardless of its significance to business. Many of the specific reasons given by the city officers were later reported to be well grounded and sufficient to warrant changes in the treaty. The attitude of opposition is stated here to emphasize the fact that at this meeting and through the press descriptions of it New York City's officials, her legal guardians and spokesmen, were neutral or opposed to the project and treated it like a vagrant.

The arguments in favour of the treaty were made by the legal representatives of the port commission which drafted it and by two other distinguished lawyers, one for the Chamber of Commerce and one for the Merchants' Association. The latter Association in its letter of indorsement asking all members to write to each member of the Board of Estimate and not to fail to write to the Mayor and the Comptroller urging approval of the pending port treaty told its members that it was a question of the city's commercial prosperity; that it "vitally affects every business interest"; that the two state legislatures were waiting only for the approval of the city authorities; and that it "is advocated by nearly all the important business associations of New York and the several New Jersey cities." Yet in the course of the hearing its counsel in answer to an almost casual criticism by an official admitted, "Yes, that article in the treaty is vicious and should be eliminated"; again this distinguished lawyer, after seeing the shreds into which impromptu questions and arguments had torn the supposedly adequate plan which the Merchants' Association urged all of its members to indorse, reminded the Board of Estimate that the plan was "simply a basis for discussion, not presented as a plan or as a workable plan until the Board of Estimate should propose amendments."

At no time during the two days of public hearings on this subject were there a dozen business men present, nor were the newly enfranchised women voters any better represented. On many an occasion the Board of Estimate room has been crowded to its capacity by citizens who wanted to debate a public improvement affecting a dozen city blocks or a half-dozen unimproved lots. Just a few weeks prior several hundred women and business and professional men appeared to urge a $50,000 appropriation for school lunches.

City officials neutral and opposed, business men vicariously represented through paid counsel, a few civic agencies vicariously taking notes through paid agents, nearly a million women voters not even vicariously present! What does it mean? It means, first, that America's first port has not yet "arrived" as a subject of vital interest to those whose bread and butter and future prosperity depend upon it. It means, secondly, the port problems are not yet part of the thought of city officials. It means, thirdly, that port opportunities will be neglected in the future as in the past unless business men's organizations study them and advertise them. Finally, it means that volunteer civic attention to the port will be ineffective if shippers, manufacturers, transportation companies, landlords, merchants, wage earners, and buyers are indifferent to the subject.

For a people who were characterized as dollar chasers before the war but are justly proud of their reputation for being practical, we Americans have been unaccountably slow in discovering that our ports are of any special value or that our officials—city, state, and national—have any particular mission with respect to them.

When the Mayor of Greater New York in 1919—the world's largest municipality with twice the population of the thirteen original colonies, about whose far-sightedness tons of books have been written—says that he is "neutral" with respect to fostering, killing, or delaying the New York-New Jersey port treaty, he is running true to type. There have been many other mayors in the cities of New York, Jersey City, Philadelphia, Baltimore, Boston, New Orleans, Chicago, San Francisco, Duluth, Buffalo, etc.; there have been many governors in our states having ports; there have been others, too, in Congress including representatives and senators from states having port cities; there have even been presidents of the United States with armies of investigators, students, and prophets available for reading the port stories which were being thrown upon screens within easy appraisal who have failed to see port problems.

The type fact about *governmental attention to the port problems* of this country is that *government has been inattentive and accidental, or actually obstructive, more often than it has been attentive, consistent, and constructive.*

Instead of insisting upon improvements for America's first port in the interest of the whole country Congress has bartered with improvements, dangling them as political bait and reward and doling them out with the patronizing smirk of the man who hands a nickel to an importunate beggar or a cheque to an importunate charity.

Instead of demanding adequate facilities and proper management of their common port, no matter what else was done by those states, the governors of New York and New Jersey have given more attention in the last twenty years to a joint Palisade Park and to odours from the New Jersey factories than they have given to port problems. Instead of vieing with one another to see which should do the most and best for the welfare of this port as a port, the political parties in Greater New York and in New Jersey's port cities, including the spasmodic reform organizations, have hardly given port problems a passing thought.

Since the days of the greater city there have been two successful candidates for mayor on Fusion reform tickets and seven platforms pledging reforms. Not a single platform as a preëlection programme has even promised or hinted at a progressive port policy. In justice to the latest two platforms, those of the campaign of 1917, it is recalled that both the Fusion Reform and the Democratic platforms promised to correct the unfavourable working conditions of longshoremen.

The simple pledges with respect to working conditions of port labourers were inserted because of special activity by a woman school principal who was persuaded by the Institute for Public Service to use her interest in longshoremen's children for the improvement of the longshoremen's working conditions.

Seth Low and John Purroy Mitchel are names

which will live long in the annals of non-partisan reform. George B. McClellan and William J. Gaynor are names which stand for efforts by insurgent democrats to be reformers while still remaining within their political organization. Yet in the five terms beginning with Low in 1902 and ending with Mitchel in 1917, what did all of them, with exceptional opportunities, exceptional personalities, and exceptional cabinets, do for the Port of New York as a port? They built docks, some of them large docks, very large docks. For this full credit is given. But it is just as true that not one of them saw the port as a problem of first magnitude; not one of them saw the necessity for treating the port as a whole; not one of them seemed to understand what was happening right under his eyes with respect to the unequal preparedness on two sides of the North River for development of this port; not one of them gave to distinctly port problems as much time or as much attention as he gave to many a local or district problem in Manhattan.

A different reputation has been earned by the recent governments of Newark and Jersey City as proved by the remarkable development of the New Jersey Meadows and Newark Bay. It is true that many of these improvements on the

Jersey side of the port were projected by the big railroad companies needing terminals; but it is also true that while New York was neglecting the Jamaica Bay advantages, dawdling with even its limited possibility and procrastinating in its efforts to secure terminals, Newark's librarian, Mr. John Cotton Dana, was drawing pictures of the port's future, or that part of it which would build up New Jersey until the two states joined in the bi-state port commission of 1917.

For this book a chapter on government and politics was first projected, the thought being that problems so consequential as the port would surely be the subject of much specific legislation and much party controversy. Many references have been read, but with the disappointing result that the Port of New York is found to have grown in wealth and stature without seriously interfering with the peace of mind of officers and politicians. Where legislation and political issues revolved about the port it was usually because of land aspects rather than maritime aspects of the port.

This is not the place for a review of political history or municipal development, nor is it of special profit to list governmental action in the past with respect to port development. To antiquarians it is of interest that on November 17, 1647, the same local council of nine men who voted funds to support the town school and build the town church also refused to provide for repairing the fortifications on the ground that fortifications concerned absent landlords, the West India Company, and ought to be paid for from funds accruing from customs, excise duties, and tolls paid at the Company's mills. This bit of history makes one a trifle more indulgent to the New York of the twentieth century for not wanting to spend a cent which ought to be spent by Congress and for not wanting to surrender any political rights over port property.

Because land problems will always be more apparent to "landlubbers" than sea and shipping problems, and because port cities will always have more "landlubbers" than seafarers, the hope of sustained and unified governmental attention to port problems lies in the New York-New Jersey treaty for joint and unified control, or in some new agency which will give attention to keeping the eyes of officials and the public alike upon port problems.

CHAPTER XI

Business Men Stimulate Growth and Trade

IN SUMMARIZING what business men have done to accelerate growth and trade in this port fairness to the future requires that we keep both sides of the ledger in mind. The credit side gives, without reservation, praise for resolutions of the Chamber of Commerce, Board of Trade and Transportation, Merchants' Association, etc., for references to their publicity, for actions by standing and sub-committees, and for legislation secured or perfected by them. More power, more members and public gratitude for the Chamber of Commerce! for the Maritime Exchange! for the Merchants' Association! May they wax in strength and influence! But for the good of their clients and of the commerce of the country, the western continent and the world, may each of them increase its attention to port problems, and may all of them combine in securing for this port an unofficial, volunteer director of advertisement and education who will think of himself as a university extension organizer responsible for making it easy and delightful for the inhabitants of this port and its hinterland to understand America's port problems and the strategic importance of America's first port to America's prosperity and progress.

The other side of the ledger, properly called the debit side, so far as future activity is concerned, lists what might have been done, what was omitted, what was sporadically undertaken, or what was tinkered at when consistent, businesslike, scientific statesmanship was required.

Had there been four hundred business men with large interests in the port at the hearing of the New York-New Jersey port treaty; had two thousand men, knowing what was at stake, written or telephoned to the Board of Estimate and Apportionment, is it not highly probable that the mayor would have been earnestly inquisitive and not merely "neutral" and that the other city fathers would have felt the importance of immediate action instead of nonchalantly arguing for delay? Had newspapers given the subject the attention which it deserved and which they would have given it if their readers had made known an interest, it seems highly improbable that the city fathers would have straightway decided at an executive session

FREIGHT PILED ON LIGHTERS AWAITING BOTTOMS

A silent testimonial to the need of adequate docking facilities in New York for the handling of the port's gigantic commerce

"TO FOSTER THE TRADE AND WELFARE OF NEW YORK"

The motto of the Merchants' Association of New York, a civic body that has done much to focus public attention upon the numerous and especially larger aspects of the port's problems. The photograph above shows a group of the Association's members on a tour of inspection of the city's docks and harbour.

to demand a complete set of plans for port development before consenting to a port board with power to draw complete plans.

The Chamber of Commerce and the Merchants' Association unqualifiedly and publicly approved the treaty which upon casual investigation was shown to need several protective clauses. Had the treaty been given the study which it deserved it would not have come before a neutral or hostile Board of Estimate with glaring defects. The holes which were so easily punctured recalled an earlier port improvement plan, which those same leaders had unqualifiedly endorsed in 1917, only to "astound" its chief advocate, Mayor Mitchel, by admitting at a public hearing that they had not carefully studied or even read the details of the plan.

Although the port treaty fared so badly at the first hearing on it, even fewer business men came to the second, third, and fourth hearings, and the Merchants' Association in writing up the results for its very large membership gave them articles and editorials on the following subjects:

1. New York Centre for the Furniture Industry.
2. Breakdown of mail service portrayed in letters.
3. Cable regulations.

4. Editorials:
   (a) The advantages of New York City for the manufacture of furniture;
   (b) Public operation of a telephone system;
   (c) The returning soldiers and to-morrow's luncheon meeting;
   (d) The Postal Service shows no improvement.
5. Many conventions in the April list.

6. Factory fires and rubbish removal.
7. Legislation affecting city's business interests.
8. Bills in Legislature affecting corporations.
9. To Palestine by the Parcel Post.
10. Officers elected.

11. Consider restoration of deferred message rate.
12. Business communication is delayed by slow cables.
13. Where diamonds come from.
14. The "walk up" houses.
15. Sheriff protests demobilization.

16. Soldier activity calls for ruling.
17. Railroad thefts.
18. Removal of barriers stimulates foreign trade.
19. Near-East trade.
20. City's business demands improvement of port.

With the greatest respect for the credit side of the service ledger, which shows work done by great civic agencies for Greater New York, the analyst and annalist is compelled to admit that the only agency which has given to the Port of New York the attention which the country needed is Dame Nature. From the very beginning there has been a tendency to consider that nature had so situated the port that its preëminence was inevitable, and that, therefore, nothing from the hand of man could add to its certainty or enhancement. To deepen a channel or broaden a cove would be as superfluous and unnecessary as "painting the lily," and equally indicative of prodigality. Is there in all the world a port with such native endowment as America's first port? Is it not obliged to take precedence of all others simply on its physical merits? Is it not more dignified and more appreciative to permit its native endowments to work out its future alone and unaided?

Two or three times in the port's history business men have awakened to the fact that New York's prominence was a matter of degree, and that if left to nature and the rest of the country, it would lose in relative superiority, even if it continued to do a greater business than any other single port. Before the Revolution this port was ignominiously pushed back to the position of fifth in business, being distanced by the ports of Boston, Philadelphia, Charleston, and New Orleans. For seventy years New England ports led New York in imports, and the ports of Virginia and South Carolina steadily maintained a commercially invulnerable position throughout the colonial period. Thanks to the World War and to the prominence of the South in the councils and appropriating committees of the majority party, Southern ports again grew much in power to compete with New York. The ports of Virginia alone have been given improvements which cost the Federal Government more than $300,000,000.

After the village of New Amsterdam, rechristened New York, outgrew the possibility of mass meetings, there were, of course, groups of business men who organized to pass or to favour this tax or that street improvement. It was not, however, until 1768, when the city's population was 20,000, that the first serious effort was made to provide continued study and attention to port problems. On April 5, 1768, twenty prominent merchants, "men possessed of unusual foresight, almost prophetic vision," met at Fraunce's Tavern and organized what is now the Corporation of the Chamber of Commerce of the State of New York. This original corporation was called "The New York Chamber of Commerce." Its declaration read:

> Whereas mercantile societies have been found very useful in trading cities for promoting and encouraging commerce, supporting industry, adjusting disputes relative

to trade and navigation, and procuring such laws and regulations as may be found necessary for the benefit of trade in general, the [twenty persons present] had convened to establish such a society.

This claims to be the oldest institution of its kind in the world. The story of its services to its city, its port, and America is a truly convincing argument for socially minded committees of citizens aiming to supplement government and to help it become more useful. For the story of the port the most helpful guide is found in the library of the Chamber of Commerce, either in the minutes of that body, or in documents which it has collected to guide its action. Our special interest is in its work for the port, to which its early activities were mainly directed.

Commercial problems with which it dealt in the early days are indicated by these subjects: Regulation of currency among neighbouring colonies; price and quantity of flour, weight of bread, encouragement of fisheries, instituting of better methods for the inspection of provisions—the first pure food movement on record in this country; bills of exchange, inland and foreign commissions, fire and marine insurance, collection brokerage, buoys for the safety of navigation, the possibility of connecting this port by artificial navigation with the lakes

(1786), an issue which later germinated when the Erie Canal opened in 1825. It was the first president of this Chamber of Commerce, Mr. John Cruger, who drew up the famous "Declaration of Rights and Grievances of the Colonies of America," to protest against the obnoxious stamp act, and who made such impressive representations to the governor against it that the order was revoked and the stamps delivered to the city authorities. After the Revolution, during which there was naturally a wide division among the members of the Chamber, it was soon reorganized, received a charter from the state legislature April 13, 1784, and was given the name "Chamber of Commerce of the State of New York."

Membership in that body has always been of individuals and not of partnerships or corporations. The budget for 1918 totalled $90,000 from a membership of more than 1,700, it has regular standing committees on its problems, and its annual report of late has been issued in two parts totalling 583 pages.

Because of the magnitude of business, of its membership and of their personality, this organization long ago became more than a city or state body. It has taken position with respect to important national projects such as the construction of a Pacific Railroad across the continent, improvement to transportation facilities, establishment of American steamships on the Pacific, simplification of laws for the collection of revenue, reforms of the customs service, freedom of the neutral flag, and other international measures for lessening the perils of the sea, settlement by arbitration of all sorts of commercial disputes and dissensions. Matters of lesser consequence have also received attention, such as harbour protection against the dumping of ashes and refuse and the need for filling in the shores, construction and improvement of canals and bridges, harbours of refuge, disinfection of rugs at foreign ports, etc. At the same time the Chamber of Commerce has studied problems incidental to New York's growth as a manufacturing and residential city. In fact, local and state questions and national issues of importance to port development, but indirectly or remotely related to actual port management, have had the greater part of the Chamber's attention. For example, during Mayor Mitchel's spirited discussions of the West Side Improvement Plan, the Chamber of Commerce, like all but two of the other organizations in the city, took its stand without specifying that attention to the distinctly port problems should be a basis and not an incidental element in settling the West Side plan.

In the line-up for and against the New York-New Jersey port treaty two other trade bodies appear: the Merchants' Association for and the Board of Trade and Transportation against. Although the interests of these groups were identical and the same as that of the Chamber of Commerce, they permitted themselves to come before the Board of Estimate with disagreements. The sad commentary is that the disagreements were of a kind which comparing or pooling of facts and suggestions would have dispelled. One was just as public spirited and conscientious as the other. Unfortunately none of them seemed to have taken seriously enough the importance of joint study by them and immediate action by the city.

The Board of Trade and Transportation dates from June, 1873, and a public mass meeting was held in Cooper Union to protest against railroad combinations which were crushing competition, compelling the payment of exorbitant freight charges, and fleecing the public and stockholders with cynical impartiality. The first name of the body, given it September 10, 1873, was "New York Cheap Transportation Association," there being a so-called Board of Trade in the city at that time. Subsequently, in 1877, the Association absorbed the Board of Trade, and adopted its present name.

In these nearly fifty years it has successfully promoted measures of material importance to business interests. In a folder entitled "Brief Comments on the Work of the New York Board of Trade and Transportation" are listed eighteen significant activities which include nine devoted to port and trade problems:

1. "CONSULAR REFORM." The Board organized the National Consular Reform Convention, and promoted the legislation which resulted in the enactment of the Consular Reorganization Act of 1906, by which the Consular Service of the United States was taken out of partisan politics and put upon a business basis.

2. "FOREIGN COMMERCE." The National Foreign Commerce Convention which was held in Washington, D. C., in January, 1907, was called and organized by this Board to promote the enactment by Congress of measures for the extension of our foreign commerce. The convention was the largest commercial gathering ever held in Washington and was addressed by many distinguished men, including President Roosevelt and Secretaries Root, Taft, and Straus. The increase of our foreign commerce since this convention has been most significant.

3. "CUSTOMS ADMINISTRATION." The Board was instrumental in securing many of the needed changes made in the Customs Administrative Law, and it was the first to urge the appointment of an additional United States Judge for the trial of customs cases at this port.

4. "FREE ALCOHOL." The Board was the first com-

mercial organization to demand relief of taxes on alcohol used in the arts and manufactures, and the first to advocate the measure providing for denatured alcohol free of tax.

5. "Canal Improvement." This Board initiated the canal improvement movement in this State, and has ever since led in this work. It has been said that but for this organization the New York State canals would have been abandoned years ago.

6. "Barge Canal Terminals." This Board drafted and secured the passage of the Barge Canal Terminals Act in 1911, by which much-needed waterfront freight terminals will be provided for New York City.

7. "Naval Militia." The Board is the father of the law creating the Naval Militia of the several states, and has urged the organization of a National Navigating Naval Reserve to supplement the U. S. Navy in case of necessity.

8. "The Sulzer Pier Head Line Bill." The Board conceived and drafted the bill introduced by Mr. Sulzer in Congress, for the extension of the Pier Head Line on the Hudson River which will solve the long pier problem and save the city millions of dollars.

9. "Local Affairs." The Board was largely instrumental in securing better pavement in our business thoroughfares. It has been foremost in urging improvement of the waterfront for our city. It was also instrumental in securing the new deep-water channel through the harbour for our shipping, and the improvement of the Harlem River to avoid the crowded condition in the water in the neighbourhood of the Battery. Its years of labour for new and increased post office facilities is to be soon rewarded.

10. Other services to the credit of this Board include: Agitation for better terminal facilities until capitalists and railway managers erected receiving elevators on the

docks of three railroads, the Erie, Pennsylvania, and New York Central; and agitation for protection of the harbour against all sorts of "dumpings."

Its standing committees include committees on: Terminal facilities, maritime affairs, canal transportation, customs administration, foreign and insular trade. There are special committees on: New York and New Jersey Harbour Treaty, Alien Labour, and Port and Harbour Development. In 1914 they discussed perfecting the harbour in five years. The *Sun*, editorially, protested against the "present dribbling operations which are largely wasteful and disastrously retarding not only to this city but to a vast interior tract of country, of which this is the natural sea-gate."

In February, 1918, Hon. Calvin Tomkins, former Dock Commissioner of Greater New York, addressed the Board of Trade and Transportation on the west side in relation to New Jersey, Long Island, and New England, and the congestion of war business and the coal crisis at the Port of New York. His proposals should be recalled when reading later the improvements still needed:

New York is the only great seaport in the world divided into two parts by an unbridged and untunnelled waterway. All other ports are either situated about the sides of a bay, or on two sides of a river easily bridged, so that their several parts can be tied together by a series of railroad freight loops connecting all the carriers, docks, warehouses, and factories.

In New York, with one exception, the transcontinental terminals are located on the west side of the harbour, while shops, factories, and population are, for the most part, located on the east side, necessitating an immensely wasteful and dilatory expenditure for lighterage. Between Manhattan and New Jersey, especially, the lighterage methods in use are archaic and absurdly extravagant. They have been perpetuated as an incident of the rivalries of the railroads and also as a consequence of the obstruction of investors in private terminals and lighterage concerns and by food distributors and local real estate speculators, all of whose property interests rest upon the existing faulty terminal system and will be adversely affected by any radical change of plan or policy.

Improved communication between the New York and New Jersey sides of the port is the crux of the port organization here, and all-rail transit by protracting the New Jersey roads over and under the Hudson River to New York and thence to New England will be the ultimate cure of our port defects, but in the interim and as a necessary step in progressive development, vehicular tunnels and modern New Jersey terminals can easily be constructed and are absolutely necessary.

The question of port organization comes under two classes—one, war organization for imminent use, and the other for peace times. Three important things to be done are: (1) Development of a great modern terminal at Jersey City, thus utilizing motor trucks and lighterage to a greater extent; (2) construction of vehicular tunnels; (3) all-rail connections either by tunnel or bridge with Manhattan.

War organization should supplement and be made to fit into a general permanent plan of port organization, to be carried out later. The present congestion is due to the fact that the railroad terminals at tidewater are insufficient for war purposes and cannot be expanded quickly enough for this use. Their too exclusive use for war shipments will seriously prejudice their commercial use, which cannot be segregated from war use. Commerce and war are daily becoming integrated, and should not be disintegrated. As an analogous case in point, note the defect of priority railroad orders which have recently been abandoned.

The back terminals of the port along the lines of the railroads, and new back terminals which can be created, afford the opportunity for a quick and cheap expansion of port facilities in connection with motor truck and barge service.

The policy at New York should be to develop temporary outlying terminals on the New Jersey Meadows and in the higher back land; along the New Haven and Long Island railroads, both on the Sound and inland, and then utilize motor trucks and lighters for effecting transfers to the ships. The ships to be loaded from lighters at moorings in the harbour and at whatever wharves may be available. Additional wharfage and pier facilities, of an emergency character, to be constructed for war uses; but it will be difficult to construct many piers or docks promptly, and stream loading from lighters will add greatly to the capacity of the port if properly organized in a military way. The outlying terminals should be equipped with widespread, open sidings and with wooden storage sheds.

In the Hackensack and Passaic Meadows district, coarse freights like rails, billets, lumber, autos, and much engineering and ordnance equipment to be stored in the open or piled on grillage or on corduroy foundations of round timber. Higher class freight to be stored on firmer ground farther inland, subject to longer motor truck hauls. The storage sheds, where necessary, to be widely separated and of light wooden construction and dependence to be placed on military guards and organized fire protection. Extensive unoccupied areas are immediately available in New Jersey, Long Island, and Connecticut, and the land should be conscripted to avoid delay, leaving the awards to the courts.

To some extent deliveries should be made by motor trucks direct to ships, but the bulk of the coarse freight to be retransferred by trucks to lighters at the nearest points, on the waterfront, and thence delivered alongside the ships in the stream.

Both land areas and water anchorage areas, to an indefinite extent, are immediately available for the coarse freights which constitute the bulk of the war exports. If existing waterfront terminals can be relieved in this manner, they can be utilized for the higher class freights.

Shipments of munitions by barges and Sound steamers can be made direct to ships at moorings from the Connecticut ports where so much of this material is fabricated. Smaller ships can load direct at Providence, New London, New Haven, and Bridgeport.

The arterial highways in New Jersey, Connecticut, and Long Island should, without delay and under Government control, be put in order and so maintained.

It is an unfortunate fact that there are only three available roads connecting the west side of the Port of New York with the continent. One is in good order, viz., the Lincoln Highway. One in bad order, viz., the Paterson road. One is impassable—the Newark Turnpike, which is the most direct and important of the three. The Attorney General's office should promptly collaborate with the New Jersey Government to overcome State Constitution inhibitions, against the issue of State bonds for public works, highways, terminals, housing, etc.

It is necessary to conduct the Pennsylvania Railroad across the Lincoln Highway between the Hackensack and Passaic rivers, and this should not be effected by a grade crossing, except temporarily, as otherwise it will disastrously obstruct the motor traffic on the one road leading out of New York, which is already crowded.

The Long Island and New England railroad terminal systems should be connected with the railroad terminal systems in New Jersey by improved carfloat service between South Brooklyn and New Jersey. This will involve the integration of the Pennsylvania and Bush terminals, and the construction of a new water terminal at Bayonne. Coincidentally, there should be developed in New Jersey classification yards for joint use and a series of exchange railroad stations at points of contact along the belt-line road connecting the trunk lines back of the waterfront.

Civic bodies and trade agencies seldom come singly. Shortly after the Board of Trade was organized, the Maritime Association was chartered, April 11, 1874. It was really started two years earlier when a number of merchants interested in shipping found themselves meeting out-of-doors at the intersection of William, South William, and Beaver streets. The necessity for shelter mothered an invention of shelter when meeting together, and within two weeks from the time the suggestion was made one hundred and forty firms had joined in the plan, and the Maritime Association started with quarters at 61 Pearl Street. To-day the membership exceeds twelve hundred, and its programme more directly relates to maritime interests of the port than that of other leading organizations. Maritime Exchange is not used in the usual sense of the term, as its business is not transacted after the manner of the stock and cotton exchanges. The "hour" of the Exchange is from 12:30 to 1:30, when a visitor will see the floor well filled with members associated with shipping interests in various capacities. There is no public transaction of business, which is solely of an individual nature. The primary function of the Exchange is to collect and distribute marine news, arrivals and sailings of vessels at the Port of New York and all United States and West Indian ports. It also reports all disasters to vessels bound to and from the Port of New York. In order to obtain marine information, all business interests in any way allied to shipping find it a matter of convenience to be identified with the Exchange. Incidentally the Exchange takes an interest in all matters of the port, particularly in the advocacy of legislation at Albany and Washington that will best serve the interest of the port.

The annual report for 1918 summarizes the action of the Exchange in marine interests:

1. We advocated the immediate deepening of our harbour channels so as to provide a depth of 40 feet from

Sandy Hook to Long Island Sound, as a measure of national defence at this time, and as necessary for the future commercial growth of our port.

2. We urged the passage of bills pending in the Legislature providing for an appropriation of $100,000 to defray the expenses of the New York-New Jersey Port and Harbour Development Commission, which Commission is engaged in the work of devising a joint plan of harbour development that will provide for present requirements and insure adequate accommodations for the future.

3. We communicated with the United States Shipping Board, suggesting that, if possible, tonnage be provided for the transportation of perishable products from the Island of Bermuda to the United States during the winter months, when there was a scarcity of same in this country, in order to relieve the food situation.

4. We were represented at a meeting held at the Chamber of Commerce on July 19, 1917, to consider the shipping situation. The conference was called for the purpose of discussing the critical situation existing with reference to the Government shipbuilding programme.

5. A conference of representatives of commercial organizations was held at the Chamber of Commerce on December 10, 1917, which was attended by General William M. Black, Chief of Engineers, U. S. Army, the same being called by Governor Whitman for the purpose of ascertaining the outlook for traffic on the Barge Canal in 1918. We were represented at this meeting by four members.

6. Considering the operation of junk boats in our harbour to be a menace at this time, we recommend that steps be taken that would make further operation of same impossible during the period of the war, and we are pleased to report that such action was promptly taken by the authorities.

7. We endorsed the plan presented to the United States

Shipping Board by the Board of Governors of the New York State Nautical School, and Columbia University, providing for the utilization of these two institutions in conjunction with the Shipping Board so as to provide for the training of 1,000 young men annually for positions as officers in the Merchant Marine, instead of 100 as at present.

8. The Committee on Piers and Bulkheads jointly considered several matters affecting our port. In connection with the appropriation for defraying the expenses of the New York-New Jersey Port and Terminal Commission, the committees recommended the passage of legislation to make same effective.

First in present-day publicity received by trade organizations is the Merchants' Association of New York, which has just passed its majority, having come into being June 21, 1897. Its purposes are stated in its simple motto, "To foster the trade and welfare of New York." From the offset, however, it has given a broad interpretation to the trade and welfare of New York and has taken up relatively small and local problems such as an anti-litter crusade and relatively large and national questions like foreign mail rates, consular service, etc. Its present membership, which is by firms as well as by individuals, is about six thousand; its annual income is at present about $300,000. Its thirty-four committees include these which deal with port problems directly: city traffic, commercial law, customs service and revenue law, federal trade commission, foreign trade, harbour, docks, and terminals, inland waterways and water storage, maritime, and transportation.

In its report of achievements it includes the following references to distinctly maritime problems:

1. Aggressive activity against efforts to make the New Jersey cities, instead of New York, the terminal for the trunk line railroads.

2. The creation of a Foreign Trade Bureau for the special development of the overseas commerce.

3. Coöperation in the effort "to secure the early completion and operation of the Erie Canal, as well as the operation of the present canal under the most effective conditions possible during the period of reconstruction."

4. "Consistent and continuous activity . . . in the effort to secure action by Congress whereby the improvements in the channels and waters of the Port of New York might be had at the earliest possible moment, in order to meet as promptly as possible naval as well as commercial needs. This work particularly applied to the effort to secure appropriations for the deepening of the East River and Hell Gate channels so as to make those channels adequate for the use of ships of the navy from the harbour to Long Island Sound."

5. Continued advocacy of the establishment of a free port.

6. Active interest in inland waterways, and the construction as "part of the new Erie Canal facilities, of a lock at Tonawanda in order to continue in service the existing Erie Canal between Tonawanda and Buffalo"; and vigorous opposition to legislation "intended to pre-

vent the construction of a high-level railroad bridge across the Hudson River at Castleton, such bridge being highly desirable by reason of facilitating the movement of freight between New York and the West, and by reason of the railroad operating economies which would result therefrom."

Invaluable as the service of this organization has been, the fact remains that its attention to port problems has in the public mind and in the membership mind been generally overshadowed by other local and national problems, many of them of tremendous consequence. During the war period, for example, when neither American business nor our national congress nor the shipping interests centring in New York should have been led to underestimate the supreme importance of advertising the needs of this port, the annual summaries of the Merchants' Association give surprisingly little space to port and maritime problems. While many topics were touched upon in ways which show appreciation of the problems by officers, the emphasis in its large reports (10″ x 7″) is not such as to instil or foster concern among the membership for large port development and correction.

Taking the year 1916, for example, because in that year before we entered the war there came to this port goods worth $2,200,000,000 and there left goods worth $4,300,000,000 under conditions which spelled great profits to American business, we find port and maritime problems reported upon under different headings as follows:

1. *Principal Achievements*, 26 lines, not mentioned.

2. *Federal Trade Commission*, assisted in formulating a questionnaire designed to gather information upon which legislation might be predicated for the development of export trade—5 lines.

3. *Maritime Laws*, opposed to the pending shipping bill "based upon the principle of Government ownership, or operation, or both, of mercantile vessels." Advocated "a proper subsidy for American-built ships only, amendments to the unnecessarily restrictive provisions of the Navigation Laws and the repeal of the so-called La Follette Shipping Law," exempting barges from compulsory pilotage charges, and continuation of the state nautical school—8 lines.

4. *Customs Service*, helped secure a modification of the construction of the statute concerning the weighing, sealing, and testing of distilled spirits for exportation; called to the attention of the Board of United States General Appraisers suggestions regarding reform of procedure before that Board—9 lines.

5. *Quarantine at Port of New York*, urged transfer of quarantine at the Port of New York from the jurisdiction of the state to that of the Federal Government—3 lines.

6. *Harbour Improvement*, urged the necessity of proper and adequate improvement of the channels and harbour of New York by the Federal Government from the standpoint of both national defence and commerce and industry —4 lines.

7. *Inland Waterways,* opposed abandonment of certain portions of the existing Erie Canal at Buffalo. Favoured the proposed bond issue required to continue without interruption the canal and terminal construction—9 lines.

8. *Rate Adjustments,* proved to carriers that discrimination in rates on certain commodities existed and should be removed—7 lines.

9. *Free Time at New York—Export Carload Freight,* opposed, without result, Trunk Line Association proposal to reduce the allowance on carload traffic, consigned to this port "for export" from 30 to 15 days—16 lines.

10. *Freight Accumulation and Embargoes,* secured cooperation from carriers in effecting many methods for the relief of freight correction—44 lines.

11. *Lighterage and Storage Regulations at New York,* successfully opposed a charge of 12 cents per ton for loading to, or unloading from, lighters other than station piers or vessels of carriers. "*No case of more importance* to the shippers and receivers of the city has arisen. Had the proposed changes gone into effect they would have cost the shippers hundreds of thousands of dollars a year."—16 lines.

12. *Freight Congestion at Railroad and Pier Stations on Manhattan Island,* studies made to interest shippers in prompter removal from carriers' terminals—

"An investigation made by the Bureau demonstrated that but a small part of the inbound freight is removed on the day of arrival and that the larger part of the freight was not removed until the last day of the free time allowed. This indicates that our merchants are largely availing themselves of the carriers' facilities for partial storage while suiting their own convenience for the removal of freight.

"The dimensions of pier stations on Manhattan Island are necessarily restricted as to length and width, so that they cannot be materially enlarged. The working capacity of these pier stations is measured by the amount of freight that can be put through them. A constant and regular flow of business, both inbound and outbound, must be maintained to secure the greatest efficiency.

"On one day in April, 1916, it was found that between 1,500 and 2,000 cars, containing merchandise for delivery at pier and freight stations, were just outside Manhattan waiting to be brought in as space for unloading could be provided. In addition, there were embargoes against the receipt of further freight for movement to New York.

"The Association has urged on all shippers and receivers that their shipping departments be required to coöperate with teamsters in the prompt handling of freight, its more even distribution through the day, and in the avoidance of the use of the carriers' facilities for storage purposes. Our experience has fully demonstrated the necessity for additional terminal facilities to care for our rapidly growing commerce, such as contemplated in the West Side improvements of the New York Central Railroad.

The final test of what leaders among business men and other organizations are accomplishing for any public service is to be found in the attention given to it by newspapers. This was not true in the early days. After the Civil War, merchants having a common maritime interest would gather together in the open street at the old Five Points, but in the Twentieth Century few public minds are affected sub-rosa, secretly, or as the result of comment limited to a handful of public-spirited men. Whether judged by the number of times when port interest has been mentioned in the newspapers of New York City and vicinity, or by the quantity of space, or by the definiteness of information given to the public, it must be conceded that while retained in the cast, the port has usually played the rôle of supernumerary. This conclusion needs to be qualified in two ways: the press has given considerable attention to such projects as the opening of Hell Gate; and the press has magnified rather than minimized the port's alleged freedom from dangerous competition.

It is not the fault of the newspaper if the shippers, manufacturers, civic interests, and trade organizations of America's first port have failed to register unmistakably a demand for news space and comment in behalf of a free port, of greater port facilities, franker publicity about threatened competition, more consistent publicity about the need for team work by New Jersey and New York, etc., which will bring about a combined port management with tunnels under the Hudson, a bridge across the Hudson, and adequate terminals.

By no means does all of the volunteer activity or stimulus to growth and development centre in Manhattan. So far as the port is concerned, Brooklyn organizations have been more port-conscious than those of Manhattan. The best discussion available of the destinies and dangers of America's first port was written in 1914 by Harry Chase Brearley and published under the auspices of the Brooklyn Civic League. So superior is this document, that by the League's consent a sample page and one of its maps are reproduced.

Another less-known agency, but because of its youth and its thirst for opportunity it has been aggressive and daring, is the Jamaica Bay Association, which, in season and out of season, for twelve years has been trying to arouse the public and officers of New York to see Jamaica Bay as an integral part of New York's harbour and as the site of the eastern seaboard's free port and the export terminal of the New York State Barge Canal. Had the same persistency and dramatic presentation been employed by the Merchants' Association or the Chamber of Commerce with their notable and well-earned prestige, no wideawake citizen of New York could now be unconscious of Jamaica Bay's possibilities.

A pertinent war-time propaganda in the interest of a merchant marine was organized in 1912 under the name of the National Marine League, the purposes of which for the first time recognize the fact that America's ports are every American's business:

To awaken the people of the United States, whether living on the seacoast or in the interior, to a full understanding of the necessity for reëstablishing an American overseas Commercial Marine, particularly America and Asia through the Panama Canal.

To bring about nation-wide recognition of the paramount need for providing export outlets for the products of our manufacturing industries, that labour and capital may be steadily and profitably employed.

By compelling force of imperative public opinion, to cause the enactment by Congress of such laws as will most speedily and effectually restore our former standing as a great maritime nation.

"Keep the flag flying" is the slogan of this popular agency. The kind of "hot-shot" popular wording in which these pages abound is exactly what must and can be successfully used to make "landlubbers" as enthusiastic as old salts in demanding a great merchant marine. The chart on the rise and fall of American shipping under the American flag on page 151 was taken from this pamphlet. Following are some of the facts and sentiments which indicate that its publicity work is on the right road:

In 1914 United States had 1,356 ships (884 steam and 472 sail) ranking below Sweden (1,466), France (1,576), Norway (2,191), Germany (2,388), and Britain (11,328).

In tonnage United States was eleventh	954,000
(having even less than) Russia	1,054,000
Austria Hungary	1,056,000
Sweden	1,118,000
Holland	1,496,000
Italy	1,668,000
Japan	1,708,000
France	2,319,000
Norway	2,505,000
Germany	5,459,000
Britain	21,045,000

Of our 884 ships only 137 had a tonnage of 1,000 or more and only 21 had the minimum of 7,000 needed now for successful competition.

One of our chief needs is to have a merchant marine, because if we have to deliver our goods in other people's delivery wagons their goods are delivered first and our goods are delivered incidentally on their routes. This is a matter I have had near my own heart for a great many years.

PRESIDENT WILSON.

So long as our competitors own the ships they make the rates, they control the service, and they determine the routes. With this power it is easy to favour their own commerce and discriminate against ours.

SECRETARY OF TREASURY MCADOO.

The problem that confronts us to-day is over-production in most of our great lines of business endeavour. We must find foreign markets for this excess or we must content ourselves with low prices, idle mills and factories, and labour out of employment. I, therefore, contend that there is no problem that addresses itself more urgently to the business man and the statesman of to-day than that of the development of foreign commerce along sound and economic lines. Yet we find our commerce to-day in much the same condition it was in the first decade of the life of the nation.

SENATOR OSCAR W. UNDERWOOD.

We are a blind and strutting fool among the nations (in our marine policy). This is not a party question, it is not a question of politics. It is a question of national prosperity, of national safety and patriotism.

REPRESENTATIVE HUMPHREY of Washington.

Ships of the tramp type are the prime necessity in international trade. Wherever freight is offered there she may go.

Germany had its marine league with more than four hundred thousand branches in its towns and cities. School children sang the praises of German ships and every man, woman, and child in Germany knew that his country's success "lies on the water." The National Marine League is established to do for America what the German Marine League has done for Germany.

We must get ships into the consciousness of every American as prominently as railroads. The American manufacturer must think of ships as a continuation of railroads which are no longer to stop at tidewater. The American community must think of ships as a local improvement. The chief thing is to weave ships into American business thinking. When American business thinks ships every day in connection with every product, transaction, and plan, there will be no difficulty in supporting ships.

EDWARD N. HURLEY,
Chairman, United States Shipping Board.

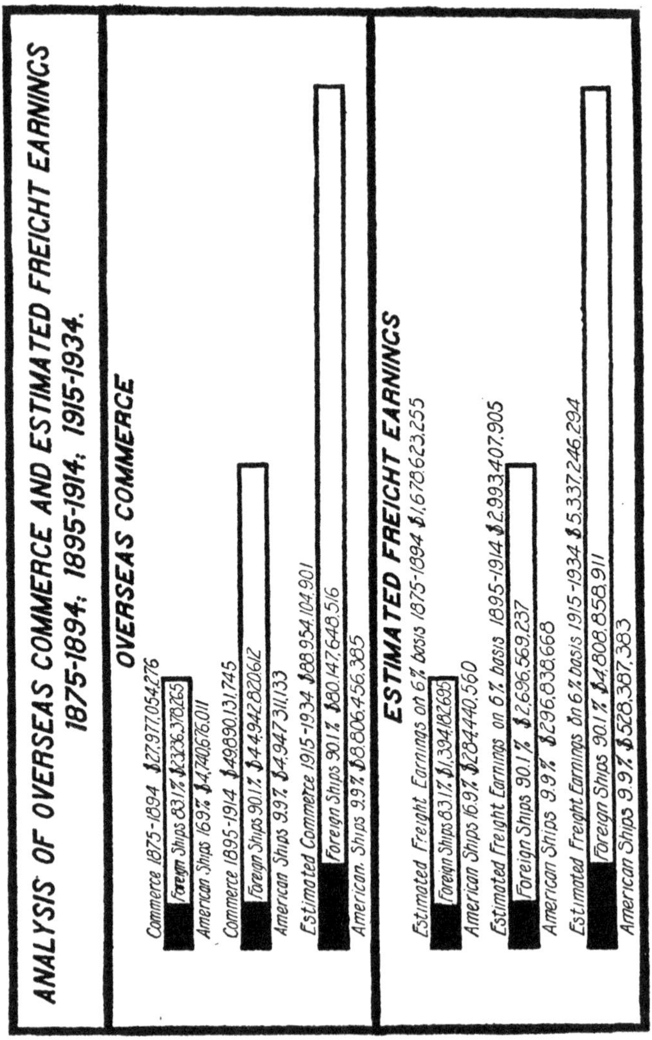

ANALYSIS OF OVERSEAS COMMERCE AND ESTIMATED FREIGHT EARNINGS 1875-1894; 1895-1914; 1915-1934.

OVERSEAS COMMERCE

Commerce 1875-1894 $27,977,054,276

Foreign Ships 83.1% $23,236,378,265

American Ships 16.9% $4,740,676,011

Commerce 1895-1914 $49,890,131,745

Foreign Ships 90.1% $44,942,820,612

American Ships 9.9% $4,947,311,133

Estimated Commerce 1915-1934 $88,954,104,901

Foreign Ships 90.1% $80,147,648,516

American. Ships 9.9% $8,806,456,385

ESTIMATED FREIGHT EARNINGS

Estimated Freight Earnings on 6% basis 1875-1894 $1,678,623,255

Foreign Ships 83.1% $1,394,182,695

American Ships 16.9% $284,440,560

Estimated Freight Earnings on 6% basis 1895-1914 $2,993,407,905

Foreign Ships 90.1% $2,696,569,237

American Ships 9.9% $296,838,668

Estimated Freight Earnings on 6% basis 1915-1934 $5,337,246,294

Foreign Ships 90.1% $4,808,858,911

American Ships 9.9% $528,387,383

CHAPTER XII

The Port Awakening of New Jersey

NEW YORK'S opponents to the Port Treaty with New Jersey profess to fear the aggression of a New Jersey bent on privateering and desiring to play with New York on the basis of "heads I win, tails you lose." For such apprehension there is the slight justification that New Jersey has of late been seeing the future of the Port of New York in a larger way than the State or City of New York. In fact, New York's awakening or near-awakening has been stimulated in a large measure by New Jersey's determination to capitalize in every legitimate way the world's need for a modern port, including a free port within New York Harbour.

How recently New Jersey became alive to our port possibilities is shown by the following letter which expresses a vision possessed by too few even to this day. The writer is the "Prince of Librarians," Mr. John Cotton Dana of Newark, who has made the position of librarian mean an out-post for teaching statesmanship. The letter was written eleven years ago, in October, 1908, to a governor of New Jersey and to a great daily newspaper. The newspaper returned it unprinted, the governor did not even acknowledge its receipt.

When the highest congestion in war-time traffic, February, 1918, demonstrated the soundness of the argument contained in this rejected ten-year-old letter, Mr. Dana sent it to the New York *Evening Post* as evidence that to those who were then condemning government officials for almost every kind of shortcoming, mental, moral, and emotional, we are:

> A little unfair to blame government officials for finding it difficult to do in haste what far-seeing, hardheaded business men failed to do during the last forty years!

The business men referred to are those captains of transportation thus characterized by Mr. Dana in 1918:

> Now the transportation companies by land and water, whose lines converge at the greatest transportation centre in this country, New York Bay, have had before them for years the opportunity to show their business competency by coöperating in the production, on the west side of the Hudson River, of a system of lines, yards, warehouses, and transportation facilities which would have made impossible much of the present traffic congestion in these parts. They have ignored the opportunity.

(Both photographs copyrighted by American Studio)

NORTH RIVER TERMINAL PIERS

Large docks have been built in the past, but on the whole neither Congress nor the city government has approached the problem of port development with anything like a true appreciation of its magnitude or its civic and national importance. Below: West Street, bordering the North River piers.

CONGESTION ON THE NORTH RIVER WATERFRONT

Forty-four per cent. of the entire nation's exports and nearly forty-three per cent. of its total imports passed through the customs district of New York in 1918. The capacity of ships entering and clearing at the port in that year amounted to more than twenty-two million tons.

Here is the picture as one seer—not a captain of industry, or a great shipper, described it in 1908, and as an unimaginative governor ignored it:

The most important commercial development in all New Jersey in the next generation will be that of the territory in and about Newark Bay.

Briefly the conditions are:

(1) The trade supremacy in North America of the Port of New York.

(2) The separation by water of Manhattan Island from terminals of all American railways save those of New England and the New York Central.

(3) The inconvenience of terminals placed on Long Island and the resulting check on attempts to develop the same on its western margin, or in Jamaica Bay.

(4) The inevitable terminal development on the west side of the Hudson, due to New York's supremacy and the wish of American traffic to reach America's greatest seaboard city.

(5) The narrow and almost crowded limits, set by nature, to terminal opportunities on the Hudson River front of New Jersey's part of the great port.

(6) The presence of a commercial community of 600,000, with great and growing industries, about Newark Bay, and of an ideal suburban residential region of almost unlimited area to the west and north of the Bay.

(7) The imperative demand, enforced by Federal authority, for the preservation of the entire superficial water area in and about Newark Bay that the tidal prism may be kept at its maximum.

(8) The ease with which the bay and its adjuncts may be deepened for dock purposes.

(9) The proximity to it of terminals of all save two of America's great lines of land transportation.

(10) The irresistible demand which will soon be made for several wheel-traffic roadways of the highest character between the Hudson and the park and residential regions to the west and north.

(11) The interest, evidenced by present large expenditures, taken in the development of Newark Bay and its adjuncts by the Federal Government.

The rapid development of this region is thus inevitable. If the development goes on at haphazard, as the resultant of many forces, without a common plan, the outcome will be conflict of interests, misplaced improvements, wasted energy, which will satisfy none of the parties interested and bring small profit to the State at large, which has most at stake.

Parties interested are:

(1) Railroad companies.

(2) Steamship and water-transportation companies.

(3) Municipalities—all that lie near Newark Bay, from Perth Amboy to Paterson, and from Morristown to Jersey City.

(4) Manufacturing companies.

(5) Trolley companies.

(6) Suburban residents.

(7) Haulers of freight by wagons.

(8) Automobiles—including all who may use self-propelled wagons on ordinary roads for whatever purpose.

The problem of development is here most difficult. The importance of this problem will cause errors in its solution to result in tremendous loss for a long term of years to all parties interested.

How shall a wise plan for this work be secured? I do not favour State commissions, for we have too many already; there is a prejudice against them; they are often quite unsuccessful. I suggest an appeal by you to the persons who, after all, are most interested in the wisest development of this great area—the business men of the several cities which lie in and about it. Let private enterprise, stimulated by a call from the highest officer in the State, secure for New Jersey the broadest and most far-seeing plan for the development of this great commercial and residential centre.

I suggest that you issue a message, setting forth the immense importance of this great problem, the gain that will come to all the State if it be wisely handled, and the loss to all concerned if it be treated piecemeal and at cross purposes. Let the message call on the business men to bring together the influences and the resources of their commercial and civic-betterment bodies, and urge that they employ at once a body of the best experts money can secure to examine this area in all its aspects, and to make, within a year at the most, a report with recommendations.

This body of experts will furnish a city plan—a plan which will suggest the most economic lines of development, not for one city only, but for all the municipalities which lie on and near the Hudson in northern New Jersey. The composite city—not a city under State laws, but a city under economic laws—we may call, in proper imitation of its sister city across the Hudson, the City of New Jersey.

I have written enough to make plain my main point—that there is pressing need of a city plan for the development of New Jersey's richest commercial and residential area, centring about Newark Bay. I believe I can make this need seem still stronger if I call attention to a few of the subjects which a committee of experts on commerce, manufacturing, transportation, engineering, architecture, and landscaping will need carefully to consider before they can formulate a plan which will, when carried out in coming years,

(1) Profit the maximum number of parties in interest.

(2) Injure the minimum number of the same.

(3) Proceed with a most equitable distribution of expense.

(4) Distribute its cost over coming generations in a proper way.

(5) Conserve for the general public the maximum of profit, welfare, and beauty for all times.

The experts would examine into and report on:

(1) The commerce of this region, including New York and Brooklyn, by land and water.

(2) The riparian rights of New Jersey in this region, and the extent of the possible control of development which these rights give to the State.

(3) The present and future suburban population of this region and the best development of its means of transportation.

(4) The power of the Federal Government in respect to the waters of this region and the policy that will probably be followed—as to bridges, for example—in the exercise of these powers.

(5) The present conditions and the future needs of all railway lines passing through this region.

(6) The probable development of water transportation here.

(7) The probable growth of population in this region in the next forty years; and the residential development as a result of that growth.

(8) The probable increase of manufacturing in this region and the accompanying increase in transportation facilities.

(9) The probable future of wheeled traffic on ordinary roadways here through the development of motor cars.

(10) The probable trolley development.

(11) Questions of drainage, sewage, water supply, parks, etc.

(12) The plans of passenger and freight transportation, including tunnels, docks, roadways, etc., now under consideration in and about Greater New York.

(13) The demands which the needs of great corporations of all kinds will compel them to make for rights and privileges in this area.

CHAPTER XIII

Harbour Improvements

THE preëminence of the Port of New York is not limited to its size, its safety, its beauty, its unparalleled shore front, and its great depth of water.

It is also preëminent in the expense of its transshipping, transferring, handling, and re-handling of freight.

As the *Marine News* said, editorially, in 1915, when the rapid increase in business due to world demand upon America had already taught us our port weaknesses, "New York is the port of circumlocution and delay."

It is preëminent in having more different governmental agencies in charge of it than any other port in or outside of America.

It is preëminent in the lack of statesmanlike attention to what it needs if it is to further and not hinder American industry. At this point Editor A. R. Smith of the *Marine News* and of the *Port of New York Annual* wrote this annotation:

Why not "roast" our senators and representatives in Congress for their indifference to appropriations for the improvement of the Port of New York? The city governments should be "roasted" for the same thing. The commercial organizations are not one tenth as active, as vociferous, and as indignant and determined as they should be. They should be rampant instead of mildly interested. And our newspapers!!! They are the chief offenders by their policy of indifference. Talk about the Federal Government being grudging and niggardly in spending its money on improvements for our port: but what of the unwillingness, the niggardliness of the newspapers of New York in saying the right thing about the Port of New York, of giving port news proper prominence? There's a fine chance for some well-deserved invective. I'm saying it, several times. Congress, as a body, is not unwilling to improve New York as it should be improved. What Congress expects, and properly, is that its senators and representatives from New York should point out what New York requires and advocate it in a united and aggressive manner—then they'd win. That's how other ports win, with delegations possessing but a tithe of the number and influence of the New York-New Jersey delegations.

It is on the way to becoming preëminent in its appreciation of port and maritime problems.

Finally, its preëminence is due "not to consecutive planning or to continuous port policy or to logical development of port facilities, but to nature's gifts."

The improvements which have already been made have their interesting history; in fact, the port started with the right kind of governmental attitude and procedure. In the days of Peter Stuyvesant it was only necessary to show that something was needed in order to have an ordinance passed providing for it and immediate action taken by the director.

In 1648–49 a wooden wharf or dock was erected on the East River "for the convenience of the Merchants and Citizens." This served them until a larger one called the "Bridge" was built ten years later at the foot of the present Moore Street, and was lengthened in 1661. That same year the municipality constructed a pier and began to collect wharfage fees, a policy to which we have only recently returned.

When the English took New York in 1664 improvements were under way which included work on a canal, street-grading, and construction of bulkheads along the waterfront. Throughout the British occupation from 1664 to 1781 much attention was given to upbuilding the port as a strictly business enterprise.

In 1676 the Great Dock was completed by the extension of the last-mentioned pier, the "Bridge," and the construction of a new pier running out from the half-moon battery in front of the city hall.

From 1686 to 1730 every person who received

a grant of waterfront land bound himself "to erect a wharf on it at the outer end of the lot granted"—a practice which has caused considerable trouble in the later days of privately owned railroad wharves. Any delinquent was fined forty shillings a month. Once the lessees were required, at their own cost, "to keep the entrances of their docks clean and free from oil, sand, gravel, or what else that shall or may 'lye' there, so that no sloops, boats, or other vessels will suffer delay or uncleanliness." Anybody who failed to do his part in building docks or keeping them clear was liable for all costs of having the city do it.

It was not until 1798 that an attempt was made to give regularity to the bulkhead line and to plans for streets and wharves. For this Federal Government intervention became necessary.

From the first, however, this Federal aid has been grudgingly given. The initial step taken in 1851, namely, the deepening of Hell Gate, is still prominently before the country as an unfinished project. By the year 1918 approximately $11,000,000 had been appropriated for improving the East River and Hell Gate, of which approximately $7,000,000 has been expended. Another improvement project still un-

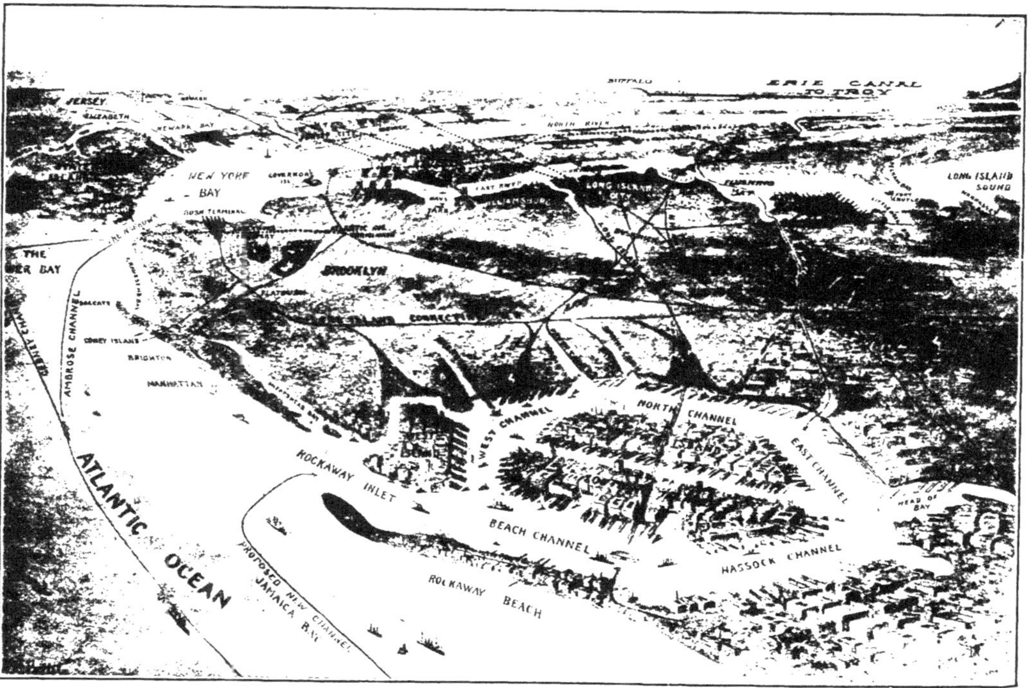

JAMAICA BAY

"Jamaica Bay has an unlimited area for railroad expansion, and through the agency of the New York Connecting Railroad acting as a Trunk Line Marginal Road, all roads will have access to the bay on equal terms. With the advent of the tunnel under the Narrows on Staten Island and thence to New Jersey, the entire railroad system of the continent will be in direct touch with the seaboard at the ocean front." Work on the Jamaica Bay project has already been started under a coöperative agreement between the Federal Government and New York State.

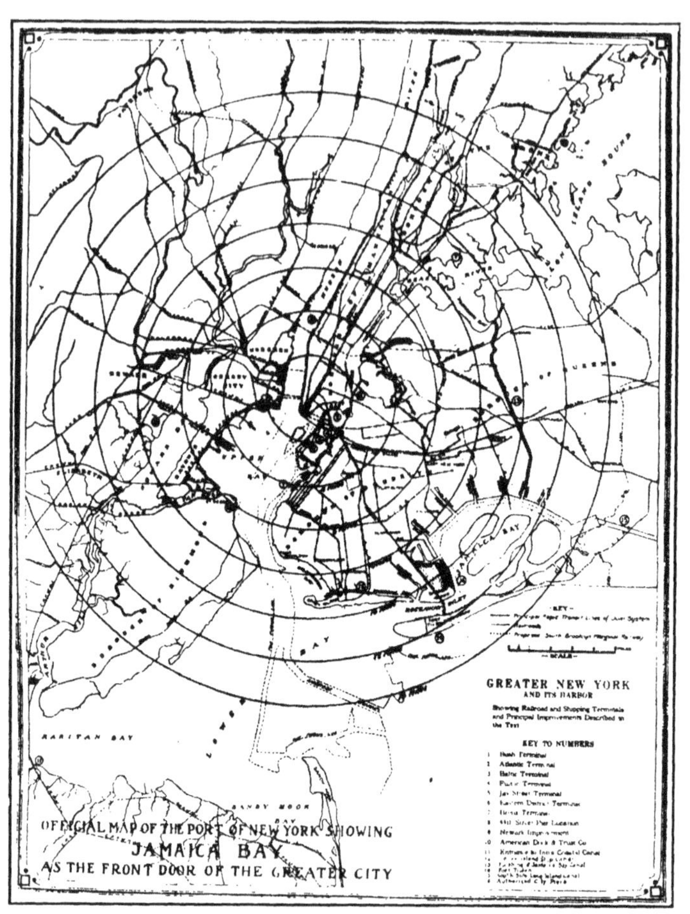

THE ACCESSIBILITY OF JAMAICA BAY

A zone map showing the desirability of Jamaica Bay as a port of entry and departure for transatlantic and coastwise ships as compared with New York Harbour.

finished is on Jamaica Bay which Henry A. Meyer, Deputy Dock Commissioner of New York City, summarizes as follows:

A plan of development has been provided under a coöperative agreement whereby the Federal Government constructs and maintains an entrance channel 1,500 feet wide and 30 feet deep, and coöperates with the City of New York in constructing an inner or main channel 1,000 feet wide and 30 feet deep around the westerly and northerly side of the bay a distance of eight miles. The total amount to be expended on the part of the Federal Government for the development amounts to $7,400,000.

The State of New York became a partner in the coöperative agreement by ceding to the city for the purpose of the development all the land under water around the bay, a total of more than 16,000 acres.

The Federal and State governments exacted of the City of New York for what they contributed toward the improvement that it provide auxiliary channels, basins, and docks, so that the entrance and main channel could be utilized for industrial and commercial purposes. As an evidence of good faith and an intention to perform its part of the work, both governments demanded that before their appropriations became available, or the cession of land a fact, the city appropriate and set aside one million dollars to be used for the purpose. This was done.

The Federal Government has performed its part of the agreement by dredging the outer channel the preliminary width of 500 feet and depth of 18 feet and reimbursing the city for its dredging of the first section, and appropriating nearly a half million dollars more for the purpose, assuming the city would proceed with main channel dredging as soon as the first section was completed. This was completed in August, 1913.

The city has created a basin at the foot of Flatbush Avenue called Mill Basin, although not yet fully completed, with a city dock 400 feet long and 30 feet wide. The channel leading to the basin is in an incompleted state, but plans have been prepared and it is expected the channel and basin will soon be completed.

Jamaica Bay has an unlimited area for railroad expansion, and through the agency of the New York Connecting Railroad acting as a Trunk Line Marginal Road, all roads will have access to the bay on equal terms. With the advent of the tunnel under the Narrows to Staten Island and thence to New Jersey the entire railroad system of the continent will be in direct touch with the seaboard at the ocean front.

The people of the State in 1911 voted that the export terminal of the Barge Canal should be located in Jamaica Bay; after the Legislative Commission had recommended that place as the ideal and practically the only location for one in New York Harbour. The State has made a survey of a direct route for the construction of a canal between Flushing and Jamaica bays as the most direct route to reach such a terminal and avoid the congestion of the main harbour. The State has also enacted a law making it a partner with the Federal Government in the construction of the Coney Island Ship Canal so as to provide a safe inside waterway from the upper bay to Jamaica Bay for canal traffic and other small craft that could not navigate the main entrance channel at Rockaway Inlet in stormy weather.

Other projects and their costs, at the Port of New York, through the year 1918, including both original and maintenance charges, are as follows, stated in nearest thousands:

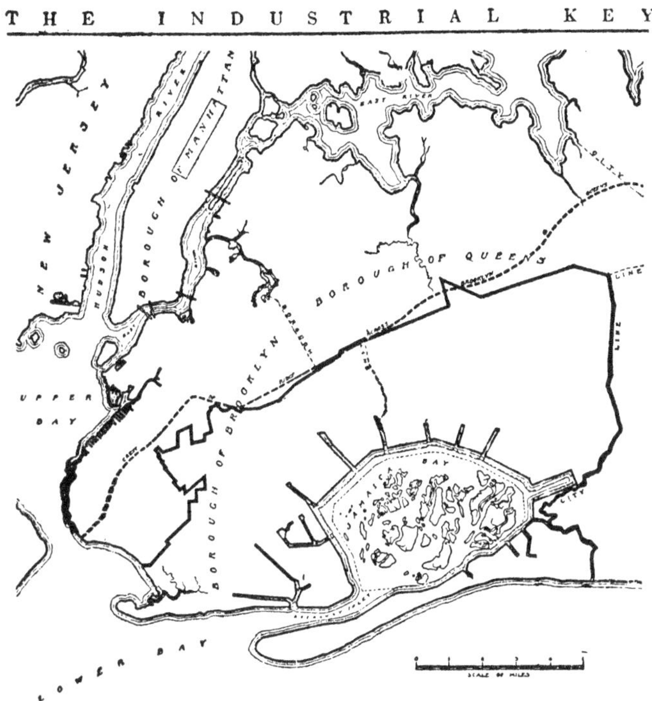

A GREAT CITY WITH AN IDLE HARBOR

The 26th, 29th, 31st and 32nd wards of Brooklyn, and the 4th and 5th wards of Queens lie in a semi-circle around Jamaica Bay. They are bounded on the west, north and east by the heavy line on the above map, and on the south by Jamaica Bay. The population in this territory in 1910 was 378,609. The rate of increase from 1900 to 1910 was 146%. Using this rate for estimate from 1910 to 1914, the present population would be 599,716. The building operations in 1913 amounted to approximately $20,000,000. The real estate taxes paid by these wards in 1914 exceeded $8,400,000. This district, in itself a great city, is unjustly deprived of its natural harbor. At present its supplies (estimated at 3,200,000 tons annually) must be trucked from the distant waterfront of the East River or Upper Bay, or else brought in by railroad under heavy tariff. The district is thus put to an unnecessary transportation expense of at least $960,000 per annum through the city's failure to carry out its agreement to develop Jamaica Bay.

TOTAL FEDERAL EXPENDITURES ON NEW YORK HARBOUR THROUGH 1918

East River, including Hell Gate, 1852-1918.	$ 6,520,000
Jamaica Bay, 1892-1918	250,000
Channel in New York Harbour, 1834-1918.	858,000
Ambrose Main Ship, Bayside and Gedney channels, including Upper Bay and Craven Shoal and channel between Staten Island and Hoffman and Swinbourne islands, 1836-1918	7,642,000
Bay Ridge and Red Hook channels, 1890-1918	4,393,000
Newtown Bay and Creek, 1880-1918 . .	527,000
Gowanus Creek and Red Hook channels, 1892-1918	148,000
Coney Island Channel, 1907-1918 . . .	123,000
Sheepshead Bay, 1880-1918	36,000
Great South Bay, Long Island, 1902-1918 .	172,000
Staten Island-New Jersey Channel, 1852-1918	2,318,000
Brown's Creek, Sayville, L. I., 1890-1918 .	51,000
Huntington Harbour, 1872-1918	73,000
Port Jefferson Harbour and Inlet, 1852-1918	180,000
Hempstead Bay, 1913-1918	51,000
Echo Bay Harbour, 1878-1918	67,000
Harlem River, including Spuyten Duyvil Creek, 1875-1918	2,120,000
Bronx River, 1896-1918	921,000
East Chester Creek, 1873-1918	211,000
Mattituck Bay and Harbour, 1896-1918 .	121,000
Raritan Bay, 1881-1918	693,000
Raritan River, 1836-1918	771,000
Shrewsbury River, 1852-1918.	478,000
Woodbridge Creek, N. J., 1879-1918 . .	95,000
Cheesequake Creek, N. J., 1880-1918 . .	59,000

Elizabeth River, N. J., 1879-1918 . . .	61,000
Keyport Harbour, N. J., 1882-1918 . . .	112,000
Matteawan Creek, N. J., 1881-1918 . . .	91,000
Shoal Harbour and Compton Creek, N. J., 1890-1918	85,000
South River, N. J., 1871-1918	204,000
TOTAL	$29,431,000

A second type of harbour improvements began in 1870 when the city government awoke to its responsibility when, by an act of the Legislature, the Department of Docks was established.

Mr. S. W. Hoag tells us that, at the inception of their work, the authorities advertised for all persons who were interested in the improvements of the waterfront, or who had any ideas on the subject, to attend hearings, discuss schemes for improvements, and to offer suggestions. The resulting "new plan" submitted to the Board of Docks by General McClellan, then engineer-in-chief, was so far superior to anything proposed by those who responded to the invitation as to place other recommendations in the category of curios.

Since then (1870–1918) the Dock Commissioner reports that $105,000,000 has been spent by New York City for acquisition of property ($40,500,000) and for construction of piers

($64,400,000). Of this total investment of nearly $105,000,000, the Commissioner says the city earned in 1918 the sum of $6,320,000, or $5,770,000 net after subtracting the operation costs ($594,400). This means a net profit on total cost of 5.5 per cent., or as the Dock Department reckons it, 8.95 per cent. on the construction cost.

In reading these figures business men who are accustomed to including interest on their investment and taxes, too, in their statements of operation costs must remember that the net profit of 5.5 per cent. does not provide for these charges.

This issue is not new. In 1831 a "Committee on Application" of the Common Council startled the Legislature and the public by announcing that "the income derived by the city government from the public wharfs of the best Harbour in the world, and of a City the most commercial and most thriving on the American Continent, is inadequate."

At that time the city's wharfage rates were unnecessarily low; one sixth those of Boston; one fifth those of Savannah; one half those of Baltimore, and only approximated Philadelphia's.

Two conclusions by the Committee of 1831

foreshadowed action by the Sinking Fund Commission of 1918: "For the last seventeen years ending January 1, 1831, the gross disbursement on the public wharfs exceeded the gross receipts by $124,338. The income might be increased without endangering commerce in the least. It is deemed a good general rule that each branch of business should sustain itself from its own income."

In 1918 a controversy arose over the leasing of Pier 69, North River, and it was offered at public auction to the highest bidder, thus calling attention to an abuse which had been a scandal for nearly two decades, of sub-leasing city-owned piers right under the city's very eyes for two or ten or twenty times the rental which the original lessee paid the city. In this first case which attracted public attention public letting raised the annual rental from $15,000 to $65,000.

Commissioner Hulbert, however, has inaugurated a new policy with reference to the development of the Staten Island shore, where he has put into execution a plan for the construction of twelve great modern piers along a stretch of one and one quarter miles. For these improvements appropriations have been made aggregating $14,562,032, and tenants already secured for the piers include such firms as the

International Mercantile Marine Company, the Pan-American Dock Corporation, the Union Transport Company, Edward M. Raphel & Company, Wessel, Duval & Company, Moore & McCormack. This substantial public improvement is directly attributable to the foresight and perseverance of the present Dock Commissioner. Another improvement for Staten Island, for which plans have been perfected, is the construction of two large dry docks by Fraser, Brace & Clark Company and the Morse Dry Dock Company.

B. F. Cresson, Jr., Consulting Engineer, New York-New Jersey Port and Harbour Development Commission, maintains that substantial earning powers should accrue through properly designed port improvements: "I have just returned from a trip to the Pacific Coast and have been greatly impressed with the eagerness with which the municipalities there are projecting port improvements. Los Angeles has just voted a bond issue for port improvements of $4,500,000; San Francisco has appropriated $8,000,000; Portland, Oregon, has available about $5,000,000; Tacoma has just voted $2,500,000, and Seattle is embarking on a $2,500,000 pier project, and boasts that her million-dollar Smith Cove pier earned 38 per cent. last year."

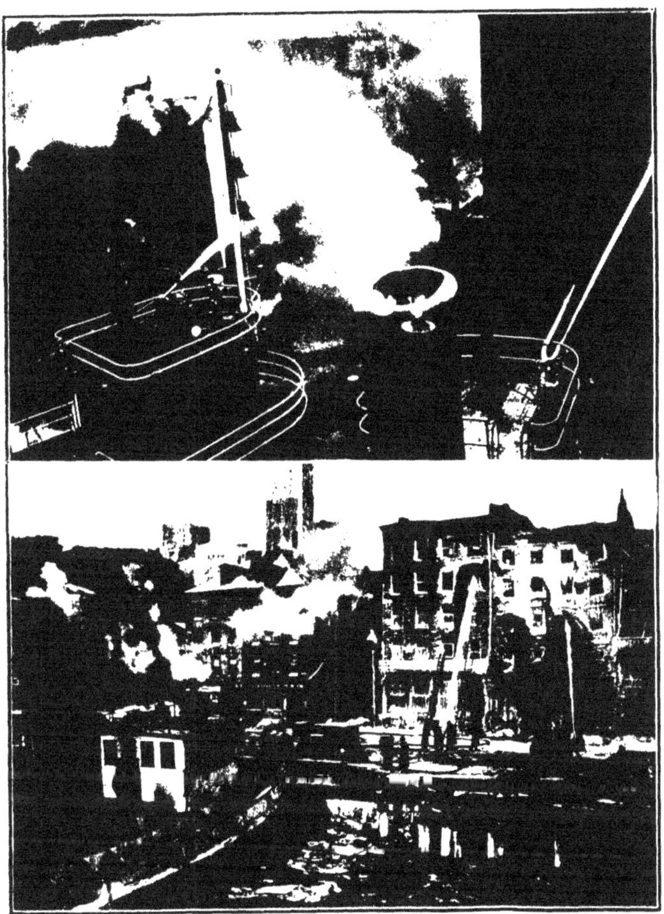

DEFENCE AGAINST FIRE

New York City's waterfront is protected from fires by one of the most efficient fire departments in the world. The photograph shows two of its fire boats in action.

(Copyrighted by the American Studio)

DOWNTOWN NEW YORK

A view looking north from the top of one of its office buildings. The bridges in the photograph spanning the East River are, from south to north, the Brooklyn, the Manhattan, and the Williamsburg bridges. Another bridge crosses the river at 59th Street, the Queensboro Bridge, and across Hell Gate is the magnificent concrete bridge of the New York, New Haven & Hartford Railroad, used almost exclusively for freight traffic.

Pacific ports have all practically eliminated charges against ships and have placed the charge against the cargo. This is an interesting comparison with the situation at New York where ships are paying three hundred and four hundred dollars a berth.

Private capital presents an interesting type of improvement, the most notable example being the Bush Terminal. Charles Molesphini, real estate editor of the New York *Evening Post*, maintains that what private capital has done in the way of freight-distributing centres along the city's waterfront is proportionately larger than what the city has done for itself, but the total combined effort has but simply scratched the surface of the possibilities. If private capital was far-sighted and forehanded while government agencies and merchants were napping, posterity would spend its energies correcting government action.

Over on the Jersey side even less has been done by government agencies. In Jersey City only 125 of 26,400 feet of waterfront, or *less than half of one per cent.*, is owned by the public. The many municipalities (40) are too poor to develop, acting singly, but through State coöperation and treatment of all ports as a whole the improvements could be profitably made.

Plans are in preparation, however, by private owners to develop 2,300 feet of shorefront on that part of the Jersey shore known as Weehawken, where it is contemplated to construct four piers together with two or more dry docks.

Lest in our eagerness to focus national attention upon improvements still needed we underestimate the advantages which the Port of New York already offers to trade, let us remember that it is by far the greatest railroad, commercial, and industrial centre on the Atlantic seaboard.

The population of the metropolitan district of New York is four times that of Philadelphia.

The port has the finest harbour on the Atlantic Coast, with 780 miles of waterfront.

Three times as many railroad trunk lines come to New York as to any other city on the Atlantic tidewater.

More manufacturing industries are located in the New York district than in the combined cities of Philadelphia, Chicago, Cleveland, and St. Louis, and the value of the products of the New York industries is nearly as great as the combined value of the products of those of the other four cities.

CHAPTER XIV

Forts and Fortifications

For months prior to our entry into the World War moving-picture films acquainted millions of Americans far from the seaboard line with the fact that ships of the enemy might easily bombard the Port and City of New York without risking fire from the longest range guns then used to defend this gateway to America. And if the enemy fleet had been ocean rovers at large instead of bottled up by England's navy, our country would undoubtedly have learned many other lessons with respect to the adequate defence of all our seaports, especially the great commercial centres. To-day we have almost forgotten the dangers which appalled us in the early years of the war, and most of us are completely indifferent to the manner in which the Port of New York was protected against submarines and battleships.

Later on, when reading dramatic summaries of steel nets and how they would have excluded submarines, how electric mines would have destroyed any intruder, whether foe or friend, how disappearing guns would have hit the enemy target with an almost uncanny accuracy, let us never forget the fact about the entrance to New York Harbour, that:

> A good-sized steamer or two sunk athwart its meagre channel would more effectively bottle up the Metropolitan area of New York with its aggregate population of 10,000,000, with its fleets of merchantmen and battleships and its navy yard, than did Captain Hobson the flotilla of Admiral Cervera at San Diego, or the English soldiers of the *Vindictive* at the German channel at Zeebrugge—that is why this channel is called "The Narrows" and that is also why the Port of New York is a haven unsurpassed.

Nothing but the determination to prepare against war will excuse our failure to keep the Port of New York fortified with the best expression of human ingenuity and to employ humanity's need for fortifications there, as a constant incentive to further invention and protection.

Eminent military authorities assert that the World War emphasizes the necessity for safeguarding our port:

1. Long-range guns for outlying fortifications;
2. Railway artillery, that is, long-range guns and howitzers mounted on railway carriages to be utilized as a

reserve in case any defences of New York Harbour require additional support;

3. Aërial defences including anti-aircraft batteries to prevent air raids;

4. Block Island as a sentinel to the defences of eastern New York should be provided with larger, longer range high-power guns;

5. Adoption of national policy to have fortifications so strong and so abreast of scientific possibilities that no one could hope successfully to attack New York or any other important American port.

In re-asserting the need for action rather than reminiscence, the same authority points out that every war, and in fact every war scare we have had since the birth of our nation, has found New York inadequately fortified against attack. Among the principal improvements added in 1917, anti-submarine nets and mines, air squadrons and anti-aircraft batteries, all might have been ready before we needed them had we displayed the necessary caution.

To be forewarned is to be forearmed, and lest our country, whose welfare requires that the port which serves half the country's shipping shall be properly fortified, should again forget this obligation, a few reminders of past shortsightedness may be cited:

1. In 1664 the port fell to the English because its Dutch promoters had failed to heed several warnings that defence and ammunition were needed;

2. During the English occupation, 1664 to 1783, improvements were due to hindsight rather than foresight, to actual attack or actual threat rather than to pre-vision and providence;

3. The residents who became revolutionists did not see the need until war was actually upon them.

"No further additions or improvements of importance to the city's defences were made until the Revolutionary War, the Americans then proceeding with the work, as they intrenched on this part of the island and the adjacent country."

General Lee was in charge of these operations, and his first act was to close Hell Gate Channel by the erection of a fort at the foot of the present East Eighty-eighth Street, and of another fort on the opposite shore. He also placed batteries at the entrance to the harbour on both sides of the river, at the intersection of Catherine and Cherry streets, on Rutgers Hill, immediately north of that point, and at Coenties Slip, a short distance south, near the foot of Wall Street.

Fort Amsterdam, which at the opening of the war a British officer said seemed "to have been intended for profit and form rather than for defence, it being entirely exposed to a fire in reverse and enfilade," was demolished on the side facing Bowling Green, so that, in the event of capture, it could not be used by the enemy as a citadel, and a battery was built under the southern walls.

Various points along the Hudson were also fortified by batteries, while the streets leading up from the water were protected by barricades, and a chain of fortifications was thrown up in the north, to defend the city from attack in that direction.

General Lee being assigned to other duties in the southern part of the country, his work in New York was taken over by Lord Stirling, who, on a special plea from General Washington, hastened the completion of the fortifications in order to be ready for the British, who were about to evacuate Boston; and it was suspected that their next move would undoubtedly be against the important northern Port of New York and its environs.

The deduction proving correct, General Washington hurried to the city to aid in prosecuting measures for its defence, which included the strengthening of the works already begun, and the erection of a fort on the Hudson shore at the north end of the island, to which was given the name of the great commander, Fort Washington.

This fort was merely a hasty expedient, having no casements, barracks, or well, or other bulwarks for withstanding a long siege, but designed solely, in conjunction with Fort Lee, erected at the same time on the Palisades opposite, to cover the communication with New Jersey. It occupied almost the highest elevation on the island, and its outworks extended in every direction for more than a mile, while west, east, and north were strong redoubts.

There were also effective works at Kingsbridge, while Long Island was defended by three small fortresses and two redoubts connected by field entrenchments and protected by abatis and other entanglements in a line extending from the Wallabout Bay across the neck of land that is now the heart of Brooklyn, to Gowanus marsh, fronting a little to the southeast. On the extreme right of this line was Fort Box, commanding the approaches from Gravesend and Flatbush, while to the left at about an eighth of a mile the most substantial structure, Fort Greene, mounting six guns, stood guard over the road to Jamaica and Flatbush. To the north of this, but on the same line, the "Oblong Redoubt" was planted, with Fort Putnam, mounting three pieces, a quarter of a mile still farther north, defending the Newtown, Bushwick, and Flatbush roads; Fort Stirling, a mile west, near the edge of the bluff now called the Heights; and on the extreme left the remaining redoubt, its northern flank covered by rifle pits, marked the beginning of the swamp ending in the "Wallabocht." These entrenchments were further strengthened on the right flank by a battery of four guns on Cobble Hill, an elevation about a half mile due west and back of Fort Box, and approached only by a lane from Red Hook, which, with Governor's Island, stood guard over Buttermilk Channel. The works of the former were armed with 18-pound guns, and those of the latter with four 32-pound guns and four 18-pound guns, both of which were manned by an adequate force.

The fortifying of Governor's Island, which had periodically been recommended from the time of the first English governors, was also begun during this period, presumably by the citizens of New York, as an old paper records that "everybody turned to with great spirit and industry," and had made considerable headway by the arrival, on April 4, 1776, of General Putnam, who carried them to such effective completion that General Washington, on May 9th, in a letter to General Lee, said: "Governor's Island has a large and strong work erected and a Regiment encamped there," while in August following Lord Stirling, in answer to a request for more men on the island, wrote: "The General bids me say that in our present situation Governor's Island is more strong and better guarded than any other post in the Army."

When the British took possession of New York after the Battle of Long Island, in August, 1776, they repaired and strengthened all defences, particularly those on Governor's Island and at Fort Washington, but they did very little actual building and only in minor operations, such as Fort George, near Washington Heights, on what is now Fort George Hill.

4. After the Revolution the fortifications were either diverted to other uses or given no attention at all and were in urgent need of repair within a short time. Finally the Federal commissioners appealed to the citizens to volunteer

for the work as a patriotic obligation. The result was that an army, including men from every profession and occupation from lawyers to labourers, was soon engaged at the task, concentrating their energies particularly on Governor's Island, and in exactly two years they had all the fortifications in such condition that the engineers reported them as completed.

5. By the year 1806 New York had again become "defenceless." After two years of agitation Castle Williams on Governor's Island was begun, and completed in 1810.

6. Our war with England in 1812 found New York again unprepared, and not until 1814 had "defences been erected at vast expense at almost every available and commanding point. Those at the Narrows, at Staten Island, and before the city, mount collectively more than 350 pieces of the heaviest artillery. . . . The different works on the island of New York which are perfected are, the City Battery, which has been raised upon a foundation of stone at the extremity of the city, and about 50 yards from the Battery or parade ground; it is a circular fort of masonry, and mounts twenty-eight long 32-pounders; it has capacious magazines and cisterns; it is connected with the shore by a regular drawbridge. The North Battery stands a mile up the Hudson and is a semi-circular work of stone, mounting sixteen 32-pounders. Fort Gansvoort is about one and a quarter miles farther up the Hudson, and is also an enclosed stone battery with magazines, extensive barracks, and furnaces for heating red-hot shot."

There were also in the city in 1812 four arsenals: the State Arsenal, the United States Arsenal, the United States Magazine and Arsenal, and the United States Arsenal on the Parade, now Madison Square.

Outside there were on Governor's Island "Castle Williams," at the west, and Fort Columbus in the centre; Fort Wood, a mortar battery, on Bedloe's Island; a circular battery of fourteen heavy guns on Ellis Island; and on the eastern shore of Staten Island the three batteries of Fort Richmond, Fort Morton, and Fort Hudson.

The old fort, now known as Fort Wadsworth, first erected by the Dutch on the heights of the Narrows, and later enlarged and strengthened by the English, was also greatly improved during this period, 1812-1815, and Fort Tompkins was begun on the heights of Staten Island, but had not progressed above the foundations. When completed, it commanded the forts of Richmond, Morton, and Hudson.

The State coöperated with the Federal Government in the construction of fortifications, the work being done as rapidly as possible, and extended to every possible point of attack.

Defences were begun on Sandy Hook in 1813 and on Telegraph Hill, now the Highlands, about three miles back of the present lighthouse, a considerable fort had already been erected, while at Hallett's Point, on the Brooklyn side of Hell Gate, work was begun on Fort Stevens, an open battery of twelve guns.

The work on Harlem Heights was commenced in July, 1813, at Mount Alto on the Hudson, near One Hundred and Twenty-third Street, the trenches for it being opened by a company of volunteer militia, citizens of New York, under Mayor Van Horn. The line of these operations extended east across Bloomingdale Road where it was a bastion called Fort Horn, and along the elevated ground overlooking McGowan's Pass, and by the ledge of rocks and the elevated ground overlooking Harlem Flats to Hell Gate.

Land attacks by way of Brooklyn were provided against by particularly complete and extensive fortifications, which, as finished in 1814, extended from Gowanus Creek to Wallabout Bay, continuing eastward as far as Nevins Street and De Kalb Avenue, thus completely enclosing the peninsula.

7. Until the Civil War a half century had passed with little attention to fortifications.

8. In the Civil War, because no sea power was engaged and because the North underestimated rather than overestimated danger from the South, improvements to fortifications were in the form of strengthening and extending rather than in erecting new fortifications.

Fort Totten was built on Willett's Point, which was designed, together with Fort Schuyler, to close the harbour against approach from Long Island Sound, and strong batteries were planted at various strategic points, these additions completing the cordon around New York, and comprising, with the old works, practically the line of fortifications that exist to-day.

9. In 1872-1873 some additional batteries were set up. The Glacis Mortar Battery on Staten Island, south of the fort on the site of Fort Tompkins, which is designed to throw a powerful vertical fire upon vessels approaching or attempting to pass through the Narrows; and between the years 1888 and 1906 extensive work was done in the way of planting batteries, but since then all efforts have been directed mainly toward repairs and the improvement of ordnance.

10. An advance in policy was begun in 1886, by the creation of the Board of Fortifications, originally called the Endicott Board and later called the Taft Board. Under this body the defences have been brought up to a very high state of efficiency, and are kept in thorough and constant repair.

The inadequacy of New York's defence in 1917 was due to lack of modern appliances, not to lack of forts; to short range and not to the small number of guns. Against short-range guns on warships it was well prepared.

Of course, the most formidable fortifications become impotent as new instruments of attack against them are invented, but, even with all the new devices that have been found during the last few years, it would be no easy task for an enemy to invade New York, or even to approach near enough for an effective bombardment. Barring the way would be Fort Hancock at Sandy Hook, Fort Wadsworth, the most powerful of the port's fortifications, guarding, with Fort Hamilton, the entrance to the Narrows; Fort Tompkins, on the heights of Staten Island, heavily armed, and flanked along the channel sides by a line of the strongest known type of water batteries; within the harbour, Governor's Island, with its strong defences of Castle Williams; old Fort Lafayette, still useful for the storage of ordnance supplies; Fort Tilden, recently established at Rockaway; and Fort Schuyler, on Throgg's Neck, with Fort Totten on Willett's Point, commanding the entrance to the East River from Long Island Sound.

On Long Island Sound, at the eastern entrance, there would also be encountered a line of four forts, some eighteen miles in length, from northeast to southeast, with Fort H. G. Wright on Fisher's Island; Fort Michie, across the Race to the south on Great Gull Island, and farther on, Fort Terry on Plum Island. Although these fortifications are a hundred miles from New York, by guarding the sound they form a part of its defences, and complete the great circle of New York Harbour defences.

CHAPTER XV

New York the Nation's First Air Harbour

THE heading for this chapter is furnished by the *Bush Magazine*, a progressively edited and delightfully illustrated magazine published in the interest of the Bush Terminal which has set the pace for port service. The article in question begins: "Practical air transportation is a reality, but the mere fact that it is possible to fly great distances with heavy loads of explosives in war proves that even greater distances and heavier loads will become common in peace. New York is the strategic base for air-borne commerce as it is for rail and ship commerce. Its total available harbour frontage is approximately 780 miles. Almost 50 per cent. of the nation's total foreign commerce passes through it. Thirteen railway systems with an aggregate trackage of more than 300,000 miles centre here. In 1916 the overseas cargoes in and out of this one harbour totalled 17,567,580 tons. It is on the basis of past performance and future promise the greatest centre of trading activity ever dreamed of, and as such it takes a natural leadership in the establishment of an aërial harbour."

Surveys have been made of the port and it is estimated that for $45,000,000 a complete terminal can be equipped including warehouses, industrial centres, complete rail communication with every line entering New York, and a system of dockage for the largest ocean carriers, which would be something more than twenty-five miles long.

Does this sound visionary? Yet it is almost at our very door. Philadelphia's mayor has plans for an air port there. With our recent experience—air raids, regular air postal service, air trips across the Atlantic, passenger service every hour from Long Island to Atlantic City commenced as an early commercial achievement, freight service close on the heels of passenger service—it is easier for us to believe in an air harbour than it was to believe a generation ago that there would be ships of concrete or Leviathans carrying 15,000 people or 80,000 tons.

A practical engineer has drawn plans to cost an initial $650,000 and an ultimate $40,000,000 for a port to be beautified to look upon and to possess these service elements:

1. Large plain for air machines with convenient landing and starting space.

2. Sheltered bay for hydroplanes with easy access to the outside. In connection with these, a number of land and water hangars with their particular dependencies, such as machine shops, instrument shops, and repair shops.

3. Quartermaster's department with storehouses to take care of raw materials, finished products, and outgoing provisions for the planes, in easy connection with railroad and starting grounds.

4. Sufficient number of sheds with yards for the quick disposal of incoming and outgoing freight, and in connection with these a building for arranging and forwarding mail and parcel post.

5. A power plant with wireless station.

6. Administration building and branch custom house.

7. Grand terminal station with facilities for the care of arriving and departing passengers, in connection with the pier system and aërial station, and for the final disposal of mail and freight.

8. Any other units necessary to the efficiency of the station.

Already our editors are worrying about how to prevent aërial smuggling. Diamonds are easier to carry than dynamite. Ships that can carry mail bags can carry laces and drugs. Once in the air, a plane has its own choice of a thousand landing places. It is too much to hope that because governments will find it almost impossible to guard their frontiers against aërial smuggling, all importers will sympathetically forswear profits obtainable by smuggling.

Taking risks costs money. Well-equipped aërial harbours will offer so many conveniences, so many ways of reducing costs and serving customers that they will thrive in spite of smuggling. As for the small number of business men who in our day will sneak and lie, and run the risk of prison and confiscation in order to evade customs duties, we may trust the Government and its port services to keep their number and their activity at a low minimum. After all, there are relatively few society women who hate taxes enough to go up in the air with their jewels or laces to some place of uncertain landing.

For the Port of New York the Dock Commissioner of 1919, Murray Hulbert, suggests that Governor's Island be set aside for an aërial landing place, terminal and port—with room enough reserved for a great war relic museum. The connection with the mainland would be by a station in the subway to Staten Island. There will be air terminals and that means air harbours among which New York will be first in size, first in volume of business, and first in service to the whole country.

So rapidly is "air commerce" taking on form and substance that within a few days after the first serious suggestion of air fleet harbours and a few days before America's *NC-4* finished the first air flight across the Atlantic, the following notice of Government plans appeared in the New York *Times* as a special despatch from Washington:

> The Government's plan for coöperating with municipalities in the establishment of airplane landing fields and creating a system of aërial highways capable of use for military, postal, and commercial purposes was announced to-day by the Air Service of the United States Army.
>
> It was also made known that the Air Service, coöperating with the Post Office Department, hoped in the near future to aid in the laying out of air terminals in at least thirty-two cities and towns from the Atlantic to the Pacific, and from the Canadian border to the Gulf of Mexico. These points range in size from New York City to Flatonia, Texas, and have been selected for their fitness as part of a national system of air lanes.
>
> The establishment of landing fields throughout the country through coöperation with the Government agencies and the cities concerned will certainly operate to the advantage of both the Government and the city, because in the rapid development of commercial aviation those cities which have provided the primary facilities for operation of aircraft in their vicinity will have paved the way for local benefits, resulting from the development of aërial, inter-city transportation, express service, mail service, emergency service, and local photographic mapping of aërial protection.

CHAPTER XVI

Free-From-Customs Zones in Ports

OUR great ports are, of course, on the ocean. Far from our inland populations they are little known as ports even to their own populations. A country which has persistently neglected its port problems would naturally fail to understand the arguments for so-called free ports and the very term, "free port." It would not be surprising if an overwhelming majority even of our chamber of commerce leaders throughout the country have studied this question so little that they still believe the words "free port" mean a port into which goods can come without paying any duty. To make it easier to remove this particular misunderstanding the term "free-from-customs zone" is used in this chapter and commended to American business men who wish to increase our ability to make money by serving other nations. It is a zone within a port, and not a whole port, which New York, Boston, Philadelphia, San Francisco, and New Orleans wish to have made free from duty.

While our interest is in liberating American industry and American shipping from handicaps that are bound to prevent expansion of our trade until we have free-from-customs zones in all our principal ports, we here illustrate the nation-wide need by the Port of New York and Latin-America's large and lucrative market for dealers in laces and embroideries. Heretofore Europe has always entirely supplied these goods. This is the way the Tariff describes the present difficulties:

> Commodities of this character are apt to be included in the same order with a variety of other goods, and the order naturally goes to the dealer who can fill it as a whole at the lowest price, in the shortest time, and in the most convenient form. The order often includes specialties covered by trade-mark that are produced in different countries. To engage successfully in this trade, therefore, the merchant must be able not only to furnish the goods of his own country but also to assemble, sort, and repack foreign merchandise for convenient delivery. This kind of commerce American merchants are precluded from entering except under the greatest difficulties. In many parts of South America merchandise has to be transported for long distances in carts or on the backs of mules or llamas. It must be packed, therefore, with the least possible weight and in such form that the packages may be evenly balanced. Furthermore, dry goods are usually dutiable in those countries at specific rates by weight; so that the lighter the carton or covering the lower the duty will be. But our bonding system does not permit the original packages received from Europe to be broken and rearranged.

And if American manufacturers of clothing use imported laces and embroideries in making women's wear, the difficulty of identification and the expense of collecting a drawback are so great that when they export such goods they frequently prefer to forego the claim. One American exporter testified that his firm found it necessary to take goods from bonded warehouses in the United States and ship them to a West Indian port where they might be repacked and thence forwarded to destination.

From transshipment trade three prospective benefits are summarized:

(1) It receives the profits on merchandising and transportation;
(2) Its producers have first choice at lowest price of the materials handled;
(3) It can sometimes gradually build up a preference for its own products in supplying foreign markets.

So little thought have we given to these tremendous resources that our transshipment trade has no separate statistical statement; instead, transshipments are put in the same column with goods which merely cross our country in bond from one foreign country to another. We once had a flourishing transshipment trade, just after the Revolutionary War, but far from doing work for other nations we stopped even our own trade until just before the war. One hundred years ago foreign products reëxported from America equalled nearly half our total imports. In our time this proportion has dropped to one sixteenth.

Another type of obstruction to trade and employment which the free-from-customs zone would remove is furnished by rice milling. We have everything in the United States for this business except a sufficient supply of raw rice. We do not grow enough to furnish employment by the year, yet this business requires expensive specialized machinery and skilled labour that must be engaged by the year. The mills are idle much of the time for want of material. If we could handle imported rice for reëxport to the West Indies and Spanish America our mills could keep running all the year round. At present if a miller imports the usual cargo of 6,000 tons he pays a duty of $60,000; eventually he will be able to get a drawback on so much of this rice as he reëxports, but the difficulty, delay, and expense of securing the drawback make him choose instead to keep his mills idle and to make the home consumption and the price for rice pay the cost of idle mills.

It is proposed that on the Jersey Meadows or on Jamaica Bay or in Staten Island, or possibly in all three, there be erected special facilities for docking, transshipping, sorting, manufacturing, and storing raw materials, or completely manufactured materials that are brought into this port only for the purpose of getting them ready to ship to foreign countries. Sometimes this "getting ready" will mean merely repacking them, so that the special tests or prejudices of the foreign buyer, like Latin-America, will be consulted to the last detail. Other goods would need some finishing touch put on them to change them from partly manufactured to finished articles; still others would come as raw material, say tobacco to be reshipped as cigars, or chicle to be used in the manufacture of chewing gum.

Each of these three steps is already being taken on a small scale in this country. There is nothing new about them except this proposal that we put our ports in condition to do the work with the utmost dispatch, the least expense, and the greatest convenience, so that we can underbid and outserve our competitors.

The cost of establishing a free zone in the Port of New York has been estimated at from $50,000,000 to $60,000,000 by former Congressman William Harris Douglas of New York City, who, for more than a quarter of a century, has strongly advocated the building up of our American Merchant Marine, and who now feels that the public is so thoroughly aroused to this necessity that we shall soon establish our lines of communication to all leading ports of the world. He has been equally enthusiastic in demanding free zones as essential and necessary for the maintenance of our commercial life and believes that the volume of business which will clear through such a free zone will also pay a proper interest on the investment plus a sinking fund for ultimately paying off the original cost.

We are already repacking, finishing, and manufacturing goods sent us from foreign countries not for consumption in this country but for ultimate consumption in the four corners of the globe. We are already recognizing the fact that on such goods there ought not to be charged an import duty, and we have three different ways of freeing them from duty:

(1) *The bonded warehouse*, where goods intended for reexport may be entered and held free of duty.

(2) *The bonded manufacturing warehouse*, where, without payment of duty, imported goods may be handled, altered, or manufactured solely for export, either with or without the admixture of domestic materials and parts.

(3) *The drawback*, which is a repayment of 99 per cent. of the duties paid on imported goods when they are exported.

Free-from-customs goods intended for reëxportation we already have; they come into ports where their freedom from customs is recognized. The importer gets his money back if he pays a duty or is granted exemption if he puts these goods in a bonded warehouse for storing or for manufacturing.

Every single question of public policy is already settled except the questions of convenience, economical management, and dispatch. And those who want a particular zone set aside in a port for cutting red tape, cutting corners, saving time, and saving expense are merely asking our nation to do well what it is now doing badly.

Against the free-from-customs zone is no argument whatever. No one opposes it on national grounds. Everybody who is interested at all wants it, except an occasional inland manufacturer who fears that the free zone would build up a serious competition. The only reason that it remains among the unmet needs instead of among the achievements is that, like many other port problems, it has suffered from deficient publicity. The case for the free zone is admirably stated in a letter dated November 20, 1918, from the United States Tariff Commission to the Committee on Commerce of the United States Senate. Few public documents are so readable; its type is large and clear; it liberally uses indentation, numbered paragraphs, and heavy, black-face centre headings; he who runs may read. After its facts and arguments in support of the free-from-customs port it gives a bill pending before Congress, with some proposed amendments and reports from the Chambers of Commerce in New York, Philadelphia, New Orleans, San Francisco, and Galveston, and closes with information respecting foreign free ports, especially Copenhagen; and copy of a bill introduced in the French Chamber of Deputies just before the war, for the establishment of free zones in French maritime ports.

There is so much ground covered respecting foreign trade and the mutual profit in international trade and urgent problems confronting American trade, that it would serve admirably as a textbook for colleges and high schools.

"Give foreign commerce wings, not shackles"; "All interests benefited by free ports"; "Helps and hindrances"; "The Pacific Ocean of opportunity"; and "Free ports as a national policy," are five headlines from the San Francisco report. These Pacific Coast business men and statesmen do not mince words or tangle them in stating reasons for a free-from-customs zone in ports; they say that the tremendous trade development, which is imminent, cannot go on "without any provision for the elimination of the intolerable friction inseparable from present arrangements"; industrial and commercial development are dependent upon transportation; efficiency of transportation is measured by the cost and speed of handling goods; inadequate harbour facilities poorly correlated with railroad transportation are prime contributors to the high cost of living because slow and expensive circulation of supplies inevitably adds to their cost; the more hands through which goods pass from producer to consumer the more the public must pay; we cannot claim or hold commercial supremacy if we are inefficient on the sea; we cannot be efficient on the sea and take advantage of our own position due to the war unless we have free zones.

Developed and properly organized free-from-customs zones (note that the Tariff Commission here quoted used the expression "free ports") in our ports would insure eight benefits:

1. Ports are the gateways through which commerce must pass. Every form of waste, whether of time or money, that can be eliminated means to that section and to the country added facilities.

2. The establishment of free zones in ports will tend to encourage new business and make land area more valuable

as a terminal and cheaper as an entrepôt. Traffic follows the line of least resistance, with saving of time, labour, and money.

3. By handling traffic more economically and expeditiously a free port or free zone will encourage and give impetus to surplus production, and benefit shippers, consignees, and consumers.

4. Free ports will be the means of saving interest on large sums of money by precluding the necessity of tying up funds for customs duties whilst goods are held in warehouses.

5. Free ports will increase the speed and decrease the cost of receiving, transferring, and reshipping of merchandise.

6. Free ports accord facilities for unloading goods which may be stored, packed, mixed, assembled, manipulated, and even manufactured within the free zone with the greatest possible freedom. Manufacturers are accorded the privilege of exhibiting and demonstrating their goods, grading and altering same for domestic or export use. Buyers can examine, test, and compare the commodities of the world before making purchases.

7. Well-developed free zones in ports in the United States stimulate the growth of exporting houses and enable them to hold goods for set periods without the payment of duties, often equal to the cost of the commodity itself. Besides supplying a more convenient outlet for American goods, free ports will aid the American manufacturers in need of foreign supplies by bringing raw material to our shores cheaply for subsequent import or export, as the needs of the trade demand.

8. The number, speed, and efficiency of cargo boats will be greatly increased, and in this direction a free port becomes a vital factor in enabling us to meet the foreign trade demands that will be placed upon us after the war.

Mr. Douglas states that the free zone would not only be of inestimable value to our own shipping, as the port would be equipped with latest machinery for loading and discharging, repairing vessels, etc., but it would also attract to the free ports established foreign shipping as well, where repairs could be accomplished expeditiously, and where ships would be of value to our export trade for recharter purposes.

The same story is told by the Tariff Commission when it lists the disadvantages of our present method of examining goods free from duty which are intended for reëxport. Four disadvantages of the bonded manufacturing warehouses are summarized as follows:

1. Production can be carried on in such a warehouse for export only. With a few special exceptions, the output cannot be disposed of in the domestic market, even on payment of duty. The most important exceptions are metal from ore smelted in bond, and cigars "made in whole from tobacco imported from one country." Minor exceptions found in a provision for the entry of Mexican peas, or garbanzo, which have been cleaned at such warehouses, and in the permission to sell for domestic consumption by-products and waste arising in the manufacture of goods for export, provided duty is first paid on such articles as if imported from abroad.

2. Before beginning operations the proprietor must file with the Treasury Department and with the Collector of Customs a statement of all the articles he intends to manu-

facture, giving the names of the articles, the exact kind and quantity of ingredients, and the formula of manufacture, and he must adhere rigidly to the formulæ set forth.

3. He must also give bond in double the value of the goods he intends to produce.

4. From beginning to end materials and operations are under strict customs supervision. A multitude of restrictions make the procedure intricate and expensive, and the penalties for violation are very heavy. Only in the most highly standardized industries is it possible to avoid frequent disputes and misunderstandings.

On the subject of drawback, the Tariff Commission says that "the privilege is so hedged about with exacting and intricate regulations that the amount of the drawback very often does not pay for the labour and cost of collecting."

1. To prove the identity of goods on which drawback is claimed requires a minute checking of imported elements entering into the manufacture, with the right and oftentimes with the need of examining into factory management sometimes threatening the disclosure of trade secrets of importance. So complicated is the procedure in making claim and proving identity that many producers do not find it worth while to apply for drawback at all. Large-scale industries, like sugar refineries and those compelling the use of large quantities of tin plate, go to the expense of employing experts permanently to look after their drawback interests.

2. Every step must be taken subject to customs inspection, and oaths are required from importers, superintendents, and exporters.

3. Even after reshipment, before drawback can be re-

covered, evidence must be given of the actual landing of the goods in a foreign country.

4. At best, under the smoothest operation of the law, that part of the owner's capital advanced in payment of duties is tied up in the Treasury from the time the goods are imported until 30 days after they are reshipped.

Now that our country has become a creditor nation and the greatest nation, and that our industries and financial leaders see that we can hope to increase our sales to other nations only by increasing our purchases from them it is inconceivable that we will longer continue restrictions upon the commerce which we have sacrificed to develop. The fact that we have heretofore done only a small business in remaking and repacking means nothing except that we have lost a great opportunity. As the Tariff Commission said, "obviously, the free zone alone cannot create commerce; it can only facilitate the operation of the forces that do create." The only open questions are two: (1) How much money shall be spent on creating free zones and providing them with the facilities for storing, shipping, repacking, and manufacturing, and (2) who shall furnish this money—private corporations, municipality, or state or national government?

To see that the money spent shall fit the prospect of business to be done, the Tariff Commission recommended a careful investigation for each port to be sure that foreign trade and not home appetite for "pork" expected by log-rolling (our euphonious American name for Federal appropriations) shall determine the location and cost of free zones and that the states or localities shall provide the funds.

In other words, a free-from-customs zone in an American port would be as the San Francisco Committee wrote, "merely a new system of customs collection and supervision. The Custom House, so to speak, is removed from the ship and wharf where it now holds sway and is set up at the gates of the free zone."

Any need so obvious does not depend upon the President for its sanction. European ports have demonstrated that free zones do remove shackles and do give commerce wings. In 1914 Spain established three free ports, at Cadiz, Barcelona, and Bilbao. The year before, Portugal named a commission to select a site for the free zone in Lisbon. Copenhagen, Trieste, Fiume, because of free zones, increased their total tonnage 50 per cent. in ten years; even Rumania has such a free zone at Sulina—three miles of the Danube. Switzerland has been considering the establishment of a free area at Basle. Germany had as long ago as 1904 nine different duty-free areas varying in size from the free port of Hamburg, with an extent of about 2,500 acres, to the free district of Danzig with an extent of less than one acre. The four free ports are: Hamburg, Bremerhaven, Cuxhaven, and Geestemunde. The five free districts are Bremen, Emden, Stettin, Brake, and Danzig.

How the free-from-customs zones will appear to us after we have established them may be judged from the following headline and clipping of March 29, 1919, announcing Stockholm's invitation to American business to use the free zone in her port:

STOCKHOLM FREE PORT OPENS JUNE 1

BALTIC SEAPORT BIDDING FOR MORE OF WORLD TRADE

American Exporters Invited to Store Goods in Stockholm in Anticipation of Enormous Demand from Russia and Sweden.

The City of Stockholm has invited American exporters to store goods in her free port, which will open June 1, in anticipation of the gigantic demand expected as soon as conditions in Russia become more settled. Herbert Hoover has predicted that this demand will reach enormous proportions forty-eight hours after the fall of Petrograd.

Stockholm bids for more world trade. It has begun the erection of warehouses and docks, in addition to its old tariff port, for a free port, primarily to serve as a distributing point for commodities from America to Russia, Sweden, Finland, and the Baltics.

	1913	1914	1915	1916	1917
Transfers of merchandise stored in bonded warehouses to bonded manufacturing warehouses	63	60	50	87	85
Export shipments from bonded manufacturing warehouses	3,002	2,395	2,299	2,853	2,442
Warehouse entries	44,897	30,950	21,159	21,172	20,018
Withdrawals of merchandise from warehouse for exportation by sea	7,508	8,951	11,910	11,234	10,998
Transshipments from one vessel to another for exportation	21,555	17,840	17,279	17,840	13,854

All of these would be affected by a free-from-customs zone in ports.

CHAPTER XVII

A Model Government Warehouse and Private Rivals

To HELP win the World War there was erected by the Construction Division of the United States Army at eastern ports of the United States seven large supply depots, each one consisting of warehouses, piers, railroad yards, administration buildings, and buildings necessary to house the mechanical plants to operate them, the purpose of these depots being to handle all shipments of material and supplies overseas. The largest of these plants was located in South Brooklyn, Port of New York, described as an Army Supply Base, and typifies the terminal statesmanship that is needed in all our ports, particularly in this port; and when one considers that less than twelve months' time was consumed in this extraordinary construction and that the governmental expenditure, made under the closest economy and supervision, was approximately forty millions of dollars, a fair idea can be had as to the extent of the improvement and its permanence as a commercial advantage, not only to the Port of New York but to the United States as a whole. The buildings, including the warehouses and piers, were erected with such efficiency that the commercial value of the project seems almost incredible, not only for war purposes but as well for the great export and import business which the *post-bellum* days will have developed in the port. It is not only the best shipping terminal in the harbour, but is regarded by engineers as the finest expression of the coördination of shipping facilities in the world.

The work was conducted under the supervision of Brigadier-General R. C. Marshall, Jr., Chief of the Construction Division, U. S. A., and under the immediate direction of Lieutenant-Colonel H. S. Crocker, of the Quartermaster Corps; with him were associated various majors, captains, and lieutenants in the Construction Division of the Army. The architect was Mr. Cass Gilbert.

The land area of reservation for this Army Supply Base is 57 acres; the water area, including that occupied by piers, 43 acres. The excavation exceeded 704,000 cubic yards and was handled entirely by steam shovels; disposal was made by team, auto truck, and narrow-gauge railroad. The dredging necessary was to provide a depth of 35 feet of water in the slips between the piers. The same depth of water was also to be provided between the ends of the piers and the Bay Ridge Channel, a distance of about 250 feet. This work required the removal of about 1,700,000 cubic yards of material, and was started May 15, 1918, and was available for use in January, 1919.

The waterfront development consists of a bulkhead wall extending along the full length of the property, of the usual platform type with a concrete quay wall of gravity section, three covered piers 150 feet by 1,300 feet, and one uncovered pier 60 feet by 1,300 feet. The slips between the piers are 250 feet wide. The pier shed consists of a double-deck steel structure with a wooden roof covered with felt and slag. The second deck is a beam and slab construction of reinforced concrete with granolithic finish, supported on transverse trusses. A steel cargo beam and walkway are provided above the roof for attaching tackle for the operation of freight-handling devices. To provide easy access to the piers from warehouses, a four-span steel truss bridge with reinforced concrete deck and housing is built. The floor of the bridge is at the elevation of the second deck of the pier and enters the warehouse at the third-floor level.

The land under development is located between Fifty-eighth and Sixty-fourth streets, the pier-head line and Second Avenue, South Brooklyn, and the site was selected after a thorough investigation of the available properties in New York Harbour, both on the New York and New Jersey shores. The preeminent advantage of the site was that the property was available for immediate development and of sufficient size to permit of the erection of very large warehouses and piers required to meet the needs of the War Department at this port. It is immediately adjacent to the Bay Ridge Terminal of the Long Island and Pennsylvania railroads, with direct rail connection with the New Haven Railroad over the Hell Gate Bridge and with the Bush Terminal property, under lease by the War Department during the war, and it had the added advantage of the Subway and Elevated Railroad facilities connecting all parts of Brooklyn and Manhattan, at the same time being located in a section of Brooklyn where the population was sufficiently large to be able to supply the labour required for the adequate operation of the base.

As will more particularly be found in the accompanying map, the total yard capacity is 1,295 freight cars, total mileage of railroad tracks, 17; the capacity of the warehouses exceeds 700,000 tons, or 100 shiploads of supplies; the slips can easily accommodate for loading twelve ships of 8,000 tons each at one time. If the bulk of freight could come in by rail or by tunnel under the Narrows, which project is being urged upon the Board of Estimate and Apportionment, eighteen of these large vessels could be loaded at one time.

The warehouses provide 6,000,000 square feet, gross, of space. The elevator installation is the largest ever attempted, a total of 96 elevators, of which six are for passenger service, in the various buildings and piers.

This Government warehouse-terminal is not without its private rivals and yet the port has a serious deficiency of modern terminal facilities. Manhattan, where congestion is more pronounced, has few available facilities either on the East River or on the North, or Hudson, River from the Battery to West Sixtieth Street. On the west side are sixty piers up to Sixtieth Street in use for terminal purposes by the various railroads. The New York Central Railroad, the Pennsylvania, the Baltimore & Ohio, the Erie, the Lackawanna, and the Lehigh Valley all have stations along the Manhattan waterfront, but the largest number of piers are those of the New York Central. Its greatest yards are in the vicinity of Thirtieth Street; its greater freight yards between Fifty-ninth and Seventy-second streets; the St. John's Park Depot on Varick Street, and the Manhattanville Terminal on the Hudson River between One Hundred and Twenty-ninth and One Hundred and Thirty-sixth streets, where the Pennsylvania and the Erie railroads distribute merchandise and foodstuffs.

Terminals on the East River frontage are small but important. The Long Island and New England sections receive the bulk of their goods from this centre by way of railroads and steamers.

Brooklyn presents the best and most modern of terminal facilities developed by private capital. Here millions of tons of freight are handled annually.

The first warehouse and pier system in the western hemisphere was begun in 1850 by the New York Dock Company. The enterprise now includes 34 piers, 159 storage warehouses, with a total capacity of 65,435,000 cubic feet; 20 manufacturing buildings with a total usable area of 1,134,060 square feet; and a cold storage plant. Its activities are divided into three terminals, the Fulton, the Baltic, and the Atlantic Basin.

Queens Borough has made rapid strides, in an industrial and commercial sense, in recent years, especially in the section around Newtown Creek. Although one of the smallest, it is nevertheless one of the most important waterways of the country, carrying a greater tonnage annually than that of the Mississippi River. In this borough are the Degnon Terminal on the creek; the Brooklyn Eastern District Terminal, north of Thirteenth Street; and the Queensboro Terminal in Long Island City, opposite Blackwell's Island.

The Bronx has no privately developed terminals, but every available inch of its vast waterfront on the East River and Long Island Sound has been preëmpted for freight stations of all the big railroad companies, especially by the New Haven Railroad which has large yards at Oak Point and Port Morris, Harlem River, where its great new connecting railroad system brings all-rail freight from the vast down-east territory. It comes through Astoria, Long Island, and down to Sixty-third Street, South Brooklyn, adjoining the Bush Terminal, for transfer across New York Bay to the Pennsylvania's Greenville Terminal.

The Bronx, however, has an important private terminal in the making where some day transatlantic steamers are expected to dock. This is the development along the lines of the Bush Terminal of a 200-acre property at the foot of One Hundred and Sixty-third Street, Hunt's Point, fronting on the East River and Long Island Sound. This development was begun a few years ago by the Bronx Terminal Corporation.

Staten Island is just beginning to develop its natural resources, which include the Staten Island Sound (Arthur Kill) and the busy Kill von Kull. The Baltimore & Ohio Railroad has until recently been the largest user of the waterfront, having a terminal with eight docks at St. George.

The only privately owned terminal of any appreciable size and prospects for future growth is that of the American Dock Company, which has four big piers and warehouse at Tompkinsville, Staten Island.

Over on the New Jersey side development has been more rapid and extensive than in New York. In fact, New York's awakening is in no small part due to the underbidding by the terminal developments on the Jersey Meadows. The War Department spent $50,000,000, which, of course, must be turned to peace uses. One large private enterprise is now building that will cost, when finished, $70,000,000. The basic facilities were summarized as follows in 1917 by Charles Molesphini, real estate editor of the *Evening Post:*

The New Jersey side of the Hudson River is most generally used by the big transcontinental railroads of the country, the bulk of American and foreign productions being handled along the frontage from the mud flats back of the Statue of Liberty up to Undercliff, which is about opposite 109th Street, Manhattan, where the New York, Susquehanna & Western Railroad has its principal marine terminal.

Terminal activities on Jersey's side of the Hudson begin with the Pennsylvania Railroad's great yards and piers at Greenville, from where a staggering quantity of freights is conveyed over Newark Bay to mainland trackage, and the Lehigh Valley's National Storage Docks, where the Black Tom Island explosion of munitions for the Allies occurred. causing the strict enforcement of the loading of munitions to be done in open water, away from piers. Above this terminal is the first of the big railroad centres, that of the New Jersey Central, whose properties in Communipaw cover approximately 200 city blocks, and include some sixteen piers in the Hudson River and the Morris Canal Basin.

Following come the Pennsylvania Terminal in Jersey City, the Erie in Pavonia, the Lackawanna in Hoboken, the West Shore, covering a stretch of frontage at a point opposite 48th to 72d Street, Manhattan, and the furthest north yard of the New York & Susquehanna at Undercliff.

The only terminal on the Jersey side so far developed by private capital other than that of railroads and steamship companies is that of the Hoboken Land & Improvement Company at 14th Street and the Hudson River.

This terminal, in which the Stevens family of Hoboken

are heavily interested, and where large industrial and food-purveying concerns are doing business, consists of six immense fireproof buildings, one of which is ten stories and is one of the largest reinforced concrete structures in the metropolitan district. The other five buildings are twelve stories and basement, and contain in all a total of 1,500,000 square feet of floor space. This enterprise largely stands on what once was Weehawken Cove, which the company filled in, making a protected basin for ships coming to deliver and take away cargoes.

Last year the city of Newark began the nucleus of what promises to become an important industrial centre, the Port Newark Terminal, in the Hackensack Meadows, at the head of Newark Bay. This consists of 256 acres near the mouth of the Kill von Kull, with a waterfrontage of 2,600 feet and extending back 5,800 feet to the New Jersey Central Railroad.

A ship canal 400 feet wide divides the developed land from an undeveloped section of as many more acres of meadow land. Newark is preparing to build a bridge over the tracks of the Pennsylvania and Lehigh Valley railroads, to provide transportation facilities to and from the mainland.

The problems immediately ahead for both sides of the river were outlined as follows by the Terminal Ports Association at a conference on terminal warehouses, May 31, 1919:

1. Warehouses of the Bush Terminal type add to railway trackage facilities, relieve congestion at terminals, and are models to improve upon for future terminal warehouse facilities.

2. Periodically railway trackage has become congested, blocking cargoes from loading on waiting ships.

3. The City of New York and the country are operating on a hand-to-mouth, made-to-order basis not only in food lines but in all lines.

4. Industrial development is impeded and its cost increased by long delays for essential standard materials.

5. If the manufacturers of this country and abroad would go on a ready-made, adequate warehouse stock of standard products then benefits like these would result:

(1) Industrial "slack" would be taken up by "stock" orders;

(2) Periods of strike or other adversity could be tided over from the storage stock;

(3) Slower methods of transportation could be utilized;

(4) Over-expensive rushing would be avoided;

(5) American merchants seeking to sell in foreign lands could list for sale and offer accustomed and established foreign products along with their own;

(6) An immediate stock supply of world products, coupled with permanent expositions of sample lines, would draw buyers from all quarters to New York;

(7) Warehouses with water, rail, and adequate facilities could be built by land owners, but the Terminal Ports Association could invite manufacturers to give assurance that such facilities would be used if provided;

(8) The storage stock for re-sale could be financed to the mills by warehouse certificates or acceptances.

CHAPTER XVIII

Creative Port Salesmanship

VISITORS to New York are of many minds with regard to the glare of lights and the jumping, wiggling electric advertisements which have earned Broadway its nickname "The Great White Way." Visitors and residents alike agree with regard to a radiant tower which even the least tutored mind calls an architectural gem, namely, the Bush Terminal Sales Building tower at Forty-Second Street near Broadway, which can be seen for blocks by day and by night.

In the darkness of New York's indifference to its harbour problems and amid the spires and towers of commercial achievement in this port, the service of the Bush Terminal stands out as brilliantly and attractively as does this tower. This service has interest if studied only as a method of facilitating future coöperation. Its interest is accentuated when one learns that it has taken its beneficiaries more than twenty years to see what now seems so simple.

The story of how America's business men,

shippers, and railroad managers allowed themselves to be helped by an idea and method for increasing efficiency and reducing cost is repeated here because with respect to many of the improvements still needed at this port there persist the same indifference, obstruction, skepticism, division of counsel, and active opposition which twenty years ago laughed out of court the ideal which has since become the Bush Terminal.

A young man of about twenty-five, joint inheritor of a considerable fortune that included a piece of property on the south shore of Brooklyn, decided that cutting coupons did not afford enough of that element of adventure which, to paraphrase Robert Wolfe, is indispensable to contentment for labour or capital. Nursing a family fortune seemed a pretty dull outlook to a man who craved activity. It became an intolerable outlook after he realized from visits to foreign ports how backward were the provisions of this port for handling world commerce with dispatch and economy. Therefore, Irving T. Bush, barely past his majority, resolved to turn part of his inheritance into "port service."

What could be easier? Given money, given a site, and given an understanding of what loading, unloading, and storing facilities in a cheap location would mean to a commerce which was suffering from congestion, what else could be done but go ahead and build the pier!

He built the pier but only to find that apparently he might just as well have built it on Lake Skaneateles. The railroads said that "not in a million years" would they ever want a pier away over toward Coney Island. Shippers said they couldn't imagine a condition of destitution and distress that would make them run a steamer "away out there" for unloading or storing. It became a disillusionment.

The sight of this perfectly good pier, with lots of room on both sides for ships and on the inside for goods, being passed day after day by scores of ships in favour of overcrowded slips and piers and inadequate pier space in Manhattan, made him ask: "Does the use of this pier depend upon my turning shipper and merchant?"

The question was no sooner asked than he answered it by chartering a ship, naming it *Independent* and heading it toward Jamaica, West Indies, where he believed it would be found easy to pick up a cargo. Like other free lances, however, this ship found at Jamaica that, while there were goods seeking ships, no traders wanted to deal with an independent; in fact, they were afraid to offend the regular line upon which their prosperity seemed to depend, so they refused cargoes. In order not to come back in ballast Mr. Bush bought a cargo of bananas. Then he began to experience some of the doubts of the shippers who declined to use his piers, because it was obvious that South Brooklyn was no place to unload a cargo of bananas, as this would only mean transshipping again to the section where banana buyers congregated. So he took his independent steamer to a Manhattan pier and auctioned his cargo of green bananas.

Another trip was made to Jamaica, and a third, until finally the line which had the monopoly on Jamaica trade came to Mr. Bush and asked him what he was "after." He said he wanted to demonstrate that a pier for handling and storing goods, which had plenty of room where Manhattan piers had none, which could take care of business immediately where Manhattan piers must delay for days, and which charged much less than piers in the congested area, not only was needed but would be patronized by port business. This company treated him with the patronizing indulgence which is frequently exhibited by other business men to whom, for some fictitious reason, we attribute far-sightedness and open-mindedness. But this

THE PIERS OF THE BUSH TERMINAL

In South Brooklyn, an independent docking project that has succeeded despite the Cassandra prophecies of railroads and other shippers. Built twenty years ago, there are now, on 200 acres, 18 piers from 1,220 to 1,350 feet long and 275 feet wide, with plenty of room between piers and room for three ships aside each pier.

ASSEMBLY YARDS AT THE BUSH TERMINAL

Back of the piers are loft buildings for manufacturing, storage buildings, and refrigerator buildings. More than 30,000 workmen are employed by the terminal company and its tenants.

AN EXCELLENT TERMINAL

Warehouses of the Army Supply Base in South Brooklyn. "It is not only the best shipping terminal in the harbour, but is regarded by engineers as the finest expression of the coördination of shipping facilities in the world."

THE INTERIOR OF ONE OF THE WAREHOUSES

Shown in the photograph above. The construction of the Army Supply Base typifies the terminal statesmanship that is needed in practically all American ports.

particular company had a reason for wanting to humour a young man with queer notions about piers. However "queer" he might be about this pier in South Brooklyn, his menace to their trade in Jamaica was the real reason. Therefore they condescendingly said they would be glad to help him make his demonstration provided he would stop interfering with their Jamaica profits. They would now and then bring him a small cargo of miscellaneous goods, not perishable, provided he would not charge anything for docking and handling these goods!

A less imaginative, less courageous promoter might not have considered this a great triumph for the new terminal but Mr. Bush had accomplished the first chain in the evidence he was seeking, namely, the ships that were avoiding this pier at least would see that the pier was doing business; eventually their curiosity would be aroused and they would want to know what inducement led their competitors to stop there instead of coming in to the congestion of the North River and its shore as they always had been doing.

To-day, a little more than twenty years later, the idea has several monuments to his foresight—the docks, warehouses, manufacturing lofts, and marginal railroad in South Brooklyn, and the Terminal Sales Building. The latter might be called a national university for buyers or a national training school in salesmanship. This same terminal corporation has brought together on the shore of South Brooklyn, on 2,000 feet, piers, storehouses, cold storage plant, assembling and manufacturing plants—not only for the portering and caring of exhibits and merchandise but also for the purpose of giving to each user the most expeditious, expert, and economical methods that money and study can devise.

"Room to burn" has been the selling slogan of the terminal proposition. In ports of more recent development like Norfolk, where there is plenty of room, this would not have the attraction which it has in the congested Port of New York. When new business comes, the terminal does not accumulate dividends by requiring customers to pile up goods on a crowded pier, but it builds another pier. Thus there are now on 200 acres, 18 piers, from 1,220 to 1,350 feet long and 275 feet wide, each with broad slips nearly 300 feet wide, and plenty of space between piers, and room for three ships alongside of each pier, with plenty of room for unloading on the second deck and on the first deck for outgoing commerce. Back of these piers are loft buildings for manufacturing (5,500,000 square feet), storage buildings, refrigerator buildings. More than 30,000 workmen are employed by the terminal company and its tenants.

Because adequate space does not of itself mean dispatch and convenience of handling, the terminal company holds itself responsible for studying the needs of trade and for furnishing the appliances and equipment which will enable it to use that space without getting lost in it; therefore we find the sections numbered and charted, and a record kept of the disposition of everything handled.

Down the centre of the pier runs a railroad (still steam-driven, however) which delivers cars opposite the section where goods are to be deposited for later delivery to a ship with the least possible amount of rehandling. Up and down, in and out, are crossing motor trucks. After the car is emptied of its outgoing goods it is moved forward or backward to a chute by which it receives, from the second story, incoming goods from ships alongside, or stored goods to be delivered either to one of the warehouses behind or to some other city, near or far, or to any railroad station in the land.

This steam railroad connects with a classification yard, where cars loaded with incoming or outgoing goods are assorted and routed for their short trips to the warehouses, manufacturing houses, or the lighters which will connect them with the transcontinental railroads or overland to the Long Island and Pennsylvania railroads. This service would be considerable even if the terminal were entirely independent of the railroads and made its own charge. Even this inconvenience has been removed, however, and the terminal's railroad is a part of the national system of railroads; its earnings come from payments to the railroad where the traffic initiates, or is set by the terminal; it is under the Interstate Commerce Commission; for all business purposes it is just as much a railroad as the longest system in the country. And to facilitate this routing there is a marginal electrified railroad two miles long. The shipper doesn't have to think about more than one railroad whether he starts his goods on their course at the Bush Terminal or at Kansas City.

That this is a fairly busy place one may gather from the fact that during our country's participation in the war 180,000,000 pounds of frozen meat were sent every month over these piers to the American Expeditionary Forces.

Besides cheaper and expert handling of goods after they reach the pier—for the ships have thus far been responsible for the actual unloading—this terminal acts as a "trouble" broker in other ways. It says to manufacturers: "Here is manufacturing space; at the front door is a station of practically every railroad or shipping line in the world; do your manufacturing here and you have all of the modern conveniences—fireproofing, automatic sprinkler protection, adequate light, cafeteria, etc.; inside your own office you are absolutely independent; after you have addressed your goods we take all the trouble and annoyance off your shoulders and sell you highly competent, regular, responsible service."

What do manufacturers save? Several instances cited during a morning's visit to this plant make a layman wonder how business with such evidence before its eyes can go on paying the penalty for failing to coöperate and failing to use cheap, ample space instead of expensive, inadequate space. One concern, which does a large business, was skeptical. Evidently they are all skeptical. So far as port progress is concerned, business seems quite frequently to have made the mistake which Missouri discovered has cost it tremendously during those years when it was proudly advertising "Show me; I'm from Missouri." So clear are these penalties that the St. Louis Chamber of Commerce, Missouri's administration and Missouri's attitude toward new ideas, is featuring the slogan "Let us show you." A big cigar company wanted a place for assembling and routing consignments. It would cost it $10,000 to move; it accordingly consented to make the experiment on condition that if after a short trial it did not like the location and facilities the terminal company would pay for moving them back to Manhattan. Knowing what it had to offer, the terminal company did not even consider that it was taking a risk. The rent was $50,000 a year. That company made during its first year as a result of its experiment $87,000; in other words, it saved enough so that it had practically free rent and $37,000 besides.

Three phases of this investment deserve mention for the promise they give of later attention to working conditions in American ports, particularly this leading port.

About $60,000 a year is set aside for what might be called labour-culture, study of labour problems and use of knowledge gained by such study. On the books of the company it is called "welfare work." Vice-President Simonds insists that in discussing this welfare service with employees the company very frankly takes the position that it is quite as much the welfare of its company and its patrons, as well as the labourer, which it has in mind. It is not patronizing the longshoreman when it sends a nurse to find out why he doesn't come to work; it is protecting its own workmen. It is not giving help to the dock labourer's family when it offers hospital, clinic, dental, surgical, and nursing care; it is protecting its own investment and advertising its wares.

The reason for giving up valuable space to cafeterias, club rooms, billiard rooms, and bowling alleys is not to throw a "sop" to labour but to keep labour in "good fighting trim," to increase its own attraction to labour, and to reduce the labour turn-over.

That good cheer is good business the four hundred manufacturers' tenants of the sales building have also recognized, for in their rental is included the cost of club rooms for buyers which rival in facilities and beauty New York's most exclusive society clubs. At no cost whatever buyers from the humblest home and business environment find here magazines, libraries, exhibits, private lunch rooms, parlours, works of art, beautiful rugs, and even "afternoon tea" and "hostess." Only the actual cost of meals or orders from the grill are exacted from the members of this International Buyers' Club.

It is building up an employment service by which it is trying to study the reason why people shift from post to post, and resources of the neighbourhood for supplying future employees.

It is coöperating with Columbia University in giving object lessons to students. It has tried to "break in" college graduates, starting them at the bottom and putting them through the simple forms of labour in the hope that they will demonstrate that the trained mind, managerial and leadership ability may be of use in the higher ranks.

As yet there has been no development of the so-called "coöperative" or "in and out" method of instruction (one week in school, one week in the field) which the public school system has inaugurated with other business concerns; nevertheless its attitude is important because it frankly says that the responsibility for making port work attractive to labour rests not with the labourer but with the employer of labour. If there is discontent it is the terminal's business to find out why.

As part of this effort to give a different reputation to port work via greater attraction, the terminal company is now planning new piers which will have the latest and best equipment and appliances. To any one visiting these largely advertised, so-called model terminal facilities it is refreshing to have a responsible officer concede unreservedly the inadequacy of present mechanical appliances for unloading ships.

It has been proved that ships require object lessons apparently before they will install the appliances that they need. Certain it is that the heyday of great profits and no competition will be ended within this year. The Bush Terminal Company not only conceives but advertises its own needs and its intention to do its part to bring America's first port abreast of, and then ahead of, all competitors. A leaf from its spirit and method should be taken by the whole port as a self-conscious ambition to do its part for world trade.

CHAPTER XIX

Advertising New York Port's Nautical School

IT IS extremely difficult to interest ambitious boys in any profession or calling whose success is not made public in the activities surrounding it. For only an infinitesimal number of American boys do home surroundings advertise the opportunities and attractions of a seafaring life. Who then shall do this advertising, who shall be the salesman? Officially, the salesman-in-chief is the superintendent of the Nautical School; it is he who recruits the boys, supervises their training, recommends them for discharge and employment. His means of advertising include letters, occasional speeches, but more particularly the annual report he makes to the legislature which, with the Federal Government, provides the support for the school; to the governor, and to the public.

Examining this advertising matter for the school which is operated from the Port of New York, we find for 1919, a year of the greatest maritime activity our country has ever known, a year when demands greater than ever before imagined had been made for men competent to take command of our Merchant Marine, the following rather deplorable facts regarding the annual report:

1. Its pages number up to forty, of which, however, only ten are editorial matter in the report of the chairman of the Board of Governors and the Superintendent.

2. Of the remaining 29 pages, more than eight are blank, leaving 21 pages for these subjects: sea routine ($1\frac{1}{2}$), port routine ($2\frac{1}{4}$), attendance report ($\frac{1}{2}$), executive officer's reports ($3\frac{3}{4}$), chief engineer ($\frac{3}{4}$), surgeon ($1\frac{1}{2}$), weights and heights (2), commencement exercises ($\frac{1}{2}$), names of governors, officers, and graduates (2), honour roll of alumni in the United States Navy, United States Naval Reserve, Marine Corps and Coast Guard ($4\frac{1}{2}$).

Accepting the judgment of the Board of Governors and the Navy Department "that the schoolship *Newport* was rendering the State and Nation as efficient service as any vessel of her class, for war purposes, in the American Navy," it does seem regrettable that the efficient service discharged by her is not more attractively and convincingly described in the annual report.

Although the Nautical School has been in existence for forty-three years, and although all the forces of Government and business were available for interesting our boys in this opportunity, less than 100 boys were in attendance during our second year in the war; although 131 boys took examinations and enrolled, 48 withdrew, 5 deserted, 4 failed to report for duty. Had this school been a small private charitable enterprise, its significance to one hundred million people or to America's maritime prowess could hardly have been presented with less allurement and conviction.

With few exceptions, the elements of successful advertising and adequate reporting are absent. Instead of thrilling the boy mind with the significance of the seaman's profession, the story even of the schoolship discusses the private university's coöperation, the use of swimming pools and baths, a shore course of instruction which might be given on shore, the trouble over ice at the pier, the condition of the schoolship when put in for repairs, etc., before it comes to the actual cruising. Fifteen lines are given to a season's cruising, but in words more likely to drive ambitious boys away from the ship than to win them. Facts like the following may be required in the report, but their setting ought to make them seem of trifling importance: "The ship was fumigated on November 13th as vermin began to appear in different parts of the vessel."

Lest the reader suspect that the foregoing

note is too severe, the following is quoted directly from the schoolship's log book. Before reading it, try to recall the state of mind of a red-blooded American boy, physically and mentally qualified to take a course in seamanship, in July, 1918, just before our Marines took their baptism of fire at Château-Thierry:

July 1, 1918, proceeded to Brooklyn Navy Yard.
July 11, 1918, proceeded to Tietjen & Lang Shipyard.
July 26, 1918, proceeded to Brooklyn Navy Yard.

The work of the two nautical schools now conducted by New York State and Massachusetts is but a drop in the bucket with what should be done for our Merchant Marine. Business men should not delegate the salesmanship necessary to securing adequate funds for our state and national legislatures to the school officers, but should proceed to "sell" the story of the country's need for this kind of training by the best methods known to modern advertising and trained salesmanship. When a boy receives an advertisement of a nautical school he ought not to have to read about any vermin, except the vermin of indifference to our commerce; he ought not to be told the details of changes in the board of management and about repairs of the ship; he ought not to be given the idea that a student attending a land university can gain even a considerable part of the advantages of attendance at the Nautical School; nor ought he to be dependent upon his imagination for light upon the attractions of the training period and the rewards in money and in what ex-President Eliot calls "the durable satisfaction in life" that can reasonably be expected from a maritime career.

The New York Nautical School, so called, has been established for more than forty-three years, first on board the old sloop-of-war *St. Mary's* and later on, in the early part of 1908, on board the gunboat *Newport* heretofore referred to, both vessels having been loaned by the Navy Department. The great naval academies of the United States and foreign countries, of course, take precedence, more as universities, while the school maintained in the Port of New York has been a sea school, as the student during his two years of service remains on board the vessel and for half of his time, at least, is in active cruising over the ocean.

Originally this school was supported by the Board of Education of the City of New York, but in 1908 the maintenance of the schoolship was transferred to the state budget. At the present time its maintenance is divided among the Federal Government and the State, the former contributing $25,000 per annum toward the maintenance of the school, approximately one fourth of the total annual expense.

Many of the boys after completing their training on the schoolship have continued their education at Annapolis and are now officers in the Navy. Many more, however, enrolled as officers in the United States Reserve Corps and in other branches of the Federal Government where their knowledge and training on the sea made them invaluable. In addition to all these, however, there were many more who followed the sea as a profession as masters and deck engineer officers in the Merchant Marine.

Considerable credit is due to Captain Reginald Fay, Marine Superintendent of the New York Central Railroad, also Secretary and Treasurer of the Alumni Association of the New York Nautical School, through whose help and coöperation laws were amended so that an American boy at the age of nineteen would be eligible to take his examination as a third officer or a third assistant engineer. But the schoolship *Newport*, which is the only school at present available for boys desirous of entering into sea service, is entirely too small for the great number of candidates who present themselves. The Navy Department is urged to allot another vessel to supplement the service rendered in this regard by the present schoolship.

Mr. P. H. W. Ross, president of the National Marine League, has been endeavouring to stimulate our young men in the advantages sought from sea service, not only by lectures but also in moving pictures. He takes the position that sea education should be in no respect a State service, but that it ought to be entirely under the laws of the Federal Government, and he impresses upon the public the fact that the National Marine League is establishing a sort of inter-collegiate branch of its activity. Because shipping is not an industry *per se*, like the making of an article in trade, but that it is a key industry, a pivotal industry.

Mr. Ross in his capacity as president of the National Marine League communicated with the governors of every state in the union, calling their attention to the necessity for uniform and united action in the direction of organizing state nautical schools, and a copy of a bill carrying out those recommendations was transmitted to the governor and the legislators of the various states.

THE DEFENCE OF THE PORT—I

An airplane escort for the S. S. *Leviathan*, passing Fort Hamilton. Military authorities, since the advent of the World War, have strongly urged, among other things, aërial defences, including anti-aircraft batteries, as an indispensable part of the defence of the port.

(Copyrighted by Underwood & Underwood)

THE DEFENCE OF THE PORT—II

A 12-inch gun at Fort Wadsworth. Long-range guns for the port's outlying fortifications and railway artillery are also considered indispensable by military authorities for the successful defence of New York Harbour against an invader.

THE NARROWS

The southern entrance to one of the greatest land-locked harbours in the world—New York Harbour

FORT HAMILTON AND FORT WADSWORTH

Located on each side of the Narrows. The only other entrance to the harbour from the Atlantic Ocean is via Long Island Sound and the East River.

CHAPTER XX

How Port Truths Are Taught

THAT democracy depends upon education is a favourite American axiom. When trying to secure money or prestige for education, petitioners and promoters usually silence argument by saying that you can't do this, can't do that, can't prevent Bolshevism, can't prevent anarchy, can't explain commerce unless you have universal education.

Quite naturally, but still rather humorously, these promoters refuse to admit either that the education needed to prevent business is education with regard to business or that they are under any obligation to teach business. What facts have been taught regarding America's first port as a port, by the educational agencies of the port itself, or of the two states immediately responsible for the port, or of other states whose prosperity depends upon the port? This question in the following form was propounded to a number of university presidents and city and state superintendents of public instruction:

As Surveyor of the Port of New York, I have come to see for the first time many ways in which this country's future welfare depends upon the development of a Merchant Marine and upon port facilities for accommodating the ships of our own nation and competing nations.

I am trying to get together for compilation and publication the more important facts with regard to America's port assets and port needs with special reference naturally to our own Port of New York.

Will your own interest in this subject justify you in helping me increase the value of this report by securing for me at as early a date as possible a brief statement with respect to instruction—undergraduate or graduate, by textbook, lecture, or field survey—which your institution offers and gives with respect to this country's maritime policy, commercial needs, and dependence upon port development? While I shall welcome printed material, I shall be especially grateful if you can place this request in the hands of the officer most familiar with your work and most interested in the country's after-war needs for an answer which I may quote as coming from your institution.

The spirit and content of the answers it is not possible to give adequately in our limited space. Among the significant facts are these:

New York University has for sometime recognized the importance of doing work along the lines suggested in the inquiry.

For Columbia University T. W. Van Metre, Assistant Professor of Transportation, writes:

Your letter to President Butler making inquiry concerning courses given at Columbia University with respect to the maritime policy, commercial needs, and port facilities of the United States, has been referred to me for reply.

The only undergraduate course which is given in the School of Business is a course on ocean transportation. This course deals primarily with the transportation service, and in doing so it naturally touches upon the port facilities and policy of the United States with reference to the development of the Merchant Marine.

Two years ago Dr. Roy S. McElwee gave a course dealing entirely with port and terminal facilities, and another course dealing with the principles of foreign trade. Dr. McElwee left the University to work for the Government, and since his departure these courses have been discontinued. It is planned to reëstablish courses of this kind next year.

The School of Business gives courses in commercial geography, international banking, and economic history, in which the topics you mention receive consideration.

For the College of the City of New York Acting Dean Carleton L. Brownson sent a letter with catalogues that described the different courses which dealt directly or remotely with port problems. They include courses in export technique, United States and foreign customs administration, foreign credits and financing foreign trade, South American sales problems, market geography, Russian markets, practical steamship operation, plus modern foreign lanuages and business courses of a general character of interest to the student of foreign trade. In the political science department, in day and night courses, attention is given to South American business methods and foreign trade from both the market standpoint and that of ocean trade and traffic. The engineering department offers courses which include dock engineering and a special course in waterfront improvement and port facilities.

The detailed announcements indicate the laying of a broad basis for understanding port problems and one or two of the descriptions include such definite references as these: "Export and import control, sources of information and surveys, foreign competition policy, terminals and port facilities, free ports, Merchant Marine," etc.

The engineering course on waterfront improvements and port facilities is described thus: "A study of Government authorities, physical characteristics, and engineering work to be accomplished in developing the port, various forms of dock and shed construction are taken up and also modern methods of tariff."

The director of vocational subjects began in March, 1919, working as collaborator for the Federal Bureau of Education in coöperation with the Bureau of Foreign and Domestic Commerce on a survey of the foreign-trade needs in Europe. This survey was investigating

1. Manufacturing concerns
2. Commission merchants
3. Forwarding houses
4. Banking and credit institutions
5. Education provisions for training for foreign trade.

Turning to the University of the State of New York, or State Department of Public Instruction, the word port does not appear in the index. The Acting Commissioner, Thomas E. Finegan, writes:

In the high schools throughout the State, under the supervision of this department, courses in history of commerce and commercial geography have been established. These courses are intended especially for those who expect to enter upon business careers. The purpose of these courses is to give the student a broader view of commercial life and a better appreciation of the principles underlying the commercial success of a people. The course in the history of commerce is an historical survey of the world's commercial development, and commercial geography treats of the present industry and trade conditions both in the United States and foreign countries. The history of the Merchant Marine and the port facilities of the United States are studied. The commercial advantages of New York State due to the development of its transportation facilities, both water and rail, are carefully analyzed.

At the present time the aim, content, and methods of teaching these courses are undergoing a great change. It has become evident that if a knowledge of the historical development of the present commercial relations of the world is desirable for our young people, how much more important is the interpretation of the past and present in terms of future possibilities. To this end the future commercial possibilities for our country and State will be brought home to our young people. *In the revised courses there will be incorporated a study of the need of a definite commercial policy of a larger Merchant Marine, the economic principles underlying that need, the need of a free port, and the natural and economic advantages of New York Harbour in so far as they relate to the future development of our State and country.*

The great difficulty in carrying on this work in our high schools has been the lack of definite concise material in adequate forms to be used in a class room. The study you are now contemplating would be of great assistance to the development of this work by giving tangible and accurate information to the classes studying these problems.

Supplementing Commissioner Finegan's letter, the department's specialist on commercial subjects, W. E. Bartholomew, wrote as follows:

It has been my practice in the last few years to send out to commercial teachers in the schools of the State various kinds of literature bearing on commercial work. Teachers of commercial geography have received from time to time publicity material issued by chambers of commerce, educational pamphlets from the Federal and State Departments, and advertising literature from some of the larger industrial concerns.

My attention has been called to your letter of inquiry regarding the efforts made in the schools to teach the industrial and commercial activities of this State and more especially New York City. If you have any literature on plans proposed for the further development of the Port of New York, we shall be glad to be the means of distributing such throughout the entire State. Our mailing list includes about 250 high schools.

These evidences of present keen interest in bringing instruction in port commercial problems up to date led to an examination of the syllabus used in New York's State's secondary schools as revised to September, 1918. While the words *port*, *harbour*, and *New York City* do not appear in the syllabus, the "natural resources" (two pages given to this subject) of the American States are mentioned: to the development of our commerce from 1789 to 1829 are given several headings which include five topics under foreign trade ending with "brief history of the Merchant Marine, 1789 to 1829," *non-intercourse*, *the steamboat*, *immigration* are given place and of course all permit the presentation of port facts. In ten pages for economics ports are not mentioned except in speaking of exports and imports in the Port of New York, although among "natural resources in New York State" "natural harbours" are mentioned. Commercial subjects are given pages 328 to 361, of which commercial geography takes four pages and the history of commerce five and a half pages. In neither of these divisions are port or port problems specified, although under New York State the advantages of New York's situation are treated under the three heads of New York Harbour, Hudson River, and Mohawk Valley, Improvement of Long Island Sound, and Improvement of Lake Erie and Lake Ontario. Transportation facilities through canals and the Hudson River are mentioned under Commercial Future. For the State three problems are mentioned: development of water power, readjustment of agriculture, development of Adirondack iron, with no mention of the port. Instructions to teachers as to maps, stereopticons, etc., do not specify ports. In the history of commerce, beyond general instructions, there is no specification of ports to account for the commerce of Phoenicia, medieval cities, modern Portugal, Spain, the Netherlands, England, France, and Germany, although it is hardly probable that teachers could discuss trade routes, colonial expansion, etc., without discussing ports. All through the topics under the United States, none specifies ports, although such topics as commercial relations, building of Erie Canal, decline of American shipping, Merchant Marine, and building of Panama Canal afford reason for discussing port problems.

The University of Chicago, through the Acting Dean of the School of Commerce and Administration, Chester W. Wright, has many courses which deal with port problems: commercial geography; transportation facilities affecting trade; the history of our Merchant Marine; America's commerce; South American resources; etc. Although these courses deal incidentally with port problems, Dean Wright believes "that from the work offered a student can obtain an understanding of the fundamental principles, as well as the specific technicalities involved in our foreign commerce." The fourteen courses marked in the catalogue as affording occasion to teach port problems included no specification of port problems under any title or detailed description, yet special attention to port problems, foreign trade, exports, Merchant Marine, and natural resources are several times mentioned and at least permit instruction in port management. By the way, the Port of Chicago is referred to as "an inland city." In the same paragraph, however, numerous live subjects are handled which would certainly give students a desire to know the facts about port limitations and opportunities.

For the Wharton School of Finance and Commerce, University of Pennsylvania, Dean McClellan wrote that "port administration is presented in an undergraduate course on ocean transportation, while in a graduate course on ocean traffic and rates fully 25 per cent. of the time is devoted to port terminal facilities and charges. Two undergraduate courses, business of American commerce and foreign-trade methods, go into practically all phases of foreign trade and have a bearing upon maritime policy, commercial needs, and port development."

Johns Hopkins University in Baltimore gives to undergraduates what is contained in an economic textbook. According to Professor J. H. Hollander, no syllabus or other printed matter is employed other than the verbal comments by the instructors. The textbook does not index *port*, *harbour*, *merchant marine*, or *shipping*. In the sixteen pages on International Trade there is nothing relating to port problems, which is not surprising, as the textbook was written twenty-six years ago and its last edition ten years ago.

Cornell University, wrote Professor Charles H. Hull of the American History Department, on behalf of President Schurman, who was ill at the time:

> There is, so far as I can learn, no course in Cornell University devoted wholly or even largely to the "Maritime

policy, commercial needs, and dependence upon port development" of the United States. These topics are, however, made part of the subject matter of courses given here in Commercial Geography, in Economic History of the United States, and in Economics of Railroad Transportation.

In all of these courses the *predominant importance of the Port of New York is of course brought out and some attempt is made to indicate the geographic factors and the canal and railroad arrangements which have contributed to give it that importance.* I fear, however, that there is none of us who feels able to deal in more than the most superficial manner with the highly complicated technical problem of the handling of goods for import and export in New York, and the conditions of competition between it and Boston or the southern ports. I tried once to learn a little about the matter, and read quite persuasive technical papers to the effect that the lack of railroad freight terminals on Manhattan Island was a great handicap, and others to the contrary effect that the harbour with its car floats was the best switching yard in the world. Who shall decide when doctors disagree?

Yale, Sheffield Scientific School, does not offer any undergraduate or graduate courses which deal solely with this country's maritime policy, commercial needs, and dependence upon port development; but at least two courses give attention to these subjects as a part of the whole work. Doubtless other courses given here deal incidentally with our country's commercial development and allied subjects. Under the two descriptions offered by Professor Avard L.

Bishop for President Hadley there is no mention of ports, but under the growth of domestic and foreign commerce and the natural resources and economic factors affecting industrial and commercial development, innumerable helpful lessons for port problems are permitted.

The Boston University gives in its College of Business Administration twelve courses in foreign trade, "besides a new course," Professor Harry R. Tosdal was good enough to write, on behalf of President Murlin, "entitled Ocean Shipping, where considerably more time is devoted to public policy with reference to the Merchant Marine, while the course is designed for better understanding of the administration and operation of ocean shipping. Further, it is planned to offer next year a course devoted entirely to the subject of ports and terminals." The last-named course is to show the relative importance and physical characteristics of the world's leading ports and the relation of port facilities to freight movement. More detailed attention is given to special facilities like harbour belt railways, lighterage, cartage, piers, wharves, and quays and their equipment, cargo transfer, warehousing, and freight handling, port customs and dues, and the nature and advantage of free ports, "with special attention to probable development in the United States."

President Alex. C. Humphreys, writing for Stevens Institute of Technology at Hoboken, sent us the following suggestive statement:

Unquestionably the development of the Port of New York and its proper administration not only greatly concerns the prosperity of New York City and New York State, but concerns the prosperity of the nation at large.

With regard to our instruction here at the Institute I might explain that we are, I think, singular in having only a single course which is designated as a course in mechanical engineering. The fact is, however, that we do not closely specialize, though we do put some emphasis on the mechanical branch. Ours is a broad course in engineering. It naturally leads through this emphasis to the training that is later applicable to marine engineering as has been evidenced during the war when the United States Navy Department established here the United States Navy Steam Engineering School.

From what I have said you can readily see we are not able to cover in our four years every subject which is important to the engineer or to the citizen. If we should attempt to do this the students would remain here until they had passed the age of usefulness.

In my course on the Economics of Engineering I do step to one side to introduce topics such as the one you suggest. I should be glad now to give further thought to the question "Can I do more in this direction without weakening the course as a whole?" In this connection, I would say that when I assumed the presidency of Stevens in 1902 I laid down the rule looking to the keeping of our course in balance that no subject or additional work should be introduced without the elimination of an equal amount of work. This was because the students were already working to the limit.

The first department of Nautical Science to be organized in this country is not at one of the great ports, as one might suppose, but at Brown University, Providence, R. I. Its announcement is headed "Opportunity for special training in Nautical Science." Its first courses began in September, 1919. Ship's Business is one of the five different courses and it will discuss headings such as tonnage, ship's papers, pilotage, trade routes, ports, and terminals. This school aims not only to interpret and explain our country's Merchant Marine problems but also to aid in their solution. It appeals to students desiring to enter the Merchant Marine or the Navy. It emphasizes the fact that the course is "suitable for any one seeking a broad education." The founders understand the problem and the spirit which will solve it. Note the following:

> Men are needed who will be something more than mere navigators. It needs men who can not only guide ships back and forth across the oceans, but who can transact any kind of ships' business in any port, men of broad education, who can hold their own with the best master mariners of the European countries. . . . The man interested in ships and shipping should pursue in other departments such courses as mathematics, English, mod-

ern languages, history, economics, and banking, commercial and physical geography, meteorology, astronomy, physics, political and social science, and biology. . . . Opportunity to get some of the necessary preliminary experience will be given the men by the U. S. Shipping Board by sending them out during the summer vacations upon the training ships controlled by the Board. Men who prefer ocean service will find summer vacation jobs with steamship companies, exporting and importing houses, shipbuilding companies, dry docks, etc.

Professor Frederick Slocum is in charge of this course. He writes that as part of their field work the students will "make a special study of the present condition and future possibilities of the Port of Providence."

Probably nowhere in this country has the subject of port problems been described for purposes of instruction as in Newark, New Jersey, where for some years the Librarian, Mr. John Cotton Dana, has been helping the schools to prove that they can best teach geography by first teaching Newark.

The first referencc to Newark as a port is in the third-grade syllabus, where children are taught to locate the river, canals, and Newark Bay. In the fourth grade they are taught the commercial advantages of Newark "arising from its situation making it essentially a part of New York, a city connected by railroad with every part of North America and by steamship with every country in the world." In the seventh grade, which means boys and girls from twelve to fourteen, more information respecting ports is given than most college graduates, even in departments of economics, ever receive. Newark is there shown as sharing in New York's commanding position in the commerce and industries of the world which makes it the point of exchange for the international commerce of the great North Atlantic basin. They learn how Newark and all cities in the metropolitan district will further gain from the Panama Canal. Under the heading "Some plans for the future" are topics which ought to be given to pupils and students everywhere if America is to hold its position in world commerce. The headings, which of course are developed in the classes, include these: The waterfront around New York Harbour, transshipment of freight; trunk lines, and a connecting terminal; docks for ocean steamers on the Newark Bay; uses of the meadows; the construction of a ship canal; bridges, and the meadow roads.

Think What It Means to Newark's Future

That in Manhattan warehouses are on the piers, in many cases necessitating exorbitant charges for wharfage and storage;

THE OLD ERIE CANAL

In its time, the largest canal in the world. It took about eight years to build, and its opening on October 26, 1825, marked the beginning of a new era in the history both of the country and of the Port of New York.

THE NEW ERIE BARGE CANAL

Which makes possible continuous water transportation from the inland markets of the country to the Atlantic seaboard. The Canal's export terminal will be located in Jamaica Bay

That in Brooklyn the waterfront is generally owned by manufacturers and railroad men (not by the public) and without adequate railroad connections;

That in Hoboken and Jersey City the waterfront is owned almost exclusively by the railroad and steamship lines and is without adequate warehouse facilities but has the advantage of railroad connections;

That while a hundred pounds of wheat can be landed in New York from North Dakota for ten cents, it costs three cents to get it from the car to the ship;

That in the Port of New York there is no central place for transshipping goods to and from railroads;

That a great railroad terminal for all railroads is needed to hurry up transshipment and to reduce its expense;

That a terminal operating company is needed to provide cars to and from trunk lines to the transshipment centre;

That "freight is *brought to* Jersey City, *stored in* Brooklyn, and *shipped from* New York," each change adding to the expense;

That in this port there are no railroad connections between the water terminals and the local industries;

That there are no belt-lines binding all transportation facilities into one system;

That the congested condition of traffic in New York is Newark's opportunity;

That the use of this opportunity will bring "possibilities of a larger civic life to a greater and more serviceable city."

Given such training for a decade, metropolitan New Jersey will need its own schoolship and will be supplying many men for the Merchant Marine.

"Sea Training for the Merchant Marine" is the title of one folder, of which the United

States Shipping Board issued 300,000 copies in October, 1918. With a companion folder, entitled "Sea Training Primer," this thirty-two-page folder, with many illustrations and convincing statements, ought to be put in the hands not only of public school boys but of young workmen in our factories and stores everywhere. It has the kind of appeal which wins, yet from first to last it breathes the spirit that is in its title—"Sea Training." Boys learn about sea life by going to sea and they learn about wages by working for them. They have a good time and they gain an education, but the good time and the education come through hard, productive work.

In January, 1918, so few Americans were going to sea that it took three weeks to get fifty American instructors for one training ship. A year later in one month (March) 7,000 men were placed, 49 per cent. of them graduates of the recruiting service. In fifteen months, prior to April 1, 1919, 23,000 young Americans went into training. The sailors, firemen, cooks, and stewards total at present 90 per cent. of the Merchant Marine officers, and one half the crews are American citizens.

The recruiting service maintains free government schools for the training of deck and engineering officers and has training ships for sailors, firemen, cooks, and stewards at Boston, Norfolk, San Francisco, and Seattle. The headquarters are at the Custom House, Boston, Mass., and the director of the recruiting service is Henry Howard, who conceived and organized this service for the United States Shipping Board.

Three characteristics of the advertising done by this recruiting service are lacking in the catalogues of the colleges and in the report of the Nautical School, namely: attractive illustration, definite statements of wages and salaries, and concrete stories of sea life. The call to service loses none of its appeal when coupled with salary facts and promotion facts, which tell what a young fellow can look forward to. Such terms as "messboy," "scullion," and "second cook" gain rather than lose when it is advertised that the salaries are $55.00, $60.00, and $90.00 a month. There are eighteen free navigation schools and eleven free engineering schools. To make clear that these schools are vocational and not academic for recruiting a service and not for patronizing textbooks, heavy black type announces *officers' schools are not for landsmen.* No man without two years' sea-going experience will be taken into these schools. The terms are six weeks for the navigation school and four weeks for the engineers. The age limits are between 19 and 56. Graduates begin with a salary of $90.00 a month plus living, and are told that salaries range from $115 to $300 as they progress—always plus living while at sea, as in talking with the men this appeal to officers begins with a call to service—but only ten lines down on the first page is the black-face headline "Good jobs at good pay."

The Merchant Marine League, with a view to inducing university-trained men to engage in occupations connected with ships, shipping, and foreign trade has offered the college student opportunity for organized field training in the summer. The plan is to coördinate their courses of study with their summer work and thus give them four years of that which amounts to the same as vocational training. Ordinarily, undergraduates have no clear vision of the mark at which they are shooting or of the business in which they will engage until a short time before their graduation. This arrangement will bring directly before the colleges of the country the problems and possibilities of foreign commerce and ocean trade, and will tie up our educational and business interests in an intimate way.

Early answers included a letter from Johns

Hopkins University, in the interest of four young men from the University of Pittsburgh, stating that it has "about thirty men who are interested in studying foreign trade courses, several of whom are definitely interested in placements of the type you suggest; from the University of South Carolina, whence one student writes for six freshmen and sophomores wishing, if possible, to secure summer work "aboard ships or in a foreign country."

The idea of coöperating with employers is explained in the following letter from the General Motors Corporation, New York headquarters, signed by W. C. Durant, president:

1. We will probably be able to give employment to about one hundred such men during the coming summer vacation, provided the applicants will accept work in factories or shops in any capacity where they may be found useful.

2. Positions will be ready whenever the men are available.

3. The majority of these men should belong to the technical class and they will be given work as nearly as possible in line with their studies. We can provide a number of clerkships for men who want to make a specialty of economics and administration.

4. The majority of the work will be in factories or shops, working on production as machine operators, helpers, and as clerks in shipping department, stock room, production office, and accounting departments.

5. The salary paid will approximate current factory wages for the work provided.

6. The openings will be created in Detroit, Flint, Pontiac, Lansing, and Saginaw, all in the State of Michigan. It will be expected of such undergraduates as shall avail themselves of these positions that they will settle down to regular work to which they are appointed and that they will accept the prevailing factory conditions governing their fellow-employees.

One of the most helpful of all teaching programmes discovered is the outline and plan of a course of lectures given in the Brooklyn Central Y. M. C. A. by Lieutenant R. E. Lambert, U. S. Navy Supply, Commissary, and Disbursing Officer of the U. S. Naval Salvage Service. Twenty-four two-hour sessions, that is, two sessions a week for twelve weeks, were given for $30.00. Most of the thirty-five young men taking the course are already in the shipping business and give as their reason for taking it: "to increase my information on every phase of this great business, and to make myself more valuable in my chosen work." Some of them are accountants and auditors, a few are salesmen. Three assigned as their reason for taking the course that they wanted to broaden their knowledge of this most vital factor in American commercial and national life.

In striking contrast with the college catalogues

and school syllabuses is the prospectus of this evening course of university extension work. This is the first night's introduction: "The soul of the sea"; and "History of shipping"; "Special nomenclature." Other titles include: "The men that man the ships that sail the sea"; "Rules of the road"; "International rivalry"; "Immigration"; "New York Harbour," and "Port and Terminal Facilities," including the following comprehensive programme for 1919–1920:

THE PORTS OF THE WORLD

Group I.—United States Ports
- (a) New York Harbour
- (b) Other Atlantic Ports
- (c) Great Lakes Ports
- (d) Gulf Ports
- (e) Pacific Ports
- (f) Mississippi River Ports

Group II.—Latin-American Ports
- (a) Atlantic Ports
- (b) Pacific Ports
- (c) Other Latin-American Ports

Group III.—European Ports
- (a) Atlantic Ports
- (b) Mediterranean Ports
- (c) Other European Ports

Group IV.—Ports of the Far East

Group V.—African Ports and Ports of Oceania.

Instead of studiously withholding or concealing an appeal to individual ambition the folder opens to this:

THE OPPORTUNITY

The shipping business is to-day crying for men of vision, men of ability, men with some degree of training in the principles and problems of shipping. Overseas traffic is one of the greatest factors in the present world strain for Reconstruction. The demand for men is positive and immediate.

This course is distinctly commercial, not navigational, not military, nor academic. It has been prepared especially for this class by the instructor, a man with years of sea-going, importing, and exporting experience. The lesson pamphlets are revised and rewritten each week to keep them right up to the minute. *The emphasis is placed throughout on shipping from the standpoint of transportation as distinct from the special interest of importers and exporters.*

The manuscript of the first lecture in this course is entitled "Imagination"; its first sentences are:

Fifteen or more years ago, when I was a mere tyro in the business world serving my apprenticeship as office boy, clerk, stenographer, and bookkeeper, I studied Arthur Frederick Sheldon's course on salesmanship and business-building. Up to that time, in my youthful lack of experience, I had looked upon the commercial world as a realm where practical shrewdness of the David Harum variety held sway.

Sheldon taught me otherwise. He taught me to appreciate the value of imagination even in practical business affairs. Recently at a Trade and Transportation Club dinner, one of the speakers was a practical shipping man of more than thirty years' experience. He owns a fleet of ships and conducts a large export business. He is a Scotchman. The keenness of the Scot in trade is proverbial, often bordering on the uncanny. And yet this man laid great stress on cultivating the imagination as a means of creating and building business.

It is with this spirit that the youth of America must be approached if we are to have a Merchant Marine and if the doors of our ports are to swing on hinges that are equally responsive to opportunities abroad and home needs.

CHAPTER XXI

Immigration's Gateway to America

FOR every individual American who thinks of the Port of New York as a place for receiving and shipping articles of commerce, perhaps one hundred think of it as the landing place of the immigrant, the home of the Statue of Liberty, and the gateway to the New World. Since the year 1820, 33,100,000 immigrants from foreign lands have entered the United States. During the twenty-seven years from 1892 through the year 1918, 17,100,000 immigrants arrived in this country, of which 74 per cent., or 12,600,000, entered at this port. The number and percentages by years are given in the accompanying table.

For receiving the immigrant who lacks a bank account and who must produce evidence of his ability to support himself in order that he may not become a public charge, as well as proof of his physical and mental soundness, the Federal Government established the immigration station at Ellis Island, where men, women, and children are

TWENTY-SEVEN YEARS OF IMMIGRATION AT THE PORT OF NEW YORK, 1892-1918

YEAR	TOTAL INTO U. S. NUMBER	THROUGH PORT OF N. Y. NUMBER	PERCENTAGE
1918	110,618	28,867	26.09
1917	295,403	129,446	43.82
1916	298,826	141,390	47.31
1915	326,700	178,416	54.61
1914	1,218,480	878,052	72.06
1913	1,197,892	892,653	74.51
1912	838,172	605,151	72.18
1911	878,587	637,003	72.50
1910	1,041,570	786,094	75.47
1909	751,786	580,617	77.23
1908	782,870	585,970	74.84
1907	1,285,349	1,004,756	78.09
1906	1,100,735	880,036	79.94
1905	1,026,499	788,219	76.78
1904	812,870	606,019	74.55
1903	857,046	631,885	73.72
1902	648,743	493,262	76.03
1901	487,918	388,931	79.71
1900	448,572	341,712	76.17
1899	311,715	242,573	77.81
1898	229,299	178,748	77.95
1897	230,832	180,556	78.21
1896	343,267	263,709	76.82
1895	258,536	190,928	73.84
1894	285,631	219,046	76.68
1893	439,730	343,422	78.09
1892	579,663	445,987	76.93
	17,087,309	12,643,448	73.99

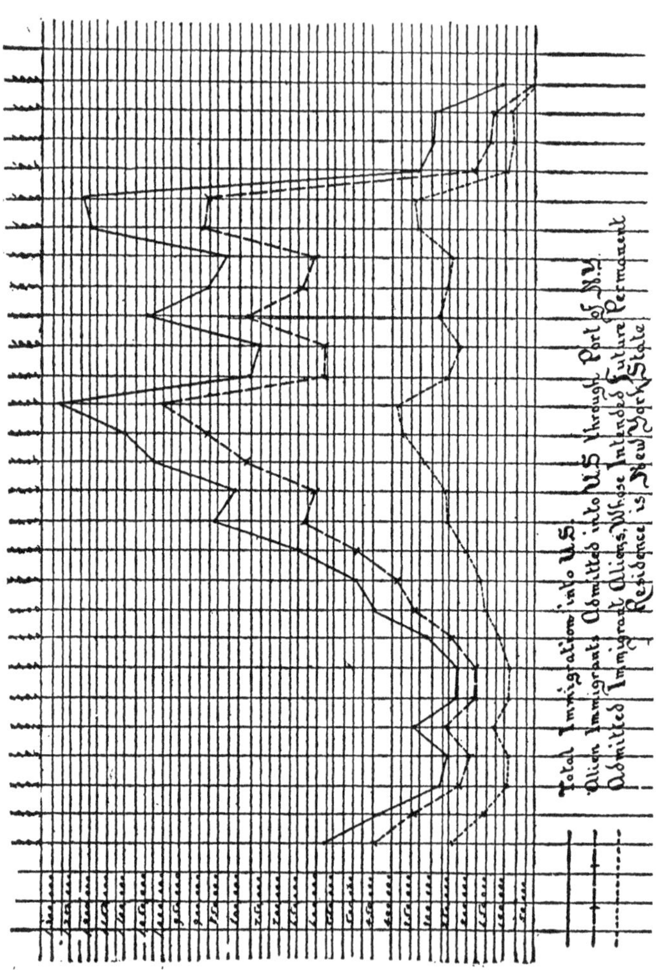
Total Immigration into U.S.
Alien Immigrants Admitted into U.S. through Port of N.Y.
Admitted Immigrant Aliens, Whose Intended Future Permanent Residence is New York State

maintained in comfortable quarters pending examination; physicians and nurses are in attendance, the Government supplying wholesome food. To prevent the exploitation of the immigrant during his first days, volunteer agencies maintain "visitors," legal aid advisers, work-finding and home-placing bureaus. After peace has been finally established and trade fully restored, many authorities believe that unless there are new immigration restrictions as to education, intelligence, and pecuniary responsibility, the gateways to this country will be overrun with Europeans anxious to come to the "land of the free and the home of the brave."

Before April, 1917, while our country remained neutral, the people of foreign lands envied us for what they thought was our security of position. After we entered the war, they were thrilled by the speed and efficiency with which we prepared; in fact, the whole world, outside the Central Powers, applauded the determined stand we had taken for world freedom. Because we began to fight after our Allies had become thoroughly tired out, it is naturally taken for granted that we shall return to full prosperity before other nations do. For this reason it is expected that, in spite of home ties, large numbers of people who can leave Europe will prefer, if permitted by their own governments and ours, to come to this country to avoid burdensome taxes at home and to seek the fabled and actual opportunities here.

Whether the possibility of such an influx is to be welcomed or regretted, it is probable that writers and speakers on immigration will emphasize the danger which will threaten our country if people are admitted who lack our standards of living and our ideals, or who are not sympathetic with our form of government, even if they respond to our education test and our standards of physical and mental fitness. The injustice and unsafety of allowing them to augment the congested sections of our great cities, when by proper distribution we might send them into country and suburban districts where more wholesome living is possible; the crime of mistreating them or allowing them to be mistreated and exploited by landlords, employers, and others who are permitted to prey upon the gullible and unsophisticated after we receive them in America—these aspects of the immigration problem are too well known to require elaboration in a discussion of America's port problems as they are found either in inland cities or in immigration's main gateway, the Port of New York.

In the following ways the immigrant is a special care to the port city: if he is allowed to come into this country without having an inland address, plus money to take him there, he will stop in or near a port city. Coming without work, destination, or funds for his support for a reasonable length of time, he is immediately in need of employment, and as his extremity precludes him from being considered a good trading asset in order to keep him alive, he cannot choose his vocation but must accept the best he can get. This would be unfair enough if it affected only the immigrant, but this also affects the alien labourers who preceded the immigrant and have already established themselves here; when the supply is greater than the demand their wages are bound to be lower because of competition; their rent becomes higher because of the increased demand for living quarters, and the same rule applies to the cost of food and clothing; finally, their work, their living conditions, and their local governments are bound to deteriorate to a lower standard because the immigrant either wants less or has less capacity to make his wants effective.

How far conditions in Europe before and after the war place the immigrant in a trading position more or less liable to wilful exploitation only time will tell. That his outlook is hopeful is the judgment of Mrs. Marian K. Clark, Chief Investigator of this problem for the New York State Industrial Commission, who says:

> He is to-day an individual who counts. He performs all of the common work of the nation. There is not an essential industry in this country that is not largely dependent upon our foreign-born labourers. Five years ago every immigrant worker who dropped out through accident or other causes could be replaced—Ellis Island could produce many more where he came from. To-day the effects of a world war have blockaded all roads to immigration; to-day, if already here, he is in a position to demand for himself and for his children all of the advantages that must make him, unit for unit, as important as the American workman, who, because of our public school system and effective labour laws, is now the most efficient worker in the world.

At the threshold of the new immigration policy it is not only expedient but possible for the Federal Government to guarantee the whole country against injuries to and from its port cities by exacting evidence from immigrants before they leave their home countries for our shores that they are going to different points in this country where industry or agriculture needs them and will welcome them, and that they are not, from misinformation, indigence, or lack of foresight, planning or hoping to find work and living room in port cities.

MATERIAL FOR THE AMERICAN "MELTING POT"

In 1914, before the outbreak of the war, we were receiving more than a million immigrants a year—1,197,892 in 1913, 1,218,480 in 1914—more than 70 per cent. of whom came through the Port of New York

ELLIS ISLAND

Where the immigrant who "lacks a bank account and who must produce evidence of his ability in order that he may not become a public charge, as well as proof of his physical and mental soundness," is maintained by the Federal Government pending examination.

BATTERY LANDING

In 1847 the State Legislature created the Board of Emigration Commissioners, which controlled immigration at New York until 1889, when the Federal Government assumed full responsibility for the admission and deportation of aliens at all ports.

This is a Federal opportunity and duty no matter how the various states may differ in the treatment of aliens after minimum and uniform requirements have been passed at the gateway. During the first years of immigration, State governments on the seaboard altogether controlled the admission of aliens arriving at their respective ports. In 1824 a law was passed by New York State requiring captains of vessels to submit detailed information to the Mayor of New York City concerning immigrants, and each alien was himself required personally to report to the Mayor within twenty-four hours after his arrival at this port. In 1847 the State Legislature created the Board of Emigration Commissioners, which controlled immigration at New York until 1889, when the Federal Government assumed full responsibility for the admission and deportation of aliens at all ports. From 1889 to 1908, when the Legislature appointed a State Immigration Commission to investigate the conditions of aliens within the State of New York, there was no official record of the immigrants remaining in this State, although from the beginning of the year 1903 up to and including 1914, when to some extent war closed the ports of Europe, the number of immigrant arrivals through this port had far exceeded the arrivals of previous years.

Another service which the Federal Government can render is to help the country determine the next steps to be taken in the programme which is now being called "Americanization."

1. It can announce to the whole country the practices best worth imitation and the mistaken practices to be avoided.

2. It can give a name which will be more tactful than "Americanization" in dealing with men who wear wound stripes and mothers who wear mourning and gold stars but who are not American citizens.

3. It can point out to the various states and to our manifold industries how to disseminate the knowledge which workers need for their own safety and the country's safety without discouraging or patronizing the foreign-born citizen or resident deficient in the speaking or understanding of the English language.

4. It can help our cities give instruction to soldiers returning from France and from our own home camps who are not citizens without absurdly questioning their loyalty to American ideals.

5. It can help employers, capitalists, and coupon cutters see the need for squarely facing and always remembering American ideals and the methods necessary to achieve these ideals.

6. Finally, Congress can make the appropriations called for in the bills which provide Federal aid to states for dealing with the immigrant and with illiteracy.

The last thing for Americans to appreciate, however, is that "Americanization" is not something which can be told. On the contrary, it is something which must be felt, acted, lived. There is no rhetoric, no eloquence, no history, no mental discipline which will make good Americans of immigrants who are indecently housed, unfairly paid, unjustly treated, or otherwise deprived when at work or at leisure of those fundamental rights to wholesome life, enjoyable liberty, and successful pursuit of happiness.

CHAPTER XXII

Port Improvements Still Needed

THE clearest way to explain what improvements are still needed in the Port of New York would be to tell the story five different ways: in order of urgency, according to ease of attainment, according to kind of improvement, in order of inexpensiveness, and according to the agency which is primarily responsible for executing the improvement. Perhaps some publicity bureau will undertake later to tell the story in these five different ways and to indicate for each step its cost. For our short review it must suffice to list the principal improvements still needed that might be carried through by the five following agencies:

1. City governments in the port area;
2. State governments of New York and New Jersey;
3. The Federal Government;
4. The New York, New Jersey Port and Harbour Development Commission, out of which will ultimately grow a unified port authority;
5. Extra governmental agencies by which the public

expresses itself through individual shippers, organizations of business men, bankers, schools and colleges, the press, and a much-needed director of port publicity.

The municipalities in the port area, without waiting for final action by the states of New York and New Jersey, which are now considering a port treaty and partnership in a unified government of the port, can take several steps of great importance:

1. They should put together facts about their interest in port development, both as to what they have to offer to a port commission, and what they ought to ask from such a central commission.

2. They should have these facts about themselves as ports so clearly stated that they can be easily taught in their schools and otherwise kept in circulation.

3. They should route the trucking and the traffic so as to invite further use of their docks and reduce to a minimum the difficulties of shipping.

4. New York City, for example, should adopt Commissioner Hulbert's recommendation to zone the shipping so that Long Island Sound boats will land their cargoes and passengers on the East River without needlessly navigating sixty miles around the island each day, thus losing more than 18,000 miles a year with a corresponding loss in coal and with serious obstruction to other navigation, and accordingly releasing North River for overseas service.

5. Similarly, the Jersey cities should go on developing their meadows and putting themselves in readiness for any coöperative government of the port which may later be adopted.

6. They should zone their activities so that wholesale

business can be centralized and brought as near as possible to water connections with rail.

7. Leases should be made not solely on the basis of rent offered, but with particular reference to the advantage accruing to the port as a whole from the lessee's business. A plan of selection should be devised which would preclude secrecy of action on the part of the Sinking Fund Commission, and in the event that long leases should be decided upon by the City, such leases should contain a provision for the cancellation of the lease before the end of the term should that become desirable from the public point of view.

8. Not only should they refuse to sell any docks or waterfront to private agencies but they should take steps to secure public ownership and control of such properties.

9. For the sake of reducing the cost of living, as well as for attracting a large business, a certain district or territory should be set aside or erected for expeditious and economical handling of fish.

10. Every city should, within its own borders, see that city-owned terminals are used as terminals, not as storage yards, and can urge railroads to do their sorting and classifying farther back, so that their terminals may be located in order that quick action can be taken and will not be always glutted with stored materials.

11. New York should urge the railroads to do their routing over in New Jersey so that they will avoid the congestion and unnecessary trucking which is shown in the diagram on page 351 and accomplish the economy of hauling and the reduction of congestion shown in the second diagram on page 352.

12. Serviceable material-handling machinery should be put on all city-owned piers and in city-owned terminals and warehouses, which would undoubtedly be an advantage in expediting the freight handling on the piers and increasing the amount of work done within a given time.

13. Instead of having ships idle for a week or more at a cost of several thousand dollars a day in order to obtain coal, a bunkering plant should be established in the harbour at some point easy of access, where ships can do their coaling. At the same time, smaller ships than those in the tramp service, many of which now take their cargo from the pier and stop at Norfolk, Virginia, for coaling purposes, would be provided with coal at the bunkering plant in New York Harbour, saving the delay and expense of stopping at any other port. If fuel lighters can be provided, there are dumping machines which will transfer coal from cars on the barges by taking a 50-ton car, lifting it, and dumping it. In our competition with England, because we have larger cars, we can unload five times as much in an hour as it can. It is said that for ships using oil New York has now bunkering facilities so complete that "if every steamship in the harbour were to change from coal to oil burner to-morrow it is probable that the demand for the new fuel could be met with little or no delay."

14. Disconnected developments should be correlated, and confused conditions of waterfronts ended, as Dock Commissioner Hulbert has planned for New York's part of the port.

15. In congested Manhattan, where the warehouses operate at their pier stations by car float service, the harbour facilities would be doubled if different locations were provided for railroad deliveries.

16. Vehicular tunnels to Brooklyn and to Staten Island are needed for the same reason that the vehicular tunnel to New Jersey was needed. While these are needed for national reasons and interstate reasons as much as the Jersey tunnel they will probably never be built except by Greater New York. When built they will greatly add to the country's ability to do business through this port.

17. The same zoning method which now prohibits

manufacturing in residential districts in Greater New York should be applied to all parts of the harbour by removing from the shore front types of business that can be done in those districts, and by developing the land back of piers for warehouse and storage as well as for manufacturing so as to reduce the haul of both raw materials and manufactured products.

18. Ice-breaking tugs should be installed.

19. Floating repair barges should be installed.

20. A harbour scavenger boat should be provided to pick up stray piles, logs, and other floating débris that now endangers and damages harbour craft.

21. There is a distinct need for efficient belt line railroads circling the port. There is not to-day a single belt line worthy of the name within the port district.

22. The best results for the benefit of the port as a whole can only be obtained by joint coördination of all commercial and shipping facilities and particularly of railroad terminal facilities.

23. Every new step taken may be planned. William J. Barney said in November, 1911, "not only for sections of the harbour but for the harbour as a whole, so as to make the port one organized connected terminal. More important even than plans is a suitable form of port administration capable of continuous port policy, and of carrying out plans after they have been once adopted."

24. *The state governments of New York and New Jersey* may contribute most to the development of the Port of New York by preparing and signing a properly safeguarded bi-state treaty which would give this port a unified management with wide vision, increased powers, and comprehensive managerial capacity.

25. The vehicular tunnel under the Hudson River has already been provided for. Its completion should be hastened.

26. These states in dealing with future proposals,

especially the revised treaty when it comes up for consideration, should expedite action without waiting for a harbour strike or a severe cold spell to discommode the people and break down their transportation.

27. The Federal Government may show in various ways that it will never again be reminded by war or other calamity that the Port of New York is of national not of local importance.

28. It may begin to understand the harbour as a whole and cease to think of it only with respect to Hell Gate or the Ambrose Channel or the sluggish Newtown Creek or Jamaica Bay as separate projects equal in importance to any of the small justifiable projects or to one of the innumerable insignificant "pork barrel" proposals that infest every Congress.

29. It should spend, not grudgingly and sparingly but competently and in proportion to the national service that can be obtained from making this port the world's best, by dredging its channels deep enough and not *almost* deep enough.

30. While it exercises limited or exclusive control over the railroads, it can give demonstrations of the "possible joint operation on behalf of all the railroads of the several existing waterfront rail terminals," which the Merchants' Association proposed in November, 1918, as a means of relieving congestion and unnecessary expense.

31. It should use the lessons of the war to give New York the most modern and perfect fortifications against accident and attack, in the form of lighthouses, coast patrols, buoys, and channel margin.

32. It should refuse to sell its Army Supply Base in South Brooklyn to any private agency, and either retain it under governmental management or transfer it to the city until such time as a bi-state unified port authority will manage it forever as a public warehouse. All other war-time port facilities in all parts of the port—and in all other ports—

should be used by the public for all shippers without exclusive monopoly to any. This includes $40,000,000 spent in the Brooklyn Bay Ridge development and $50,000,000 spent in the Jersey Meadows.

33. It should authorize at this port first one free-from-customs zone and then a second and a third.

34. Without waiting for a free zone to be authorized by Congress and established by private or local governmental initiative it should simplify its method of handling goods imported for reëxport so that drawbacks may be more quickly collected and needless delays and other expenses eliminated.

35. If the Government retains the Merchant Marine under its own control and operation it should erect in this harbour dry-docks numerous enough to care for the increment of business which the country expects and large enough to take vessels of the *Leviathan* type, and provide the mechanical ability which will excel the rest of the world in dry-dock service. Ten new dry-docks are needed at once.

36. It should consider establishing great cold-storage facilities and food terminals. This has been recommended by the Federal Trade Commission. Everyone who has studied port problems has emphasized this necessity, although usually assuming that either private or municipal capital and control are needed. Since the Port of New York is a world port it offers opportunities and reasons for Federal control of food terminals, wholesale markets, and refrigerators.

The port authority recommended by the New York, New Jersey Port and Harbour Development Commission under which both the plan of port development and administration may be effective, will, of course, fall heir to all of the opportunities,

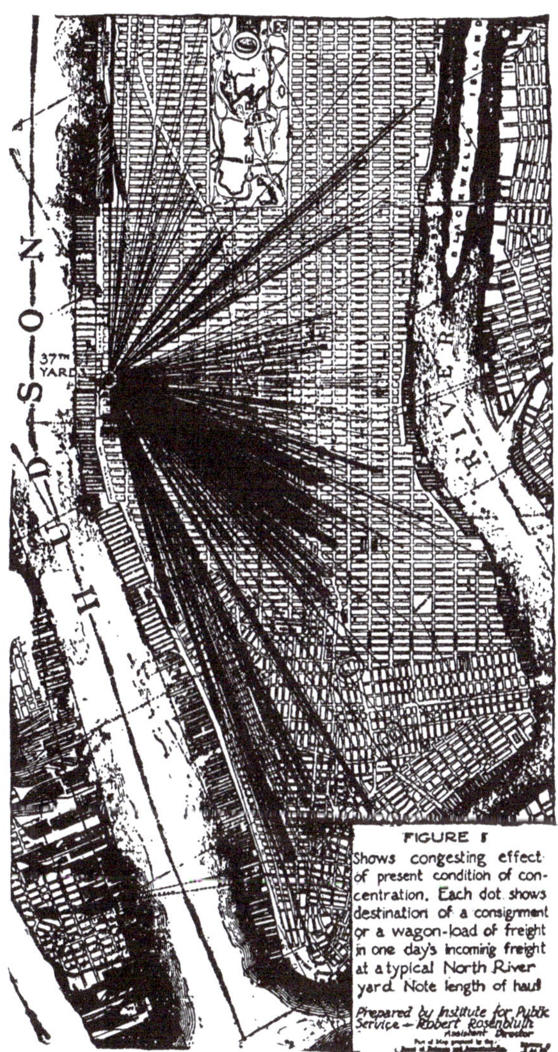

FIGURE 5

Shows congesting effect of present condition of concentration. Each dot shows destination of a consignment or a wagon-load of freight in one day's incoming freight at a typical North River yard. Note length of haul

Prepared by Institute for Public Service — Robert Rosenbluth Assistant Director

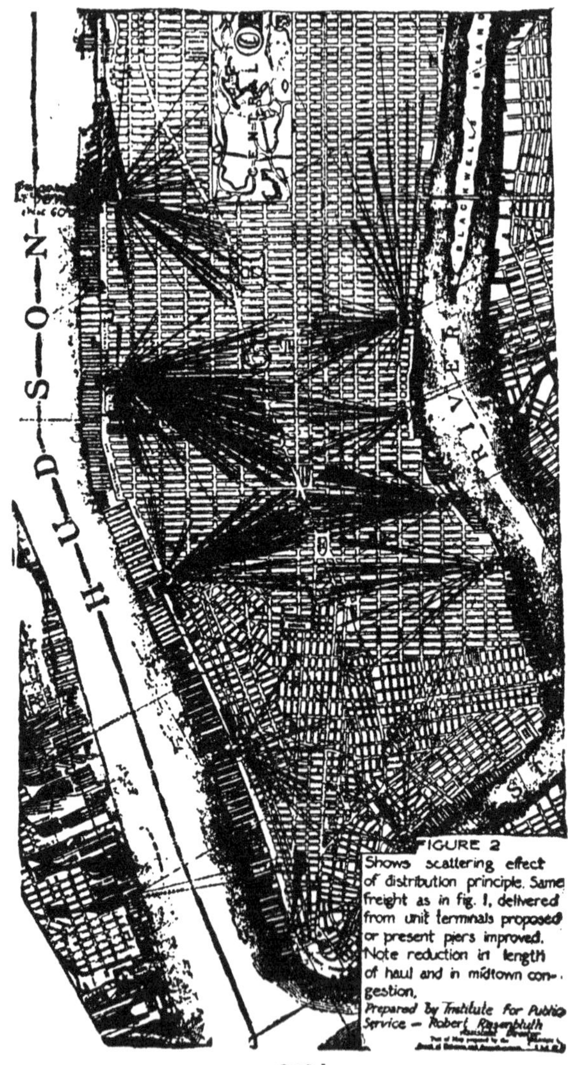
H—U—D—S—O—N
BLACKWELLS ISLAND
RIVER
FIGURE 2
Shows scattering effect of distribution principle. Same freight as in fig. 1, delivered from unit terminals proposed or present piers improved. Note reduction in length of haul and in midtown congestion.
Prepared by Institute for Public Service — Robert Rosenbluth

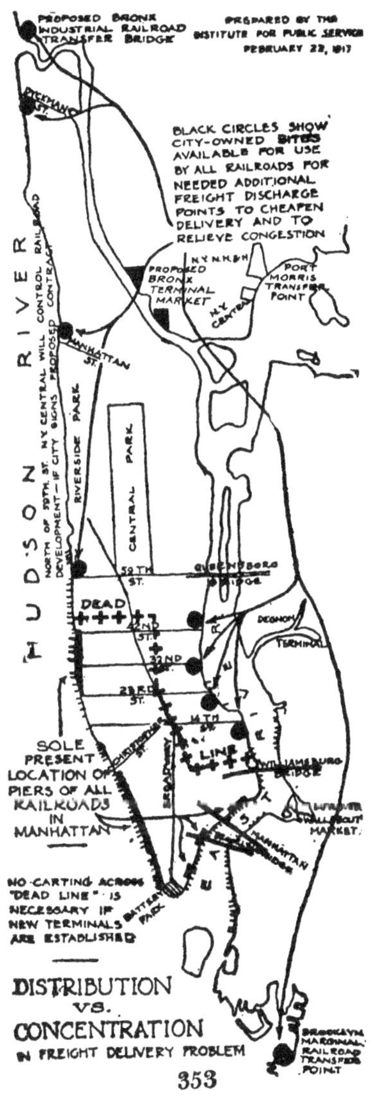
PROPOSED BRONX INDUSTRIAL RAILROAD TRANSFER BRIDGE
PREPARED BY THE INSTITUTE FOR PUBLIC SERVICE FEBRUARY 22, 1917
DYCKMAN ST.
BLACK CIRCLES SHOW CITY-OWNED SITES AVAILABLE FOR USE BY ALL RAILROADS FOR NEEDED ADDITIONAL FREIGHT DISCHARGE POINTS TO CHEAPEN DELIVERY AND TO RELIEVE CONGESTION
N.Y.N.H.&H.
PROPOSED BRONX TERMINAL MARKET
PORT MORRIS TRANSFER POINT
N.Y. CENTRAL
MANHATTAN ST.
HUDSON RIVER
NORTH OF 59TH. ST. N.Y. CENTRAL WILL CONTROL RAILROAD DEVELOPMENT—IF CITY SIGNS PROPOSED CONTRACT
RIVERSIDE PARK
CENTRAL PARK
59TH ST.
QUEENSBORO BRIDGE
DEAD LINE
42ND ST.
32ND ST.
23RD ST.
14TH ST.
DEGNON TERMINAL
EAST RIVER
SOLE PRESENT LOCATION OF PIERS OF ALL RAILROADS IN MANHATTAN
CHRISTOPHER ST.
BROADWAY
WILLIAMSBURG BRIDGE
WALLABOUT MARKET
MANHATTAN BRIDGE
NO CARTING ACROSS "DEAD LINE" IS NECESSARY IF NEW TERMINALS ARE ESTABLISHED
BATTERY PARK
DISTRIBUTION VS. CONCENTRATION IN FREIGHT DELIVERY PROBLEM
BROOKLYN MARGINAL RAILROAD TRANSFER POINT

obligations, and deficiencies of the helter-skelter and conflicting control of the municipalities, states, and Federal Government, which are at present exercising a certain degree of control over the port.

Such a port authority may be an administrator, planner, investigator, promoter, teacher, and publicity agent for the Port of New York and for the industrial and social interests, which are trying to express themselves through this port. For this chapter the present bi-state commissions Consulting Engineer, B. F. Cresson, Jr., has formulated the services which can reasonably be expected from a port authority properly manned and adequately financed and empowered:

A. It should be an informing and guiding spirit in developments both public and private, and as such will cause the creation of facilities of the best type to handle the business presented and at the most suitable location, taking into account the business of the port itself, as well as the responsibilities of this port to the business interests of the entire country.

B. It should be the agency through which conflicting interests at the port may be harmonized. There is practically no joint operation of facilities at the port. Each railroad has developed its own terminal system and carries on its business in competition with each other railroad. Some roads have better facilities than others, and in the past it has been impossible to bring the railroads together in a joint operation, which is bound to save them money, because there is no general authority or medium to bring them together. This is an immensely important and vital function of the proposed port authority.

C. It should furnish information as to methods of operation, costs of operation, volume of traffic, character of traffic, that must be provided for at the port.

D. It should furnish the best information available as to the most modern methods of port developments and design, of pier, dock, warehouse, and railroad facilities. It should recommend the most modern determination of material-handling machinery which will lessen the cost of handling freight and decrease the time a ship must necessarily be at her dock.

E. The port authority having jurisdiction over the character of developments to be placed will be able to point out the error in a proposal and prevent it, either by its own authority, or by the operation of public opinion. Certain terminal facilities have been created at the port entirely unrelated to other facilities near by, which should not have been permitted to come into existence.

F. All new projects as are planned will be submitted to the port authority for its approval, and improper developments, improperly laid out or located, would be prevented.

G. The port authority will continue the bi-state commission's lead in studying not only piers and wharves but also warehouses, markets, belt line railroads, marginal railroads, and other matters like the West Side Manhattan Railroad problem, and the question of bridges and tunnels spanning the harbour waters in many parts of the port as included in the general plan. There are questions of doubtful ownership of waterfront in sections of the harbour which the port authority working in combination with the local authorities may be able to reclaim possession for the states.

H. Under the jurisdiction of the port authority it may

be possible to create a free port zone or zones, and only through such an authority can any form of store-door delivery be inaugurated.

I. By adoption of proper rules and regulations the port authority may compel more efficient use of existing terminal facilities, thus increasing the capacity of the harbour.

J. The port authority with the support of the two states may with greater prospects of success call upon the Federal Government to do the dredging that is necessary for the full operation of the facilities at the port.

K. There is no subject of more vital interest to the citizens of the metropolitan district than that of markets and the distribution of food; the many interests concerned must be brought together on a better plan of operation than that at present in effect. The port authority by effecting this may do much to reduce the high cost of living.

L. While the harbour waters are not now infested the pollution of the same will make it necessary for a port authority to develop a modern sewage disposal system.

M. It is impossible now definitely to outline the general character of construction that it will recommend, but with the background of the painstaking investigation by the bi-state commission it is felt with a unified port control New York will be made the best, cheapest, and quickest port of entry and exit in the world!

BIBLIOGRAPHY

Chapters II and III.

I. N. P. Stokes, "Iconography of Manhattan."

J. Grant Wilson, "Memorial History of New York."

Martha J. Lamb, "History of the City of New York."

Thomas Janvier, "The Dutch Founding of New York."

Charles Hemstreet, "The Story of Manhattan."

Charles Burr Todd, "History of the City of New York."

David T. Valentine, "History of the City of New York."

Mrs. Schuyler Van Rensselaer, "History of New York in 17th Century."

Theodore Roosevelt, "Historic Towns in New York."

Daniel Van Pelt, "Leslie's History of New York."

John Austin Stevens, "Colonial Records of New York Chamber of Commerce."

Dr. E. B. O'Callaghan, "History of New Netherland."

Chapter IV.

J. Grant Wilson, *supra.*

Martha J. Lamb, *supra.*

Rufus Wilson, "New York Old and New."

Thomas Janvier, "The Sea Robbers," *Harper's Magazine*, November, 1894.

W. L. Penfield, "International Piracy in Time of War."

Maurice Prendergast, "Modern Piracy, 1914."

Chapter V.

Daniel Van Pelt, *supra.*

John F. Watson, "Annals of New York."

James Q. Howard, "Modern Smugglimg," *The Forum*, 1896.

Chapter VI.
Martha J. Lamb, *supra.*
I. N. P. Stokes, *supra.*
J. Grant Wilson, *supra.*
W. W. Pasko, "Old New York."
Daniel Van Pelt, *supra.*

Chapter VIII.
Chauncey M. Depew, "One Hundred Years of American Commerce."
W. Hamilton Benham, "Trade and Trade Centres of History."
J. McDonald Oxley, "The Romance of Commerce."
Daniel Van Pelt, *supra.*
J. Grant Wilson, *supra.*

Chapter IX.
David Wells, "Our Merchant Marine."
John R. Speares, "The Story of Our Merchant Marine."
Martha J. Lamb, *supra.*
J. Grant Wilson, *supra.*
Edith M. Phelps, "The American Merchant Marine."
William G. McAdoo, "The Naval Auxiliary Merchant Marine."

Chapters X, XI, and XII.
Chauncey M. Depew, "One Hundred and Fifty Years of the Chamber of Commerce."
Alexander E. Orr, "Commercial Organizations."
Journal of Commerce, "One Hundred and Fifty Years of American Commerce."
Reports of the Chamber of Commerce, Merchants' Association, Board of Trade, *Maritime Marine News.*

Chapter XIII.
I. N. P. Stokes, *supra.*
R. A. C. Smith, "The West Side Improvement Plan."

CHARLES BURR TODD, *supra.*

OLIN J. STEVENS, "Harbour Improvement." Address, "North Side Board of Trade," January, 1917.

H. McL. HARDING, New York *Evening Post,* June 20, 1917

CHARLES MOLESPHINI, New York *Evening Post,* June 20, 1917.

J. GRANT WILSON, *supra.*

MURRAY HULBERT, New York *Evening Post,* June 20, 1917.

Chapter XIV.

MARTHA J. LAMB, *supra.*

J. GRANT WILSON, *supra.*

REV. J. F. RICHMOND, "New York and Its Institutions."

R. S. GUERNSEY, "New York and Vicinity During the War of 1812."

MAUDE WILDER GOODWIN, "Fort Amsterdam in the Days of the Dutch."

REV. EDMUND BANKS SMITH, "Governor's Island."

FRANK BERGEN KELLY, "Historical Guide to the City of New York."

JOHN M. HAMMOND, "Quaint and Historic Forts of North America."

BLANCHE M. BELLAMY, "Governor's Island."

STEPHEN JENKINS, "The Greatest Street in the World."

THOMAS M. STANFORD, "A Concise Description of the City of New York."

Chapter XVI.

EDWIN J. CLAPP, "The Port of Hamburg."

FREDERIC C. HOWE, "The Free Port of Hamburg."

FREDERIC C. HOWE, New York *Evening Post,* June 20, 1917.

"The Coming of the Mechanically Perfect Port," *The Americas,* published by the National City Bank, May 9, 1918.

BIBLIOGRAPHY

Reports, San Francisco Chamber of Commerce, New York Merchants' Association, Department of Commerce, United States Tariff Commission.

Chapter XXII.

H. McL. HARDING, New York *Evening Post*, June 20, 1917.

F. J. H. KRACKE, New York *Evening Post*, June 20, 1917.

LIEUT.-COL. H. W. STICKLE, New York *Evening Post*, June 20, 1917.

DR. NATHAN A. WARREN, New York *Evening Post*, June 20, 1917.

Much important information was obtained from monthly magazines and other periodicals and from the minutes of the proceedings of various civic and political organizations: *Scientific American*, *The Forum*, *The National Marine*, *The Nautical Gazette*, *The New Republic*, *North American Review*, *The Independent*, *Marine Engineering News*, *Real Estate Bulletin*, *Review of Reviews*, *The Nation*, *The National Magazine*, *Engineering News Record*, *Railway and Engineering Review*, *Railway Review*, *Journal of Commerce*, *Town Planning Review* (The Port of London, Past, Present, and Future); *Records of New Amsterdam*, edited by Berthold Fernow; magazine section of the Sunday newspapers; digest of data collected in relation to the sanitary condition of New York Harbour by Metropolitan Sewerage Committee; proceedings of the New York State Waterways Commission; reports of City Club, reports of the Bureau of Foreign and Domestic Commerce, reports of the Chief Engineer of the War Department, reports of the Treasury Department, reports of committees Traffic Club of America, records and reports of the United States Shipping Board; public papers of Daniel D. Tompkins; various publications and bulletins issued by National City Bank, Guaranty Trust Company; proceedings of Engineers' Club of Philadelphia on ports and terminal facilities; proceedings of the Pacific Coast Association authorities;

proceedings of the Galveston Commercial Association; reports of the New York Produce Exchange; decisions of the Secretary of War on the extensions of harbour lines; William Joshua Barney's Selected Bibliography on Ports and Harbours; public addresses, Charles F. McLean on New York Harbour Improvement, Robert P. Bass on Marine and Dock Labour; report of the New York, New Jersey Port and Harbour Development Commission; New York Committee of Defence Minutes, 1814-1815, in New York Historical Society; GOODRICH's "Chronological History of New York"; *The Port of New York Annual* by A. R. SMITH. Also from HARRY CHASE BREARLEY, "The Problem of Greater New York and Its Solution"; THOMAS F. DEVOE, "The Market Book"; JOHN WILLIAM LEONARD, "History of the City of New York"; ADRIAN VANDERDONK, "Dutch Development," "Journal of Jasper Danckaerts"; MARY M. BOOTH, "History of New York From Its Earliest Settlement"; PETER ROSS, "The History of Long Island"; REGINALD PELHAM HOLTON, "Relics of the Revolution"; FRANK MOSS, "The American Metropolis From Knickerbocker Days to the Present Time"; IRA K. MORRIS, "Memorial History of Staten Island"; MRS. BLEECKER BANGS, "Reminiscences of Old New Utrecht and Gowanus"; EUGENE L. ARMBRUSTER, "History of Long Island"; EDWIN J. CLAPP, "American Problems of New Construction"; MOSES KING's "Hand Book of New York City"; "Historic New York" (The Half Moon Papers, published by Putnam & Sons).

THE END

THE COUNTRY LIFE PRESS
GARDEN CITY, N. Y.

www.ingramcontent.com/pod-product-compliance
Lightning Source LLC
LaVergne TN
LVHW020600110826
845149LV00002B/322